FLAT FLIP FLIES STRAIGHT!

True Origins of the Frisbee®

By
Fred Morrison
Inventor of the Plastic Flying Disc

Plus

THE ESSENTIAL GUIDE TO COLLECTING FLYIN' DISCS

By
Phil Kennedy
Editing, Design & Graphics

Wethersfield, Connecticut

FLAT FLIP FLIES STRAIGHT!
True Origins of the Frisbee®
By Fred Morrison and Phil Kennedy

Published by: **Wormhole Publishers**
181 Ridge Road, Wethersfield, CT 06109-1045

Orders: Use order form at back of book or visit www.FlatFlip.com

All rights reserved. No part of this book may be reproduced or transmitted by any form or by any means, including mechanical, electronic, photographic, recording; nor may it be stored in any storage and retrieval system for public or private use without the express written permission from the authors/publisher, except for brief quotations in a book review.

Book One: *The True History of Plastic Flyin' Discs*, ©2006 Walter F. Morrison (All rights reserved)

Book Two: *The Essential Guide to Collecting Flyin' Discs, The Colorful History of Flyin' Discs*, Appendices data, photos of discs, ©2006 Phil Kennedy (All rights reserved)

Editor: Phil Kennedy   Assistant Editor: Pat Kennedy
Photography: Phil Kennedy
Design & Production: Phil Kennedy, Graphic Images, www.GoGraphicImages.com
First Printing: January 2006
Printed in U.S.A.

Publishers Cataloging In Publication Data.

Morrison, Walter F., 1920–

Flat flip flies straight!: true origins of the frisbee / by Fred Morrison—1st ed.

SUMMARY: The inventor of the original plastic flying disc corrects and refutes erroneous published history by relating the actual events as he lived them. The co-author explains flying disc collecting and introduces a new and improved system for identifying and cataloging antique plastic flying discs.

Includes indices and bibliography.

1. Flying discs (Game)   I. Kennedy, Phil, 1947–, joint author.   II. Title

Dewey Decimal System Number: 796.2

Library of Congress Control Number: 2005936445

ISBN: 0-9774517-4-7 (pbk.)

The name Frisbee®, as used throughout this book, is a registered trademark of Wham-O, Inc., U.S. Trademark Reg. No. 679,186 issued May 26, 1959 for flying discs used in toss games. References in the title and text of this book to Frisbee and Frisbee discs and saucers are intended to be and are limited solely to the disc products manufactured and sold by Wham-O, Inc.

TABLE OF CONTENTS

PREFACE 7
INTRODUCTION 9

BOOK ONE — THE TRUE HISTORY OF PLASTIC FLYIN' DISCS
PART I   **FROM SO SIMPLE A BEGINNIN'**

Chapter 1	Who Were Those "Guys"?	17
Chapter 2	Scratchin' the Itch	22
Chapter 3	The "Hail" You Say?	25
Chapter 4	The Ultimate Disc "Who's Who"?	29
Chapter 5	The Birth of "Lid-dom"	34
Chapter 6	The Ascension	36
Chapter 7	Lids to Wedlock	38
Chapter 8	"Pan-dom"onium	42
Chapter 9	How Good Could It Get?	45
Chapter 10	The Real World	47
Chapter 11	Prudence	49
Chapter 12	Life Before "Discdom"	52
Chapter 13	The Birth of Plastic Discdom	55
Chapter 14	The First Disc Design Refined	58
Chapter 15	Elephant Whachamacallems?	60
Chapter 16	Flyin-Saucers Become Real!	62
Chapter 17	What's a PIPCO?	64
Chapter 18	Horror Story	67
Chapter 19	Instant Success Denied!	71
Chapter 20	Sal(i)vation?	74
Chapter 21	Deftly Devious	77
Chapter 22	Prelude to Culmination	83
Chapter 23	Quittin' Time	86
Chapter 24	Back to a Future	89
Chapter 25	The Awesome Foursome	92
Chapter 26	A Mold of Our Own	97
Chapter 27	Pluto Platters Enter Discdom	100
Chapter 28	Who Was That Guy?	105
Chapter 29	The Amalgamation	107
Chapter 30	Hoops and Platters	112
Chapter 31	Pre-Frisbee Fun 'n Games	115
Chapter 32	Unexpected Happenstances	118
Chapter 33	The Inventor?	121
Chapter 34	The Morrisons Take a Hit	127
Chapter 35	The Man Who Made It Happen	130
Chapter 36	Speculation	134
Chapter 37	Getting Personal	137
Chapter 38	All Did NOT Go Well	139
Chapter 39	The Bombshell	143
Chapter 40	Exceptional Representation	146
Chapter 41	Horsin' Around	151

PART II THE YELLOW PAGES

Chapter 42	Mr. Eye-Opener. 156
Chapter 43	Distortion and Unhappiness 159
Chapter 44	An Open Letter to Coszette Eneix. 161
Chapter 45	Dwindling Interests 164
Chapter 46	A Date to Remember. 166
Chapter 47	Lying in a Field of Dreams 169
Chapter 48	Li'l Abner Fallacy 177
Chapter 49	PIPCO Reconstituted 181
Chapter 50	Introduction to Frustration 187
Chapter 51	The Patent Letters 190
Chapter 52	Edward L. Kennedy, Exposed!. 199

PART III FRISBEE FOLKS REMEMBERED

Chapter 53	Stancil Johnson, 'Super Shrink' 208
Chapter 54	'The Boys'. 216
Chapter 55	Ed 'Steady Ed' Headrick. 224
Chapter 56	Goldy Norton, PR Man 231
Chapter 57	Other Major Players. 236

EPILOGUE 242

THE COLORFUL HISTORY OF FLYIN' DISCS 245–276

BOOK TWO — THE ESSENTIAL GUIDE TO COLLECTING FLYIN' DISCS

	FOREWORD 278
Chapter 58	The Thrills of Disc Collecting 280
Chapter 59	Getting into Disc Collecting 290
Chapter 60	Grading a Disc's Condition. 309
Chapter 61	A Disc's Condition…Categorically Speaking. 322
Chapter 62	Important Discs to Collect 331
Chapter 63	Tools of the Trade 334

APPENDICES

	INDEX TO APPENDICES 353
Appendix A–W	Documents from *The Yellow Pages* and More. 354
Appendix X	Timeline of Events 397
Appendix Y	Spinnin' Yarns, 30 Events That Never Happened 405
Appendix Z	Glossary of Terms. 410

BIBLIOGRAPHY. 422

INDICES   Book One 428
                 Book Two 433

ACKNOWLEDGEMENTS. 435

ORDER FORM. 436

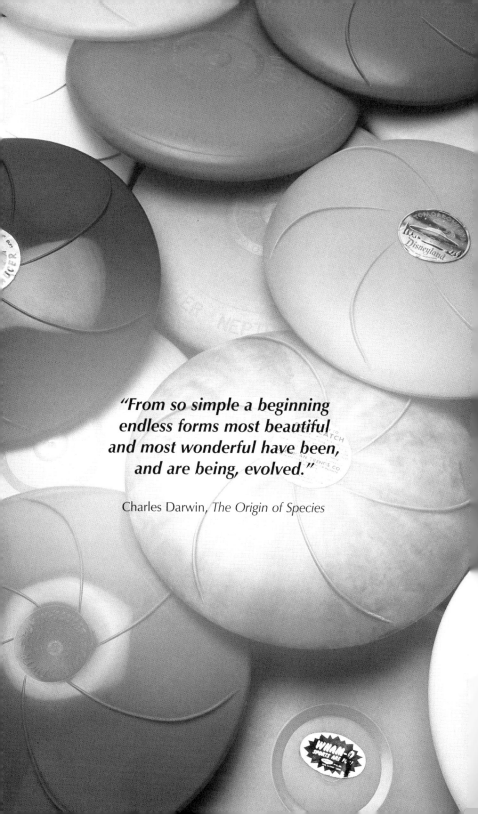

"From so simple a beginning endless forms most beautiful and most wonderful have been, and are being, evolved."

Charles Darwin, *The Origin of Species*

This book is dedicated to

Lu Morrison

whose early willing sacrifices and always active participation made possible the evolvement of Frisbees.

PREFACE

WAY BACK WHEN *(1937)*, two young lovers played catch with a large popcorn can lid that would fly after a backhanded flip. It was fun! Popcorn lids were scarce. Available cake pans replaced the lid. The lovers believed the flight characteristics of a cake pan could be improved on. It came to pass that when the reconfigured shape of a cake pan was molded in plastic (1948) it *did indeed* fly better.

I'm the guy that did the reconfiguring.

Who could have conceived at the time that those early plastic discs were the forerunners of the most money-making PLAYTHING of all time…the FRISBEE®!

During 1958 the Patent Office issued a patent for the "Flying Toy." My name was on the patent. Does my name on a patent certify me as a legitimate INVENTOR? For years I've been referred to as the "Inventor of the Frisbee." Whether I'm legitimate or not, I've happily gone along.

Being called an *INVENTOR* has such a nice ring to it….

ABOUT THE BOOK—

Within these pages is the history of "FLITTIN' DISCS" as I experienced it. Related in factual and, at times, in nauseous self-serving detail are the goin's-on that led to the phenomenal success of "AIRBORNE CROCKERY." It's the intent of this book to correct, once and for all, the media's distorted history of events that led to the evolution of plastic FLYIN-SAUCERS, and ultimately to FRISBEES.

It's the fervent hope of this author that the real facts of that evolvement will satiate the hunger of those Frisbee aficionados that have so long hungered to know the truth about how Frisbees came into being. It's the author's further hope that The Book will be taken to readers' bosoms, slept with under their pillows and be cherished forever…and recommended to their friends!

Fred Morrison

This book is printed on paper that has *not* been approved for book burnings.

INTRODUCTION

ONCE UPON A TIME, quite recently in fact, the guy I've had to live with all my life was driven to write the true history of a round piece of plastic that people enjoy throwing at (and sometime to) each other.

The guy that came up with the Flittin' Disc "idea" wasn't a rocket scientist. He was just one of those everyday, not-too-incredibly-handsome, effervescent, athletic, All-American-type boys that marries the girl-next-door. The type of chap that everybody expects will achieve success early on, DOESN'T, and more knowledgeable people take over his "idea" and make it a phenomenal success.

The "idea" had always had merit but needed promotion to bring it to financial fruition. The more-knowledgeable people provided the promotional wherewithal and know-how that made the "idea," a flying plastic disc, a national plaything. The promoted "idea" was given the name Frisbee. Today, Frisbees are *international* playthings.

The success of the Frisbees has turned out to be, over time, a financial bonanza. Some of that bonanza rubbed off on the not-so-really-All-American Boy and the Girl-Next-Door.

WHAT'S THE BIG "IDEA"?

What is the universal appeal of Frisbees? The disc is simplicity itself. It doesn't have any moving parts. It doesn't make any noise. Launching one successfully requires self-imposed coordination. When it leaves a snapped hand (flip) in a flat spin, it's supposed to fly straight. With variants of the hand's release, curves, skips, hovers, and boomerangs can be accomplished.

Few people have achieved perfection with a disc—possibly no one. Experience helps develop accuracy, but the elements (breezes), when present, and other indefinable factors, can and do interfere with a disc getting to its intended destination.

The delights of "discing" aren't limited to humans. Dogs leap for joy when given the opportunity to catch a disc as it nears the completion of its flight. (It's been observed that dogs have difficulty picking up a disc when it's laying flat on the ground!)

Not all animals are seduced by the allure of Frisbees!

Has the pride in a well-cast launch, or the unpredictability of a disc's flight, or the catcher's possibility of making a circus catch served as the catalyst for the Frisbee's amazing success? Damn if I know! (I *do* know that wagering on the outcome of a disc's flight can be costly!)

FLAT FLIP FLIES STRAIGHT!

Book One

The True History of Plastic Flyin' Discs

(As I Lived It)

By Fred Morrison

FLAT FLIP FLIES STRAIGHT!

Part I

From So Simple a Beginnin'...

"Imagination is more important than knowledge."

John R. (Rick) Pruitt, Counselor
Richfield High School, Richfield, Utah

"It doesn't hurt to get lucky."

Fred Morrison

1

WHO WERE THOSE "GUYS"?

*F*LYING DISCS ORIGINATED IN ANTIQUITY. Now it's the year 2006. This book is the history of *modern* flying discs. I'm what's left of the three people that participated in the development of the modern plastic flying discs.

The modern version of "flittin disc" history, as I recollect it, began November 25, 1937.

Disc historians have never got their history of the discs *RIGHT!* Soooo...since I'm the only person left living that participated in the actual creation of the modern discs, if an actual, factual history of the modern airborneable discs is ever gonna get writ, it's gonna have to be me that writs it!

(Unfortunately, the history includes a glut of trivia.)

THE OTHER "FLITTIN' DISC" DEVELOPERS

LUCILE MORRISON

The input of Lucile Morrison's contributions in the early and later development of flying discs has been completely overlooked by disc historians. Lu knew from the moment she flipped her first popcorn lid in 1937, then cake pans, that there *HAD* to be something better. Her willingness to gamble on, and actively participate in, the development of a plastic disc that might fly better, and maybe make a buck, are the reasons sailable, sellable plastic discs first came on the market. Without Lu there wouldn't have been Flyin-Saucers (the first plastic disc). Without Flyin-Saucers there wouldn't have been Pluto Platters (the Morrisons' second disc). Without Pluto Platters there may never have been Frisbees. Lu's handprints are all over the original discs.

Lu had become an accomplished cake pan flipper before WWII. She was well-qualified to participate in the trial flippings of the first "Flittin' Disc" prototypes. Her opinions of the flight possibilities of the prototypes were primary in the final selection of the prototype that became the Flyin-Saucer. A few short years later her input was equally as important as together we (the Morrisons) developed the Pluto Platter. It was the Pluto Platter that Wham-O Mfg. (with alterations) renamed Frisbee.

The following "How To" instructions are molded in the underside of every Pluto Platter and original Wham-O Frisbee. No "How To" instructions have ever been more explicit nor more succinct. No "How To" instructions have ever been copied more. They've been plagiarized by many of the subsequent Frisbee knockoff manufacturers. Lu wrote 'em!

Chapter 1 — Who Were Those "Guys"?

**PLAY CATCH – INVENT GAMES
TO FLY, FLIP AWAY BACKHANDED
FLAT FLIP FLIES STRAIGHT
TILTED FLIP CURVES – EXPERIMENT!**

LUCILE MORRISON — Wife of me.

Lu was a constant participant throughout the developing history of the discs. Through it all she kept an immaculate house, raised three trouble-free kids, maintained a contagious sense of humor, and tolerated me much longer than she should have. Lu was an exceptionally beautiful, bright, fun-loving, and loving mother and wife. Does she deserve recognition as a plastic flyin' disc innovator? Absolutely! Future Frisbee historians take heed!

She passed away during 1987. *The memories linger.....*

WARREN FRANSCIONI

The other person involved in the development of the first plastic flying disc was Warren Franscioni. He participated in every phase of the first plastic disc's development, except the actual designing of the prototypes. He provided the money that created the Flyin-Saucer's plastic injection mold. Without his financing the first flying discs would most likely never have got off the ground.

> "Several weeks ago I indicated in a phone conversation that I was interested in sending you a photo of my father, Warren Franscioni. After further discussion with family members I have changed my mind. ...Thank you for your interest.
>
> Sincerely,
> Coszette Eneix"

Space reserved for photo of Warren Franscioni

Warren was a natural "flipper." He picked up on flippin' cake pans the first day he flipped one in 1947. The approximately two years we spent developing, then demonstrating the Saucers at various public events (mainly fairs) are memorable. He was the first to make a "Flittin' Disc" skip. When publicly demonstrating the Saucers, he made the "Invisible Wire" come alive. (More about the "Invisible Wire" in a following chapter.)

Disc historians haven't given Warren Franscioni the credit he deserves as one of the first flyin' disc innovators. He was a great guy to work with. I liked him.

Col. Warren Franscioni died during 1974.

2

SCRATCHIN' THE ITCH

I'D HAD A COMPUTER FOR SEVERAL YEARS but used it only to keep personal and business records. It wasn't until the latter part of 2001 that I learned there was a lotta Frisbee stuff on the Internet that included my name. Curious, I got on-line, and pecked in "FRISBEE HISTORY."

The result was incredulity! There was so much of it, in so many places. About the ONLY thing the histories got right was my name! The Internet histories of the Frisbee were pure blather. Even worse, in one especially lamentable instance that professed to be Flittin' Disc history, I was libelously slandered and inflammatoriously vilified. I was, and am again as I write this, more than somewhat incensed.

In previous years the nonsense fabricated in articles by interviewers and by self-appointed Frisbee "historians" has always been an aggravating irritant…kinda like an itch you can't reach to scratch. The inordinate amount of twaddle that's been splashed on the public is (to put it politely) unmitigated, fetid, equine effluent!

Chapter 2 — Scratchin' the Itch

Also over previous years I'd often been bugged to write a book about the "History of the Discs." *THAT* suggestion had no appeal. To write a book I'd have to overcome my innate lethargy—it takes *so damn many* paragraphs to make a book.

The Internet bilge changed my attitude. *Now I had a cause.*

I would write the true history of the plastic flyin' discs that culminated with the advent of the Frisbee, and in the process, take to task the cretan disc historian who had so impugned my character on the Internet. Psychologically the exercise was supposed to act as a mental cathartic, and in the process, get some of that aforementioned itch scratched.

The scandalizing article on the Internet was originally written by some guy named Jeff McMahon. Its title is: "Where the Frisbee First Flew: The Untold Story of the Flying Disc's Origin 50 Years Ago." (He didn't even get the title right!)

Check it out. (Reprinted in its entirety with his permission. *See Appendix W*)

FRIVOLOUS McMAHON TRIVIA: At one point McMahon writes that I changed my name from Fred to Walt for some unstated but implied devious reason. Such a drastic accusation can blow a person's suppositories. For about as long as I can remember, I've said, "Hunh?" to both Fred and Walt.

By what possible figment of McMahon's warped imagination could such a name change have benefited me in any way? I've been accused of being a lot of unflattering things by unrefined, unenlightened, and unwashed detractors, but McMahon really crossed the line with his name-change accusation. He desecrated my internationally-exalted Super Luminary image...!?

TO FUTURE DISC HISTORIANS

For the record and absolute clarification, my birth certificated name is "Walter Fredrick (there's no 'e' after the 'd') Morrison." An inattentive mother let me write my name with the "e."

Frederick was a poor choice of names. While I was a prepubescent youth, my mother always called me "Frederick"—mostly at the wrong times. Most memorable: One day she called loudly from across the main street in our small town, "Frederick… FREDERICK!…Say good-bye to your playmates…Bring your football!" (Public relations at their absolute worst!) My startled playmates looked up—"Frederick? What's a Frederick?"

It didn't help that I had the only football in town.

3

THE "HAIL" YOU SAY?

*J*EFF McMAHON HAS PROVIDED an abundance of grist for my mill. There's so *freakin'* much of it! Doing this chapter now will give the reader a brief preview of what's included in his absurd twaddle.

McMahon's opening paragraph paraphrases a quote attributed to one of Franscioni's daughters, Coszette Eneix:

> Two men held a circle of plastic over a heater in a San Luis Obispo garage [Eneix actually said the basement] in 1948, trying to mold a lip onto the disc's down-turned edge.

COMMENT: I never even knew *where* they kept the water heater! Who were those guys? The mystery of who was goofin' around the water heater smacks of intrigue. Was there something going on behind my back? Only the San Luis Obispo locale is fact!

McMahon continues:

> One of those men would...die unknown, just as he began to fight for a share of the credit and millions in royalties the Frisbee generated.

COMMENT: I've never added up what the Frisbee royalties have amounted to, but they've never amounted to McMahon's implied *megamillions*. Certainly the royalties have treated the Morrisons *very kindly*. Whatever it's been, it's been spread over half a century. Had Franscioni lived long enough to initiate a lawsuit hoping to gain a share of the Morrisons' royalty millions(?), our attorneys would have eaten his lunch!

Another McMahon quote has Stancil Johnson, an author of a Frisbee history book and an important player in the history of Frisbee sports, offering this irreverent play on words:

> Franscioni died and never was able to come back and get his share of the profits.

COMMENT: There's only *one* Person I'm aware of who's ever been expected to "come back" (as in resurrect). According to the quote, Franscioni tried to make it back more than once to "get his share." Bully for Franscioni...he gave accomplishing the unlikely a shot.

McMahon, who is credited at the end of his article for "hurling amazing whirling adjectives for New Times," avows:

> One of those men [around the water heater] would be hailed as the inventor of the Frisbee.

COMMENT: *Hailed...?*

ADJECTIVAL FUN AND GAMES

My concept of a "hailing" conjures up the scenario of a returning, victorious Caesar. His barrel chest is thrust forward, his handsome physiognomy beaming broadly as He acknowledges His self-perceived, universal importance. He's leading an entourage of elegantly-uniformed, sycophantical generals and an extended phalanx of bare-kneed, spear-toting, shield-brandishing warriors up the red-carpeted thoroughfare leading to the steps of the stately Forum. A bevy of barefoot, young, wonderfully-endowed virgins, clad only in the scantiest of gauze, are sprinkling rare, imported flower petals in the path of our all-conquering Hero.

On each side of the regal procession, throngs of venerating citizens have created a blanket of upraised, multi-colored Frisbees as they applaud His resplendent passing.

At the top of the Forum's luxurious marble steps Caesar turns and faces His rapt subjects. A solemn hush falls over the expectant multitudes as He raises His muscular arm aloft, fist gripping His wondrously-bejeweled Frisbee. Following the obligatory stately pause, He proclaims to the worshipping masses…"Beware of cheap imitations!" His message is "right on!" Thunderous, approving pandemonium erupts! In that instant—with only four carefully chosen words—Caesar has insured his place in the Ænnals of Frisbee History.

(So much for "whirling adjectives.")

Today we "Hail" Caesar! Caesar's bejeweled Frisbee would be the most coveted, most treasured possession a Frisbee collector could ever hope to own. Not many could afford it. It'd be worth millions on eBay.

All Hail Caesar!   All Hail Wham-O!   All Hail Frisbees!
What the hail…Hail me!

I may have been the subject of a momentary "hailing" once. At the 1974 Wham-O-sponsored Rose Bowl International Frisbee Tournament I was asked to electronically address the forty thousand fans in the stands. My one sentence was brief and succinct—same as Caesar's. Holding a Frisbee aloft in one hand and the mike in the other, I proclaimed in my most stentorian voice: "Beware of cheap imitations."…Got a standing "O."

On a subsequent occasion I was definitely "hailed"…but for the wrong reason. In a crowded McDonald's, having just ingested a cheeseburger and fries, there erupted from deep within me an unintentional but monumental oral, gastric expulsion. A hush fell over the crowd. The shocked, sitting chompers stopped chomping. The standees—in stunned disbelief—turned to see *WHAT* was capable of producing such a reverberating, antisocial noise. All eyes focused on me. After a brief, pregnant silence, thunderous applause broke out. Shouts of approval shook the building. I graciously acknowledged the ovation…and split! (Imagine…being "hailed" for a belch?)

Wham-O arranged for me to appear on TV programs, to give interviews to reporters, and make appearances at Wham-O sponsored events. I've been the guest speaker at colleges and numerous service organizations. My presentations were always met with friendly acceptance. No one was ever aroused to a fevered pitch. Nobody was ever stirred to a frenzy.

Gauze-draped virgins have never sprinkled flower petals in my path!

4

THE ULTIMATE DISC "WHO'S WHO"?

I'VE BEEN TOLD that in the world of "Flittin' Discdom" an early champion of some renown named Victor Malafronte is considered to be the ultimate "Disc Authority"—the "Who's Who" of airborne crockery....

I first met Vic at some Frisbee event early on—then on and off again at later Wham-O sponsored events. He was friendly and easy to like. I remember that at one point he was hoping to market his "Spin Thimble." (The "Thimble," when stuck on an upright finger, would serve as a landing point for a hovering, settling Frisbee.) I wished him well. I wonder what happened to that idea. I've never seen a "Spin Thimble."

We were merely nodding acquaintances until the 1982 Frisbee Hall of Fame installations at Houghton, Michigan. We became better acquainted during those goin's on and sat next to each other on the return flight to L.A. Vic seemed smitten with my affiliations with Wham-O Mfg. and how it had come about. The entire flight was spent answering his questions. I had no reason to deceive, or withhold, or obscure anything. The flight ended. We went our separate ways. The friendly inquisition was forgotten.

Wizard Enterprises Presents The newest item on the Frisbee scene.

FLYIN' DISC RING

rotating bead
stabilizer
adjustable band

Des. pat. applied for

Send to: **Wizard Enterprises**
2910 Newbury St.
Berkeley, Ca. 94703
415-843-0446

Currently used by Frisbee Champions in three countries. Very easy to use, simply catch your Frisbee on the tip or Stabilizer, the rotating bead will allow the Frisbee to spin, thus minimizing drag and prolonging the rotation of your Frisbee, while you create new dynamic catches. Such as flipping the Frisbee behind your back or around your leg. Experiment! The possibilities are endless.

Please send your name, address, and age (important), and a $10.00 money order or cash. No checks please.

All Flyin-Disc rings are hand made by the Original World Frisbee Champion – Victor Malafronte. Rings are made of metal with a plastic rotating bead.

If not satisfied return the ring within 90 days for full refund. 3 weeks for delivery.

Ad for Victor's "Spin Thimble" — *Frisbee World*, Vol. 1, Issue 1, 1976

During the mid-nineties, Vic sent me a coupla extensive and probing questionnaires. He said he was gathering data for a history book about Frisbees. I responded with detailed accounts of my best recollections regarding the Flyin-Saucers, the Pluto Platters, and my relations with Wham-O Mfg. Again, there was no reason to withhold, deceive, or obscure anything!

A short time later I received an autographed copy of *The Complete Book of Frisbee*. I should have read the book before I called and complimented him on his accomplishment. I expected that Vic had incorporated my answers to his questionnaires in the book's text. Such was *not* the case! Portions of my contributions for his disc history had been corrupted. Vic had opted to incorporate non-factual disc history by people that were less than knowledgeable about "Flittin' Disc" reality; and I was the subject of some uncalled for malignment. I was somewhat chagrined.

Chapter 4 — The Ultimate "Who's Who"?

Vic's *The Complete Book of Frisbee* is an attractive book on the outside, and page after page of brilliant pictures of "flittin' discs" inside. I was amazed by the incredible number of Frisbee knockoffs that have been marketed over the years. Overlooking the history errata, the colorful pictures of knocked-off Frisbees are enough to commend the book.

Excerpted from Vic's book:

> Some people with direct knowledge of "what happened" have been all too vague and conveniently forgetful about dates, places and people involved, leaving a blurred composite for these essential events of the dawning of discdom.[1]

COMMENTS: What a delightful, beautifully composed sentence full of blatant nonsense. Only three people had actual, direct knowledge of "what happened" during the "dawning of discdom": me, Lu, and Franscioni. It's unlikely Lu was ever asked to contribute data for Vic's book and Franscioni died long before Vic started writing his book. It's fair to assume Vic was referring to me.

Vic, you plucked me like a chicken with your questionnaires. You extracted every scintilla of my recollective capabilities relative to your classic expression "dawning of discdom." You were provided with everything that might be construed as an *essential event*. What did I omit? Fifty years is a long time to remember *every* minute detail of minutia. Nothing was "conveniently forgot." Vic, *YOU* strayed from my factual, historical data that I so graciously donated. *YOU'RE* the "composite blurrer."

For shame!

Not in Vic's book, but quoted by McMahon[2]:

> I had asked Fred about his partner Franscioni, and he owns up to it.

COMMENT: Vic, where in hell were you coming from when you said that? Your implication that I had at some time denied that Franscioni and I had been partners is so stupid it's not worth further refuting.

More McMahon quoting Vic:

> Morrison has always been cagey about the facts of the Frisbee's birth.

COMMENT: Vic, I've always had to be "cagey" because the truth just isn't in me: I wasn't asked to approve of, nor was I present to midwife the Wham-O operation that altered the Pluto Platter mold, thereby giving *birth* to the Frisbee. That's a *FACT*. Vic, I couldn't tell you what I didn't know.

Want more?

> I think Fred has a lot of stuff he can lose and nothing to gain by talking.

Vic, I couldn't have risked telling you *E V V V V V V E RYthing*. You might have blabbed the unsavory, sordid details of my private life to others. Now it can be told. Vic, I was sinning! I was romancing a cluster of uncloistered nuns. Had Lu found out, the divorce would have left me worthless. Yes, Vic, there was "a lot to lose."

Chapter 4 — The Ultimate "Who's Who"?

To sum up: *The Complete Book of Frisbee* didn't do Frisbee history any favors, and Vic's belittling references to me were contrived and unjustified. Is Victor Malafronte the Ultimate Disc Authority? The "Who's Who" of Discdom?

I think his "Disc Authoritativeness" is disputable.

Victor Malafronte
World Champion, Author

---

1. Malafronte, Victor A. *The Complete Book of Frisbee: The History of the Sport & The First Official Price Guide.* Alameda, CA: American Trends Publishing Co., 1998. Page 69.

2. McMahon, Jeff. "Where the Frisbee First Flew: The Untold Story of the Flying Disc's Origin 50 Years Ago," *New Times Weekly*, San Luis Obispo, CA, July 24-31, 1997. Pages 10-13. (*See Appendix W*)

5

THE BIRTH OF "LID-DOM"

*J*OHN MARSHALL HIGH SCHOOL had a pretty good football team in the Fall of 1937. We wound up playing in the L.A. Coliseum for the city championship...and lost.

Something (providential?) brought me to the attention of a comely miss named Lucile Nay. (Maybe it was that padded uniform?)
It was easy to focus on Lu. She was a beaut! We got so "focused" on each other we became a steady thing. Lu was the best thing that ever happened to me!

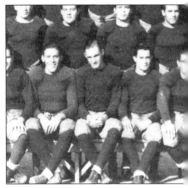

Fred...front and center.

It all began during a '37 Thanksgiving Day family gathering at the house of one of Lu's sisters. I remember it like it was yesterday! The after-dinner overeaters had assembled on the front lawn. The sister's husband, Joe, produced a large popcorn can lid. That lid would *FLY* when it was flipped spinning away backhanded. Adults and kids alike were finding joy flippin' and attempting to outwit the unpredictable flight of the can cover.

That lid led to an unforeseen financial bonanza that's made a lot of impossible things possible for a hell of a lot of people. Who'da thunk a thing as simple as a popcorn can lid would be metamorphed into an international, history-making plaything?

Chapter 5 — The Birth of "Lid-dom"

A brief, sad history about Joe. Joe was one of those pompous asses whose overbearing demeanor makes being in their presence dreadful. When Frisbees began producing the "big bucks," Joe convinced himself that it was *HIS* popcorn can lid that had germinated the emergence of plastic flying discs and the success of Frisbees. He yearned for recognition… *and compensation.* He was threatening a family-disrupting lawsuit when he up and conveniently died.

Poor Joe…. Until now, he's been completely overlooked as having played a part in the origin of "flittin' dishes."*

Joe aside…isn't it amazing what an afternoon's brief flipping of a tin can's "lid" has led to?!

Who in the world doesn't know what to do with a Frisbee?

---

*Joe, however marginal, you deserve *some* degree of recognition. Wherever you are out there, *if* you *are* out there, I want you to know how pleased it makes me to have mentioned you in this book. Your place in the Ænnals of "Flittin' Dish" History is hereby established and confirmed. You're now a "footnote."

35

6

THE ASCENSION

*I*N THE SPRING OF 1938, I was a recently-graduated, jobless and therefore penniless suitor. Income was going to be necessary if the relationship was to continue blossoming.

Clarence Nay, Lu's dad, was the construction superintendent for a large transit-mix concrete company. The company had its own sand and gravel pit. I wondered aloud in his presence, "Is it possible there might be a position…?"

Clarence may have had doubts that I was the most promising of son-in-law prospects. I would be tested. He put me to work in the bottom of the sand and gravel pit.

All day long a bulldozer pushed sand and rocks down the sides of the pit onto a rail grate. The smaller stuff fell through the grate onto a conveyor belt. The belt took the droppings up to the crusher. Boulders too large to fall through the grate needed reduction. My job was to apply, as many times as necessary, a twenty-pound sledge hammer against the oversized "donikers." When the targeted boulders finally fractured they'd fall through the grate and make the trip up to the crusher.

Chapter 6 — The Ascension

Spending eight hot, summer hours, five days a week, in a hole without a view was a challenge. It was a miserable job; hot, dirty, and physical. But…a paycheck was required to maintain the desired squiring of the superintendent's daughter. I persevered.

Did I prove myself? Clarence began to indicate a hint of benevolent acceptance when Lu and I were in his presence. Did I become a valued employee worthy of less labor-intensive work up top, closer to the crusher? The answers were gratifying Yeses. Clarence gave the timekeeper an approving nod and I arose from The Pit!

Shortly after my "ascension," with Lu's approval, less arduous, more financially rewarding employment was sought and found elsewhere…away from that God-awful hellhole in the ground.

7

LIDS TO WEDLOCK

*A*FTER THAT THANKSGIVING DAY HAPPENING, Lu and I really got into flippin' with the "borrowed" popcorn can lid. After the lid got bent out of shape, we discovered pie pans. Cake pans replaced the pie pans. (Cake pans have a right-angled flange, are more stable, and fly better'n pie pans.) We'd flip pans when we should have been doin' somethin' else. We flipped on weekends, out in the street, public parks, at family gatherings…no place was exempt! The constant flippin' developed a fair degree of expertise. Passing people would stop to watch. The two of us were making nondescript cake pans look pretty damn GOOD!

The commercialization of airborne cake pans began one weekend on a Santa Monica, California beach. We were workin' up a sweat flyin' a pan, when an athletic-type sunbather (probably an admirer of Lu's physical attributes in addition to her flippin' ability) approached and offered to buy our plaything. We parted with the pan for twenty-five cents. A light came on. What a fantastic deal! A drive-in hamburger cost nineteen cents. If we could sell two pans we could both have a burger, and split an order of fries.

At that time cake pans cost about a nickel. Trading nickels for quarters had possibilities. A business was born! Henceforth, our weekends and holidays were spent mostly on beaches.

We kept a ready supply of cake pans and a blanket in the car. The spread blanket was our showcase. A cardboard sign advertised our wares: "Flyin' Cake Pans, 25 Cents."

A typical "flyable" metal cake pan

The sign and our deft flippin' created a demand for the pans. The pans sold best on southern California beaches. Public parks were good also. The most important factor in the sales equation was people. The fairer the weather, and the more people there were, the more merrier we were.

It got so that meeting the demand for the pans was a problem. We'd buy all the cake pans in all the dime and hardware stores on the way to a beach, or wherever, then have to take a different route the next weekend to find stores that had pans. We solved that problem by having a close-to-home, cooperative hardware store manager buy 'em for us in quantity.

Pre-war prices weren't what they are today. A gallon of gas for the car cost nineteen cents. The pans paid for gassin' my mom's borrowed car and our entertainment. Life was good and kept getting gooder. The gravity-defying cake pans financed a thirty-five dollar diamond engagement ring.

My dad had higher expectations for his eldest son...like a college education. That I would want to get married before that happened was definitely NOT in Dad's playbook.

The marriage license required blood tests. We submitted to the blood lettin' then waited two weeks for the test results. While we waited, piles of prenuptial advertising filled my folks' mailbox. Mom approved of Lu and knew about the marriage license application. She deliberately kept Dad out of the loop. Dad never saw the incriminating advertising.

April 3, 1939: We were married in the L.A. Hall of Records by a one-armed (true) justice of the peace. Nice guy. Ten bucks to get his name on the license and ten for his verbiage. When the deed was done I tipped him five. The fees and the gratuity were appropriate for the times.

Lu's folks witnessed the "I do's" then took off for two weeks on what should have been *our* honeymoon. We found bliss in their house while they were gone. They returned and almost immediately relocated to some place called Baywood Park up in central California. We didn't have to move. Our honeymoon cottage became our first abode—we didn't have to find a place to rent.

Mom's car was a Durant. I'd had almost exclusive use of the Durant. The morning after the marriage I called Dad to tell him the last thing he wanted to hear: "Hi Dad, Lu and I got married yesterday." There ensued a moment of silence.... When he finally *could* speak, he was vehement: "NO, YOU'RE NOT!" (Obviously an inaccurate assessment of the fact.) Another pause...then: "BRING THE CAR BACK...*NOW!*" End of conversation.

Dad's vengeance had an effect. Not having a car in southern California presented problems. There were places streetcars and buses didn't go. Getting to and from a job could be difficult. Friends and Lu's relatives helped with transportation for necessities. Not having the use of Mom's car eliminated our cake pan peddling. Maybe that was just as well—it wasn't long before Lu began to bulge. In due time a baby girl graced our premises.

It didn't take long for Lu's winning persona to undo Dad's iron-assedness. It didn't happen overnight but when it finally dawned on Dad that a jewel had been added to his family, the ice melted and my relationship with him was restored. We were father/son friends again.

Nobody didn't like Lu very long!

Fred in 1939

Later, while I was in the Air Force, Lu went to work for Lockheed Aircraft. Mom and Dad baby-sat during the day while Lu was at work. Dad generously helped Lu financially during that period, and Lu had exclusive use of the Durant for the duration. How 'bout that.

8

"PAN-DOM"ONIUM

*A*LWAYS, FROM THE TIME of the first flipping of the cake pans, Lu and I believed that streamlined cake pans could be merchandised. With that thought in mind, I approached my dad. Dad had manufacturing experience and friends in the manufacturing business.

We considered all the available materials, including plastics. Bakelite was being used to make ashtrays and other hard items. A flexible plastic that could take the beatings of a flying "pan" didn't exist, so we were stuck with metal.

The first idea was to manufacture pans with only the upper half of the outer rim radiused. The flange would then continue on down at a slight outward angle. A flat, round blank of tin would be pressed against a spinning form the same way aluminum nose cones for aircraft engines were being formed. The slightly outward flange would allow the pan to be slipped off the form. People who knew about those things advised against the use of tin. Tin didn't have the same malleable characteristics of aluminum. So ended *that* idea.

The next idea was to create tin pans with fully-radiused outer rims. This could be accomplished by two punch-press operations. One die would stamp out round tin blanks. The other die would stamp the blank with the top half of the rim radiused. Additional, more complex tooling would fold the disc's sharp edge down and turn the rim under, thereby forming a fully-radiused rim. Dad financed the first two relatively inexpensive dies. The dies did their jobs. We had samples of partially-complete flying pans. The lack of money for the rest of the "complex tooling" put the project on hold. During the financial hang-up, along came a war.

(The project being on hold turned out to be the best thing that could have happened. Flexible plastic would become available after the war. We'd have been stuck with expensive, antiquated manufacturing equipment.)

DECEMBER 7, 1941

I was working for a metal heat-treating company making forty-two cents an hour when the radio reported the Pearl Harbor attack. *Total disbelief!* An insignificant country whose commerce was limited to exporting cheap "Made-in-Japan" toys had attacked the *United States?* America was gonna have to kick some butts!

Now that we were at war, better-paying defense jobs were available for the taking. The heat-treating experience on job applications led to similar jobs at Lockheed and Douglas Aircraft companies. I wasn't at all averse to going where the money was more. Shipyards were offering the most pay, so I went to work in one.

I became draftable…. Dad, a WWI pilot, held strong opinions about being a participant in the military, to wit: "Flyin's better'n walkin'." I enlisted in the Air Force, became a P-47 fighter/bomber pilot, was sent to Italy and in mid-December '44 was assigned to the 350th Fighter Group, 347th Squadron… "The Screaming Red Asses."

FLAT FLIP FLIES STRAIGHT! — Book One, Part I

On the 57th mission, March 19, 1945, I got hit by ground fire, bailed out and became a POW. I was transported to Germany, held in a Stalag a few miles outside of Nuremberg until the day after President Roosevelt died. That day, along

Lt. Walter F. Morrison   Fred with his P-47 "Thunderbolt"

with a couple hundred British enlisted POWs, we marched out of the camp. The rest of the war was spent being traipsed around Germany at night; always away from advancing Allied armies. The total POW experience lasted only forty-eight days. (The actual time didn't amount to much, but a guy on a limited POW diet can develop a hell of an appetite over forty-eight days!) The "flyin' part" of my time in the service, especially the brief three-month period I was privileged to be a "Screaming Red Ass," was a lifetime high. If I could do it again, I'd do it in a heartbeat.

During my time in the service, the thought of continuing the development of flying discs was always niggling in the back of my mind. With the war's end and me back home, it was time to think again about developing "Flittin' Discs."

9

HOW GOOD COULD IT GET?

THE WAR IN EUROPE WAS OVER. I came home to a family that Lu had increased by one…another baby girl.

Having been a POW, the Air Force treated Lu and me to a lifestyle that bordered on that of the rich-and-famous. We were quartered in the super-luxurious Santa Monica Bay Club. The Air Force had confiscated the beautifully-appointed building to assess and correct the possible mental and physical disabilities of returned POWs. That I was mentally alert and physically fit didn't matter…it was mandated that I submit to the rehabilitation program.

What a life! Hardly any demands on our time. Available were free tickets and transportation to anything and everything. Lu and I felt *obligated* to take advantage of all kinds of government-sponsored freebies. We rode horses, played golf, went to stage shows, danced to big bands, and slept late. We took advantage of everything; even went to an opera. Alas, too soon duty called and our paradise evaporated.

The war with Japan was still on. For a few months outside Bakersfield, California I flew bombardiers and navigators around so they could collect their flight pay. When the war ended, the Air Force rationalized that they had too many pilots. I was discharged during late-December 1945.

One of the forms I had signed while at the Club allowed that I didn't care about volunteering for additional service in the South Pacific. The war with Japan was being won without me. That form went into my (permanent military) 201 file.

During 1951, I attempted to re-enlist and fly in the Korean War. The interviewing generals reviewed my 201 file and noticed that there was a flaw in my military past: "We see you opted not to serve in the South Pacific. If we should ever run out of pilots...."

The denial turned out to be the most fortuitous thing that could have happened. I got to stay safely at home, and in time, develop an improved, round plastic thing that became the Frisbee.

10

THE REAL WORLD

With the air force subsidy canceled, it was necessary to find another source of income. Having only *de*construction experience breaking rocks in a rock pit, I lied about my construction experience and joined a carpenter's union as a two-year apprentice. (There are times when one must exaggerate one's experiences in the furtherance of one's career.) Lu's dad had to show me what tools to buy.

My first day on the job did *NOT* go well. I was teamed with a cooper—a journeyman carpenter whose entire construction experience was limited to constructing barrels. He could build barrels. I could break rocks. We made a most formidable construction team.

Under the supervision of the carpenter foreman, we hammered together a wooden, pyramid-shaped concrete form and installed it in its dirt hole. When filled with hardened concrete the pier would support part of a multi-storied building.

The form *should* have been secured firmly to the ground....
It wasn't!

As wet concrete poured into the form, it created side pressure which lifted the form out of its hole. (Why hadn't the foreman noticed that the form wasn't properly anchored to the ground?) The cooper and I became instant victims of the laws of liquid physics. The job supervisor didn't wait to hand us paychecks representing one day's labor. The construction team of barrel-maker and stone-breaker hadn't made it through their first day. How humiliating....

If journeyman carpenters (barrel-makers) didn't know any more about construction than I did, shouldn't I get the same pay? In another part of the city, at a different union hall, I lied again and became a highly-inexperienced journeyman carpenter. In those days labor unions would accept anything that was warm and able to come up with the wherewithal it took to join!

11

PRUDENCE

THE WAR HAD CURTAILED our redesigning cake pans. The war was over. There still burned within our three communal breasts (Lu, me and Dad) the desire to build a better flippin' device.

Someone had suggested that to protect an original idea, it might be prudent to have dated drawings of the idea mailed (registered and postmarked) to three different individuals. The suggestion was taken seriously.

Courtesy of the Air Force, I had learned the rudiments of what makes things fly. I took pencil to paper and diagramed what I believed would be a flying disc far superior to that of a flying cake pan.

The rim's rounded profile resembled the leading edge of an airplane's wing. I envisaged that the weight of a wire (possibly spring-tempered) located in a spinning disc's rim would add greater gyroscopic stability to a disc in flight. Then, in a moment of divine inspiration, six "arcuate vanes" were added to the top of the sketched disc. The vanes would act as a turbine, spinning air off the top of the disc, which would increase lift,

FLAT FLIP FLIES STRAIGHT! — Book One, Part I

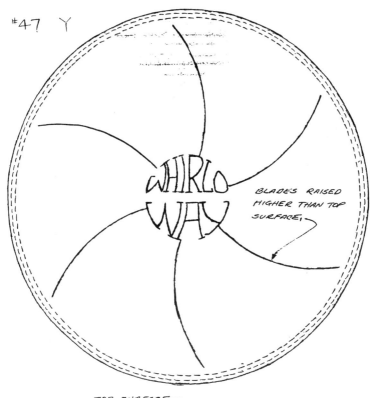

WHIRLO-WAY — The draftsman's rendering of Fred's original design for a flying disc — 1946
This drawing became the blueprint for the 1948 Flyin-Saucer—the world's first plastic flying disc.

thereby prolonging the duration of its flight. The addition of the wire and the vanes was *not* based on sound aerodynamic principles.

The envelope in which Fred sent the Whirlo-Way drawing to himself at his dad's address.

The disc in the drawing was given the name Whirlo-Way. (The name "Whirlo-Way" was a double-entendre—one meaning referring to the launching of the disc, the other relating to "Whirlaway," a racehorse making a name for himself at the time.) The dated sketches were given to a draftsman to professionalize. Registered/postmarked copies were then mailed to my dad, to me, and to a third party (whose name is long forgotten). Dad's address was used as my "permanent address."

A benevolent father let me take sole credit for "A device designed by Walter Frederick Morrison, Sept. 10th, 1946."

It's come to pass that the registered mailings had indeed been "prudent." Until someone shows up with an earlier-dated, registered drawing , I'm the original flying disc "dreamer-upper."

12

LIFE BEFORE "DISCDOM"

AFTER THE WAR available rentals in the L.A. area didn't exist. People put their names on waiting lists hoping for a vacancy. We were fortunate. We had been living in Lu's folks' home, but when they sold the house, we had to locate elsewhere. Lu's parents had built a home in Baywood Park. Baywood Park was a small, slowly-developing, sandy subdivision located midway up and on the California coast, across the bay from Morro Bay City. San Luis Obispo is eleven miles inland.

Clarence, Lu's dad, sold us on the idea of moving to Baywood Park. Lots were cheap: twenty-five dollars down and twenty-five dollars a month mortgage. Clarence suggested we buy a surplus 16´ X 16´ army tent to live in while I built a house. Clarence would see to it that his favorite daughter lived in the best of a very restrictive environment. He would help me put the tent together and later provide the know-how and assist in the construction of the house.

Chapter 12 — Life Before Discdom

Space in the tent was limited (very limited) for a family of four, but we had everything it took to make the place livable. It had a wood floor up off the sand, double-hung windows, and a framed, lockable front door. There was everything you'd find in a small (very small) house including an add-on for a shower, hot water heater, and a thing to sit on when required. The septic tank was two wooden barrels fastened together with bolts. The lights came on at the flip of a switch. It did get cold in the winter and ungodly hot in the summer, but the tent kept the rain off. The wigwam served its purpose for about a year and a half.

Baywood Park was *NOT* cosmopolitan. Only the two-lane road leading into and out of the sparsely populated settlement was paved. Building permits were unheard of. The "Civic Center" consisted of a small grocery store run by an Indian, a two-gravity-pumps gas station, and a small, corrugated tin office that housed the real-estate agent who had sold us our lot. The bay itself was scenic when the tide was in; a stinkin' mud flat when it was out! The area had one redeeming factor: construction was booming and people to do the constructing were scarce.

Just north of Morro Bay was a recently discontinued naval station. Post-war construction materials were hard to come by. Result…the buildings were being picked clean for their reusable building materials. Lumber was available for the nail-pulling. Electrical wire, pipe, and plumbing fixtures for the yanking. The major portion of our future home's building materials came from that naval station.

(So, I was a vandalizer…the price was right!)

When the unfinished two-bedroom house became livable, we abandoned our tent for the more expansive abode. Baywood Park's inhabitants were a friendly lot. At night we played canasta and bridge in neighbors' homes. We had enough space to host square dancing in our dining room. (It helped stick the tile down.) Life was definitely on the improve!

How does all this relate to the eventuality of Frisbees?

HEAT!

We needed heat in the tent for comfort, and hot water for its multiple uses. Butane was the most economical source of heat. A company named Franscioni and Davis was supplying the area's butane. A guy named Warren Franscioni sold us appliances for the tent, personally installed the butane tanks, connected the appliances, and then furnished the gas—first for the tent and later for the house.

That's how the Morrisons came to know a person who would become very important in our lives.

It's inconceivable what the future would have held for the Morrisons if Warren Franscioni hadn't had gas....

13

THE BIRTH OF PLASTIC DISCDOM

IT WAS A GREAT TIME for inexperienced construction workers (like me). Building was booming. Contractors had a hard time getting building materials, but they'd hire guys (like me) anyway, and hope that when some building material was delivered, the guys (like me) could be taught what to do with it. It was a great learning period for me—one that wouldn't have been available under current conditions.

1947—Franscioni had seen the progress I was making on our house. He hired me to make the foundations for two large butane storage tanks, liked the results, and put me to work making his butane installations. A company pickup was provided to do the company's business and for my personal use.

(The job had one extremely unpleasant aspect: crawling under old houses through the residue left behind by generations of varmints!)

The exact time and date Warren Franscioni flipped his first cake pan isn't important. That it happened while I was working for him is. Warren took to pan flippin' like a duck takes to water. The guy was a natural.

I told him about my unsuccessful prewar attempts to come up with a marketable metal flying disc. He perked up when I showed him the Whirlo-Way drawing and I suggested molding 'em in plastic. He liked the idea and agreed that if a suitable plastic were available, manufacturing plastic discs for the market had merit. He wanted to find out if a suitable plastic might exist. We decided to see if there was such a plastic.

Neither Franscioni nor I knew anything about plastics. The plastic industry was still in its infancy. (Milk still came in glass bottles.) We *did* know that new plastics were being formulated all the time. What we were looking for was a flexible plastic that could withstand constant pounding. Was there such a plastic? An answer likely lay in metropolitan southern California. We went looking.

We stumbled on Southern California Plastic Company (SCP) in Glendale, California. We told Ed Kennedy, vice-president of the company, what our mission was about. He gave us a tour of the plant, all the while explaining the basics of injection molding. He then steered us to Eastman Plastics, a company that produced raw plastics. Eastman's engineers assured us that such a suitable flexible plastic *was* available. They donated eight large-enough and thick-enough, lathe-compatible blocks of hard plastic we could use to make prototypes.

(I've never thought the name of that hard plastic needed remembering. It's been widely spread around that it was

Chapter 13 — The Birth of Plastic Discdom

"Tenite"? If that's what it was…okay…whatever. The only time we ever used the stuff was to make the prototypes.)

Assured that producing a flexible plastic flying disc was doable, Franscioni committed to financing an injection mold. We had agreed to a partnership. It was time to make the agreement legal. Franscioni, his mother, and mother-in-law would finance the disc mold and all future expenses, until such time that the business was self-supporting.

Franscioni's attorney drew up a draft for a fifty-fifty partnership agreement between the Franscionis and the Morrisons. We reviewed the draft with our attorney and suggested some changes (more about that later). With nothing invested but an unprotected idea, Lu and I weren't in a position to be too critical of the draft's terms. Franscioni was eager to get going with the creation of the flying disc mold. The go-ahead was given to create the mold without a signed contract between the interested parties.

The absence of a signed contract had diverse unintended consequences.

14

THE FIRST DISC DESIGN REFINED

*B**EING FORMER AIR FORCE PILOTS,* both Franscioni and I had been exposed to the basics of flight. We knew why an airfoil (wing) creates lift (Bernoulli's Principle). We knew that some of a plane's instruments were controlled by gyroscopes. A Frisbee disc is basically a rotating airfoil stabilized by the rim's gyroscopic action; simply put, a "gyroscopic airfoil."

Bernoulli did good coming up with the laws of physics that govern flight. Unfortunately he didn't concern himself with torque. Torque is present in everything that rotates—engines, propellers, etc...including flittin' discs. Torque becomes a major factor when a Frisbee loses its forward momentum and begins to slow its spin. Torque takes over and causes a hovering disc to go twisting off in some direction other than where it was meant to be caught.

(The "wire idea" included in the Whirlo-Way drawing was meant to increase gyroscopic stability and delay the effects of torque. When Ed Kennedy at Southern California Plastic was shown the drawing he advised: "Molding a wire hoop in the disc's rim may impair the disc's flexibility and certainly, *CONSIDERABLY* increase the cost of molding."
The "wire idea" was dropped!)

Chapter 14 — The First Disc Design Refined

Having taken drafting in high school, I volunteered to take on the task of designing the perfect flying disc. The goal was to combine a rotating wing with a gyroscopic rim in a proportion that produced the most desirable flight characteristics…in an affordable product. First, since the Whirlo-Way drawing had no dimensions, we had to agree on a diameter for the disc. That done, and using French curves (yeah!), I proceeded to envision and draw out maybe a dozen different cross-sections for a disc. Surely *ONE* of the designs represented the ultimate flittin' disc?

But we had only eight blocks of plastic to work with. So the eight cross-sections we divined had the best chance of producing the best flight characteristics were selected to be made into prototypes. Stiff cardboard templates were copied from the chosen drawings. A lathe operator would then use the templates as patterns for the prototypes. The prototype that produced the very best test results would be the one that would become the first plastic flying disc.

15

ELEPHANT WHACHAMACALLEMS?

*S*OMEONE RECOMMENDED a local San Luis Obispo machinist as being highly competent. I expected to see a spotless machine shop complete with all sorts of metal-working equipment. Inside the garage behind the lathe operator's house stood a lathe. The lathe was the *ONLY* piece of metal-working equipment in the dirt floor garage! That was cause for concern...but the guy *did* come highly recommended.

Budding inventors are a cautious breed...sagaciously secretive. I had labeled the drawing accompanying the templates "diaphragm for elephants." Manufacturing opportunists would *not* be allowed to know what it was that would soon be inundating the nation. If we were to protect ourselves from the business world's predatory "knock-offers," secrecy had to be uppermost. We were playing our cards "close to the vest"!

The lathe operator was no fool. He recognized right away that the finished product was not going to be used to protect lady pachyderms from pregnancy. The guy was blessed with a sense of humor. We decided to trust him with the truth.
His eyes lit up! He would be a fellow conspirator and keep our secret.

Chapter 15 — Elephant Whachamacallems?

The machinist's wife was something else! She was an incredibly curious nuisance. That she was naive is an understatement. She would look at the drawing's title and then ask questions like: "Why would an elephant need a contraceptive? Would the final product be flexible? Did one size fit all? Was there really a demand for such a device?" The machinist had a hard time keeping a straight face.

All did *not* go well! Our lathe operator had a problem justifying his reputed competency. He had trouble maintaining the thin tolerances required across the tops of the discs. Two of the prototypes were ruined when he cut through the thin upper surface. (He complained that the plastic didn't have the same turning characteristics as metal.) The number of testable prototypes had been reduced from eight to six.

(A nagging thought: Did the best configuration for our flying disc wind up on the machinist's cuttin' room floor?)

On the day we picked up the finished prototypes, to further magnify the wife's frustrations, I mused aloud to Franscioni that a marine biologist had called, inquiring if the diaphragms could be adapted to whales? We left with the prototypes, leaving the wife to ponder the feasibility of birth controlling the world's largest mammals in an oceanic environment.

16

FLYIN-SAUCERS BECOME REAL!

WE HAD SIX PROTOTYPES TO TEST. Lu, Franscioni and I gave them a real good flipping—indoors and out—on calm days and not-too-windy days. In the process, two of the brittle (Tenite?) prototypes didn't get caught, and shattered. Attempting to repair the fractured discs would have been a pointless endeavor. The best performer of the four remaining prototypes would be the "Chosen One"...the one that Southern California Plastic (SCP) would duplicate with an injection mold. With the creation of the mold and its installation in a plastic injection press, the first editions ever of plastic flying discs, *hot off the press,* would inaugurate the "Dawn of Discdom."

A lot of unidentified flying objects (UFOs) were being reported by the national media in 1947. The term "flying saucers" was being used to define the sightings. We were developing a saucer-shaped flying object. Ergo, we had a name for our disc: "FLYING SAUCER." In the process of SCP's creating the mold, the name "FLYIN-SAUCER" and the six arcuate vanes were engraved in the top of the mold.

As related in Chapter 11, the vanes were supposed to act as a turbine while the disc was spinning in flight, thereby reducing the air pressure on the top of the disc to increase the airfoil's lift. More lift would extend a disc's flight time. Right?...

Chapter 16 —Flyin-Saucers Become Real

WRONG!

When we had actual Flyin-Saucers to flip it was clear the vanes weren't performing as anticipated. The finished product didn't fly any better than its prototype. The expected benefit of the vanes was an assumption without foundation and an unnecessary expense while the mold was being constituted. The vanes might have given the Saucers the appearance of serving a purpose and added a degree of glamour. To have potential customers think otherwise would have been imprudent.

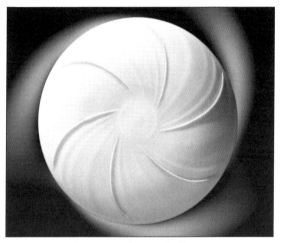

The "Rotary Fingernail Clipper"

Besides being dysfunctional the vanes were capable of causing injury. The slightest breeze could cause a Flyin-Saucer to suddenly lift as it was about to be caught. A tardy reaction to an abrupt lift and the rotating vanes could peel back one's fingernails. Later, having experienced the pain, we began referring to 'em privately as "Rotary Fingernail Clippers"... a feature of the Saucers that didn't need advertising!

17

WHAT'S A PIPCO?

WHILE WAITING FOR THE SAUCER MOLD to be developed, the Boys from Obispo weren't idle. Since the Los Angeles area was where we were going to introduce our flippable marvel, obviously we were gonna need an office where we could process the anticipated flood of Saucer orders.

We rented an office in the Glendale, California Post Office building. The Postmaster required the name of our business for his records. We didn't have one. Flyin-Saucers were going to be our only product for now. But we had to consider the future! After extended and anguished deliberation a carefully-crafted string of words was opted for that would appropriately describe our future business operations, to wit: *"If it's a PIPCO Product It's a Pip."* "PIPCO" would be the acronym for our newly-founded company. The acronym PIPCO was given to the Postmaster for his records.

Having satisfied the Postmaster with a name for our business, we opened our away-from-home "office." It was a relatively small "office." There was only one door. The walls and floors were bare. The single room was unfurnished and phoneless, but…we had an "office"!

Chapter 17 — What's a PIPCO?

Remembering back...contrary to our expectations, orders for Flyin-Saucers never flooded PIPCO's office. Fact is, I never saw any kind of mail delivered to our office. If orders for Flyin-Saucers, or mail related to the Saucers ever found its way into our office, I wasn't made aware of it. It's possible Franscioni picked up mail when I wasn't present. Had there been anything pertinent to the Saucers sent to the office, I'm sure he would have shared it with me. We *DID* get one piece of "junk mail" every month: a statement from the Postmaster for the rental of the PO Box we were using as PIPCO's "Main Office."

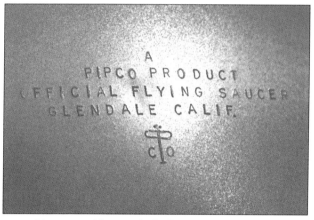

PIPCO name and logo on the back of a Flyin Saucer (FS8/D)

Franscioni did the bookkeeping. I was content not to be involved in that end of the business. I never saw the checks he used to pay the bills, so I don't know if "PIPCO" was printed on the checks(?) Was the name PIPCO ever registered as a legal entity? Not that I was aware of during the time I was associated with Franscioni. When was the PO Box Office canceled? I don't know that either.

The acronym PIPCO has been erroneously interpreted on the Internet and other published places as "Partners In Plastic." If the clock could be rolled back, I'm sure Franscioni and I would have preferred that PIPCO be the acronym for "Partners In Plastic." Back then, we were bent on promoting the product and letting the World know that future PIPCO products would be the greatest. "If it's a PIPCO Product It's a Pip" seemed like an appropriate slogan for the business.

(I'm ashamed to admit it, but the corny slogan and its acronym PIPCO were my ideas.)

A sudden appalling thought! "Partners In Plastic"? Who'd want to spend eternity with some guy encased in a solid block of plastic?!

18

HORROR STORY

SOMETIME DURING 1948, SCP's injection molding press began moving back and forth injecting hot, liquefied plastic into our mold and ejecting the finished product: flippable plastic FLYIN-SAUCERS. It took twenty-eight seconds to mold a single Saucer. That computes to approximately 3,000 every twenty-four hours. The mold worked perfectly.

The first production run of Saucers was one of overwhelming frustration caused by the incredibly stupid selection of colors used to mold the Saucers. I wasn't present at the time the color decisions were made. Franscioni denied having been involved in the color selections. Kennedy didn't lay the blame on Franscioni nor did he take responsibility for the molding debacle. I'd expected the molded Saucers would be bright, eye-catching colors like red and orange, or yellow. I was nearly traumatized when I saw what we were stuck with: one thousand "black" and one thousand "powder blue" Flyin-Saucers! Gawd....

The first run of Saucers was meant to be the grand introduction of the first flippable, catchable plastic entity that was going to set new standards for the nation's playtime pastimes— and what they were was an unattention-getting *black* and *blue*. Had we been smart, we'd have refused to accept the first batch of Saucers. Why we didn't demand that they be replaced with brightly-colored Saucers escapes me.

To avoid that occurrence from reoccurring, it was made specifically clear to Ed Kennedy and all at SCP that, unless otherwise specified, in the future only eye-catching, brightly-colored Saucers would be acceptable!

During the molding process, an unfortunate circumstance occurs which we had to accept. When changing from one color of disc to another, the new colored plastic granules are poured on top of the previous colored granules in the molding machine's hopper. The gravity-fed granules liquefy and combine as they enter the mold's injection nozzle and fill the mold. The result is a casting that's a mixture of the two colors. The end product is called "variegated." Generally, variegated Saucers were eyesores. Black and blue variegated Saucers most resembled great big, round, ugly black and blue bruises. Not pleasant sights to behold. Ugh!

There was one notable exception. When changing colors from red to white, or vice versa, the variegated Saucers resembled something good enough to eat—like liquid strawberries poured over vanilla ice cream. *Yum!*

Since most variegated discs resembled an unpleasant digestive eruption, we soon referred to 'em as "Vomit Models"...or just plain "Vomits." Fortunately the number of Vomits we had to

Chapter 18 — Horror Story

get rid of after each color change was limited. Later, when demonstrating the Saucers at fairs, we learned that people tended to buy the same color Saucer that was being demonstrated. People watching the demonstrators and listening to our pitch were given the option of buying the Vomit Models we openly referred to as "airsick, seasick and carsick." The unexpected irreverent references to the discs invariably evoked vocal expressions of jocularity (laughter). Of course, the Saucer being demonstrated was a Vomit!

A typical later Style "Vomit Model" (FS7/AT)

Once, later, the horror story got retold. While demonstrating the Saucers at a fair, we were in danger of running out of discs. In desperation we had Kennedy mold us two thousand Saucers with whatever colored plastic they had on hand. Something got lost in the translation. Either that or SCP seized the opportunity to clean out their plastic dregs! What we got were two thousand yellowish, greenishly-brown mottled Vomits that were so repulsive we willingly drastically cut the price just to get rid of 'em.

Ordinarily, we never sold 'em for less than a buck. The two thousand super-ugly Vomits were got rid of at our cost: twenty-five cents. It was a happy day when we saw the last of those dreadful Vomits. I'd have gladly trashed 'em!

Butyrate, I think(?), was the name of the plastic used to mold the original Flyin-Saucers. Whatever it was, it was tolerably flexible when it was warm. After sundown, when things cooled off, it was a different story: the plastic lost its flexibility. When demonstrating the Saucers at night before a crowd, catching an incoming disc became *very* important. The cooled Saucers—not always, but often enough—fractured when impacting a hard surface (like asphalt). A broken Saucer, lying on the ground, sometimes in pieces, was NOT conducive to sales…and once-attentive crowds tended to quickly disperse.

In the beginning, when we placed a Saucer order with Kennedy, we had to stand in line waiting to get 'em. Other previous orders had priority. When Kennedy realized he had a mold in his factory that was making his firm a killing every time a Saucer popped out of the mold, our orders for Saucers were filled forthwith!

19

INSTANT SUCCESS DENIED!

NOW THAT WE HAD SOMETHING TO SELL—two thousand less-than-attractive black and blue Saucers—the time had come to get crackin'. Expectations ran high. We had a great product. We were impassioned with the desire to introduce and promote it. Get ready America! Get ready for an item so novel that it would alter the recreational lifestyles of millions of people. The masses were about to experience *"The Happy Way to Flip Their Lids!"* We were champing at the bit to get started.

To be properly merchandised, the Saucers needed to be displayed in eye-catching, see-through plastic bags. Kennedy had lined us up with an advertising agency that designed and produced such bags. The finished bags would depict a handsome young lad backhandedly flipping a Saucer. Off to the side would be "How To" flipping instructions. The young lad and instructions were to be printed in royal blue. I thought the bags were sure to do exactly what they were supposed to do: favorably show off the Saucers. Unfortunately the bags were still in the design stage as we prepared to sally forth and spring our airborneable prodigy on the populace.

We had a plan. We would give sporting-goods store managers the opportunity to be the first to display the Saucers on their counters. When we eventually had bags we would contact chain-store buyers. Once Saucers had established a healthy bottom line, we would consider signing up with a major distributor—one who could handle national distribution. Brilliant? (We were *SO* naive!)

So we went calling on sporting-goods store managers. We weren't received with the enthusiastic reception we had anticipated. We were met with unexpected and disturbing resistance. We got the same reception from other store managers. Getting store managers and chain-store buyers to get off their duffs and witness the wondrous capabilities of a demonstrated Flyin-Saucer never happened. The general response to our sales pitch was: "No unheard-of, ugly black or blue, round pieces of plastic were going to clutter up their valuable counter space! Thank you...*NEXT!*"

Ed Kennedy was aware of our problem. He believed the Saucers had considerable potential. Naturally he wanted his company to be molding the item when the demand for Saucers went "big-time." He suggested we go talk to the manager of the Woolworths store in downtown Glendale. (Kennedy may have had an influencing relationship with the store's manager?) We went.

The manager watched us demonstrate a Saucer on the sidewalk outside his store. He was impressed. Possibly career-oriented, he allowed us to erect a five-foot-high chicken-wire barricade inside and across the front of his store. The chicken-wire would keep customers from interfering with our demonstrations.

Chapter 19 — Instant Success Denied!

The store opened at nine. Naked Saucers had been stacked next to the cash register nearest the store's entrance. (The plastic display bags still hadn't been delivered.) We commenced flippin'. The Saucers in flight attracted onlookers. We explained the basics of flippin' and let those who wanted to try it out. Out of the corner of our eyes, we watched the stack of Saucers diminish. More Saucers were placed next to the register. The store manager was all smiles. He had shown initiative and exceptional business acumen when he allowed the Saucers to be introduced in his store. Surely he had enhanced his future with the Woolworths chain-store hierarchy!

Our high expectations were finally being gratified. We were witnessing, for the first time, the public's near-spontaneous, favorable acceptance of our product when it was demonstrated. Enormous financial rewards lay just over the horizon. We were on our way to joining the rich-and-famous.

Suddenly...*DISASTER!* A mis-tossed curving Saucer (mine) dove into and wiped out a fingernail polish display. The formerly-delighted store manager came unglued. His career was in jeopardy. He was traumatized by what seemed to us to be a minor, restorable mishap. Mollification didn't work. Reconciliation was out of the question. Here, paraphrased, are his near-incoherent terminating remarks: "Take those (expletive deleted) plastic things and get the (expletive deleted) out of my store! And, take that (expletive deleted) chicken-wire monstrosity with ya...*NOW!*"

Woe was us! We had tasted (but oh so briefly) the euphoria of budding success. The mere collapse of a fingernail polish display had done us in.

We were out of the store in time for lunch!

20

SAL(I)VATION?

*S*O IT WENT. The only way the Saucers were gonna sell was if they were demonstrated. To help pay expenses, we'd been demonstrating the discs on weekends at beaches and public parks, but the sales weren't offsetting overhead—like motels, eating, gas for the car, etc. Income was becoming a pressing necessity. Throwing in the towel and going home was becoming a distinct possibility.

We had considered approaching Knott's Berry Farm, a theme park in Anaheim. The Farm was open every day and attracted a lot of people. We'd come to realize that people—in large numbers—were a vital necessity if the Saucers were going to bail us out of our pending financial crisis. If the Farm's management would let us work there…?

We opted against the Knott's Berry Farm idea. We'd have to rent a place to live. Working full-time meant we'd be separated from our families for long periods.

A possible solution to our financial dilemma developed when someone suggested we try getting in the L.A. County Fair. The '48 Fair was coming up shortly—the first three weekends of September. We went to see the Fair Manager.

Chapter 20 —Sal(i)vation?

A fair manager has two very important obligations to the organizations that sponsor fairs: make 'em money (through the sale of space to concessionaires), and protect 'em from lawsuits.

We approached the Fair Manager, showed him a Saucer, and explained how we would like to demonstrate 'em. The Manager had instant visions of potential lawsuits. He was vehement: "Are you guys *NUTS*?! Throw the equivalent of a boomerang in and among my fair attendees? *NEVER!*" Disappointed, we left the Manager's office knowing that our Flyin-Saucers had no chance of being demonstrated where we might do some good.

Just for the hell of it we went to flippin' a Saucer in the street between two huge exhibit buildings. An exhibitor, who had a booth in one of the exhibit buildings, watched us doing our thing, and observed how the Saucers grabbed the interest of passersby. He approached us and struck up a conversation. The conversation got around to our mentioning the Fair Manager's negativity. The exhibitor offered that he had "friends" in the front office. For a piece of the action, he would "speak" to his friends. We were desperate. We agreed to pay the exhibitor a percentage of our sales. All sales would be made from his booth. He went to speak to his friends.

He came back. "Go see the Manager." We went. The Manager's demeanor had undergone a remarkable reformation. He was apologetic. He wanted to "talk." Flyin-Saucers no longer resembled boomerangs. "Now, what was it you wanted? Of *course* space is available for you to demonstrate your discs. Would space alongside one of the exhibit buildings be satisfactory?" It would! The assigned space just happened to be across the street from the exhibit building in which our benevolent exhibitor had his booth. (Our boy had been thumking ahead when he "talked" to the Fair's management.)

Turned out we had been given a great location. The two exhibit buildings were separated by a hundred-foot-wide street. Opposing twenty-five-foot-wide access doors in the middle of the buildings allowed people to walk back and forth between them. People passing between the two buildings couldn't miss us. Our space, alongside the building and starting at the edge of the access door, extended to the end of the building. (We had more space than we could use.) Permanent floodlights attached high on the side of our building, with a little adjustment, made our space the best-lit area in the nighttime street.

The Fair's attendance the previous year had been a record-setter. If the '48 crowds were equally large, if the weather cooperated, and if the people liked what we had to offer, we believed we had a chance of making out. Considering our financial situation, it was make out…or else!

The fair opened. We went to demonstrating. Everything worked in our favor. The black and blue Saucers had been sold. We had bright red, yellow, and orange Saucers. The flow of people passing between the buildings was beyond all expectations. The sight of plastic discs flittin' through the air demanded their attention. People during that era had money and were willing to spend. Our exhibitor in the building was kept busy exchanging Saucers for dollars.

Demonstrating Airborne Crockery at fairs had found us a way to go!

21

DEFTLY DEVIOUS

*D*URING MY YOUTHFUL, TEENAGE PAST, I'd interrupt a passerby, point down at his or her feet and with authority warn: "Hold it! Watch it! Step over the wire! Step over the wire, please!"

Invariably the passerby would look down and become confused trying to avoid the nonexistent "wire." When the light came on and he realized that he'd been had, the reaction was almost always the same: "Oh, YOU…!" More often than not there'd be a friendly punch on the shoulder. I only did it in front of friends. It invariably produced some sniggerings. Try it some time for laughs. (Of course, there's the risk you might get knocked on your ass.)

At the '48 L.A. Fair, occasionally it was necessary to stop demonstrating and talk to the distributor at the Saucer Booth. Getting there was difficult because of the closely-packed crowds. One day, for no good reason, I held my hand aloft and pretended I was pulling a wire: "Let us through, please!

Watch out for the wire!" Franscioni embellished the deception. Following a few paces behind me with a hand held high keeping the imaginary wire taut and glancing up at the nonexistent "wire" he'd warn: "Watch the wire. Watch it, please." People would look up, "see" an imagined wire and peel out of the way. It was absurd—and remarkably effective. The way to the Saucer Booth was expedited. The people who had complied with our warnings to "Watch it" and then realized they'd been conned were more often then not amused by the absurdity of it all.

We began using the "wire" in our demonstrations. A "pitch" evolved that matched our demonstration. (For those who don't know what a "pitch" is, it's the over-selling vocalizing a "pitchman" lays on the "tip." Tips are the people that stop to watch and listen as the pitchman expounds the glories of his product.) All it took for us to build a tip was to start flippin'.

A Flyin-Saucer being flown on an "invisible wire" must have been an irresistible force. Watchers just naturally congregated at the sight of the "Airborne Crockery." When a fair amount of people had assembled to see what was going on, one of us would turn, face the tip and begin the pitch. "Folks, what you're witnessing being demonstrated here, today, is something you've *NEVER* seen before!" Holding the "wire" stretched between our hands, and moving the "wire" up and down, we'd declare: "This is Invisible Wire. You don't see wire like this every day!" Then, pointing down to someone standing close, assert with authority: "You're standing on the wire! Please…Get off the wire…Please!"

We began the Saucer demonstration by showing the tip how the Saucer was "attached" to the "wire" and declaring positively

Chapter 21 — Deftly Devious

that "Wherever the wire goes, that's where the Saucer goes." Fifty feet away, and simulating a tightly-held "wire" was the catcher (me or Franscioni). "If the wire is kept taut between us, the Saucer will fly straight!" A Flyin-Saucer was then flipped "straight" to the other end of the "wire." He reattached the Saucer to the "wire" and flipped a straight flip back. "Isn't that a-MAAAzing…"

Following the straight flip, it was explained how an appropriate amount of "slack" in the "wire" permitted skips and curves. Skips and curves were then demonstrated in the same manner as the straight flip.

We tried to synchronize our movements while maneuvering the "wire." The more we worked the "wire," and our accuracy improved, the more realistic and convincing the demonstration became. So convincing, in fact, that on one occasion, we had convinced a less-than-perceptive, possibly myopic individual that there was indeed a wire. He became argumentative when a more-perceptive observer of the "wire demonstration" tried to explain that the "wire" was an illusion. The verbal exchanges between the two became more than heated—they were about to become combatants! Pacifiers stepped in and ended the confrontation. The scene wasn't real. Anybody with an ounce of intelligence and tolerable vision had to know that there warn't no wire.

There were times when a head-down, unobserving person would wander between us. Visualize the individual's antics after a Saucer had just whisked by his head, and he's being yelled at: "Hey! Watch out! You're interfering with the wire!" The poor guy looks around, is confused, doesn't know what he's doing wrong, and doesn't know which way to turn.

Impolite? Yep…but it got a laugh. Sometimes the picked-on individual joined in the tip's laughter. Sometimes we were the recipients of a finger-wave.

After we'd finish demonstrating the capabilities of a Flyin-Saucer, the one holding the other end of the "wire" was "pulled in" and the "wire" was left lying tangled on the asphalt. Our closing spiel usually went like this: "Folks…what you've been witnessing are the wondrous capabilities of Invisible Wire. This wire comes in hundred-foot rolls. We charge a cent a foot and give you a free Flyin-Saucer with every purchase. Wait! That's not all! You have your choice of your Saucer's color. We have red, yellow, blue, and green—and three lovely shades of vomit: airsick, seasick and carsick." (It's not normal for pitchmen to refer to their merchandise in such unflattering terms. Our shocking reference to our product got laughs.)

Continuing: "Saucers are available across the street, through that big doorway, turn left, and go down the aisle to the large beer display where they're giving away *FREE BEER*. Our Saucer booth is across the aisle from the *FREE BEER* display."

(The guys running the beer exhibit were prohibited from selling their elixir, let alone *giving* it away. Doing so would have ended their employment. We knew that. Being regular guys, they went along with our deception. I think they enjoyed saying "No" to the freeloaders, and telling them where to go… even if it was only across the aisle. Complimentary Saucers went home with every one of 'em!)

With that we sat down in our deck chairs and watched the crowd of watchers head over to the doorway. Once they were gone, we got up and commenced to build a new tip.

Chapter 21 — Deftly Devious

Our demonstration, along with the pitch, was like nothing ever seen before. The size of the crowds the Saucers attracted were at times astonishing. We had fun doing it. The verbal interaction that went on with the people watching the demonstrations was part of the fun. We liked hearing the oohs and awwes when we pulled off something spectacular. Best of all: watching the Flyin-Saucers justifying their existence.

The fair ended. We had moved an extraordinary number of Saucers. Our benevolent exhibitor got his percentage—part of which, I assumed, went to the fair's management. The fair's management hadn't been threatened with lawsuits. We were told we'd be welcomed back the following year. I even got to send a little money home (a first). Obviously demonstrating Saucers at fairs was the way to go if the Saucers were going to produce immediate resources.

Our next stop was the ten-day Ventura County Fair. Our location wasn't the greatest. Wind off the Pacific Ocean discouraged the use of the "wire." We managed to do some good at night after the wind died down. But sales didn't equal expenses. The somewhat discouraging message we got from that fair was that not all fairs were Saucer sellers. The wind was a killer.

Fairs attract other fair managers looking for new exhibitors for *their* fairs. During the L.A. Fair, the Arizona State Fair Manager had introduced himself and suggested we go over to Phoenix and work his Fair. He assured us of a good location, and that the crowds would be sizable. We went, pulling a trailer-load of Saucers. We were given a fantastic location just inside the Fair's main gate. The streams of people coming and going couldn't help but see us. The weather was ideal. The crowds were receptive. The Saucers, the "wire," and our "pitch" combined to sell us out before the Fair ended. Everything had worked in our favor. The Fair Manager booked us for the next year's Fair. We left Arizona with money for the creditors.

For us the '48 fair season was history. We'd been away from home much too long and our asses were draggin'. No matter how lucrative the fairs had been, there never seemed to be a surplus. Franscioni blamed it on "overhead." I had no reason to doubt him. Molded Saucers, buying space at fairs, and living away from home were expensive. I needed to get home and get to providing some income. We went home and got reacquainted with our families.

The plan was to do it all again next year. Maybe next year a Promotin' Distributor would recognize the Saucer's latent potential, and make 'em what they were predestined to become…a national sensation!

22

PRELUDE TO CULMINATION

*T*HE 1949 FAIRS STARTED UP. We worked our way through those fairs we thought had the most potential. Some were moneymakers, some weren't. The L.A. County and Arizona Fairs were exceptionally good to us again. But the good ones didn't offset the not-so-good ones. A worthwhile bottom line seemed always to be just a kiss away. Almost in desperation we decided we'd try the fairs in Florida. New York snowbirds go to Florida to winterize. We loaded up the trailer with Saucers, and headed for the Sunshine State.

Florida believed in licensing. We had to buy state licenses for both the car and the trailer. Seemed like no matter where we started to flip—public parks, parking lots, wherever—a representative from some sort of agency would descend on us and require a license. Unless there was a glimmer of hope that there was a chance to sell a reasonable number of Saucers, we'd say "Thank you…No," and go elsewhere.

It's SOP that fair concessionaires (like us) would be charged a "nut" (fee) by a fair's management to display their wares. Only in Florida were we ever required to get a business license in addition to the "nut." Florida's licensing policies were an unanticipated nuisance and expense.

The first fair was in Tampa. Tampa was populated mostly by elderly retirees...not the type of people who get enthusiastic over Flyin-Saucers. Flippin' for the old folks didn't pay. We left before the fair was over. Next, we worked the fair at Orlando. We did a little better, but nuttin' to write home about....

Our only remaining hope to salvage anything from the trip was about to start at the Dade County Fair in Miami. Maybe the Miami Fair would be the bonanza that would help bail us out. We went truckin' down the Tamiami Trail to Miami and paid the Fair's entry fees. We were given space that we thought would be profitable. The Fair had a history of attracting sizable crowds. Hopes were running high.

The day the Fair opened a hurricane-type wind blew through the area. The ferris wheel was blown over. The carnival tents wound up in a neighboring county. The fairgrounds looked like a disaster area. There was no point in stickin' around. We left Florida worse off than when we arrived.

The road back to California passed through Lincoln, Nebraska. Their state fair was about to start. It was breezy, but we decided to gamble...maybe we'd get lucky? Overnight the breezes grew to a howling wind. We listened to the wind howl for a coupla days and gave up in despair. Adios Lincoln, Nebraska!

Back in southern California we worked the ten-day San Bernardino County Orange Show. Did real good there, but there was no way we were ever going to overcome the costly excursion to Florida. The hoped-for solution to our financial problems hadn't happened. The '49 fair season had been a disaster! It was "back to the barn" (carnival talk meaning "going home for the winter").

Chapter 22 — Prelude to Culmination

I was discouraged. Two years of chasing Saucers and there was nothing to financially justify the effort. I doubted that the Saucers had a future. Lu and I still didn't have a written Flyin-Saucer agreement with the Franscionis. The grind had certain physical drawbacks—one of 'em being the hole the Saucers had worn in the middle finger of my flippin' hand.

WHAT to do…?

23

QUITTIN' TIME

TWO YEARS OF EXPOSING FLYIN-SAUCERS to large numbers of fairgoers and the interest and sales they had created had, we believed, proven that the Saucers had the potential of being a mass-marketed item.

Saucers sold where they were demonstrated. So we had gone to beaches and public parks and done our thing—demonstrating and selling black and blue Saucers. Ridding ourselves of the ugly discs (which was good) helped pay our away-from-home expenses. Our lucking into the L.A. County Fair had shown us a way to sell the Saucers in quantity.

We realized early on that running our butts off chasing Saucers at fairs wasn't gonna make us millionaires. We had hoped that some enterprising promoter/distributor would come forward, offer to take over the promotion and distribution of the Saucers and make 'em a success. No such company, that I was made aware of, ever came forth.

Chapter 23 — Quittin' Time

It had been apparent for some time that Franscioni was experiencing financial difficulty. During late-1949 or early-1950 I had flown to Sacramento with him to meet with three potential financial backers. I didn't know who those people were, nor how he had become aware of 'em. Franscioni had handled all the Flyin-Saucer business stuff, so it was best that he did the talking. That meeting was made memorable when one of the potential financiers made the comment: "I don't have any faith in the present management." He was looking at me when he said it. The meeting ended. Nothing had been accomplished that I was aware of that would have resulted in the Saucer's salvation.

Workin' the fairs had kept me away from the family for extended periods. My contributions to the family's welfare had been miniscule. Lu had kept the wolves from the door bookkeeping for a "big-time" farmer. She'd kept the faith but her faith was wearing thin. The situation stunk! We sat ourselves down at the kitchen table, and did some serious evaluating. The Saucers hadn't provided the income we'd at first anticipated. Lu's and the kids' existence had been near the poverty level. Too much time was being spent away from home. The house was still in an unfinished state. There still wasn't a legal Saucer partnership agreement with the Franscionis. There was damn little positivity to consider.

Lu and I agreed. Opting out of the situation with Franscioni was the way to go. Early in 1950 I gave Franscioni the word that the Morrisons were bowing out. Franscioni accepted our decision without comment. I got the impression he was relieved. For over two years we had worked together without any major disagreements. The absence of a formal Partnership

Agreement had caused some uncertainty, but I always believed that would be worked out. The parting was accomplished without animosity.

Not having a legal Partnership Agreement made dissolving the relationship uncomplicated. There weren't any contractual entanglements (whereases and wherefores) to undo. There was no need for attorneys. The separation was simplicity itself.

The Flyin-Saucer mold was the major asset. Whatever other assets we had generated had been bought and paid for by Franscioni. It was fair and right that he should have total ownership of all the assets. That was it. The future of the Flyin-Saucers—if they had a future—depended solely on Franscioni.

Franscioni had been a major in the Air Force during WWII. He had mentioned that he might try reenlisting. On a February day in 1950, we shook hands and wished each other the best. The relationship was over.

I never saw, nor heard from Warren Franscioni again.

(So the ersatz Saucer Partnership failed to accomplish anything significant. I still find it astounding how the idea for the original flying disc—the "Whirlo-Way"— has metamorphosed into what it is today…it's called the Frisbee!)

24

BACK TO A FUTURE

CONSTRUCTION in the San Luis Obispo area had dried up while I'd been doing fair stuff. Work was so scarce I was having to leave the area to find it. The union hall had some jobs out in the California desert that nobody wanted. Why not soon became understandable. It was a two-and-a-half hour commute to an inferno; but putting beans on the table had a higher priority than waitin' it out for a comfortable work environment.

The job site was located close by a barren spot in purgatory called Cuyama. The spot consisted of a few sun-baked shacks and a small greasy-spoon cafe. Water had to be trucked in. Extravagantly-priced meals included a glass of water. By itself a glass of water cost a nickel. The construction had something to do with repressurizing an oil field.

During the week an open flat-bed trailer furnished with a sleeping bag served as a boudoir. On weekends it was home for a shave, shower, and a good meal. After several weeks spent laboring in a hotter-'n-hell wasteland, a fisherman friend in Baywood came to my rescue.

The cook on a shark boat my friend worked on had suddenly quit. The friend had recommended me as the cook's replacement. The boat's captain offered me the job: cookin' for a crew of three on his sixty-foot boat. The opportunity to escape the desert heat and labor in the ocean's cool breezes was irresistible. I gratefully dropped my hammer and grabbed a spatula. (I didn't know beans about cookin'!)

The boat's sole-purpose profitmaker was soup-fin sharks' livers (a major source of vitamin B). All night the boat drifted, dragging a five-mile-long gill net. My job was to prepare a dawn breakfast, then go topside and help the crew haul in the net. A lot of different types of oceanic livestock got itself tangled up in the net during the night. Only soup-fin sharks were kept—everything else was dumped overboard. After that there was lunch and dinner to put on the table.

After several trips out (usually lasting from two to three weeks each), I was beginnin' to get an occasional compliment on my cookin' (in lieu of uncomplimentary threats) when synthetic vitamin B came on the market. Demand for sharks' livers evaporated. The captain had to find a different use for his boat. The boat's new use didn't require a cook. (Or had he engaged a more accomplished chef?)

A future in the San Luis Obispo area was bleak! Lu and I had been considering moving back to southern California. I went south to L.A. and landed a carpenter job working on a multi-storied hotel whose construction was just getting started. Supposedly I'd be drawing a check for quite some time. A house was rented. Lu sold the Baywood house, gathered up the offspring, and joined me in Smogland. Finally a muchly desired permanent togetherness with a fairly dependable income had been reestablished.

Chapter 24 — Back to a Future

Payin' rent seemed like a financial dead end, so we made a down payment on a fairly good-sized lot on the rural fringe of a city called San Dimas. San Dimas is twenty-five miles east of L.A. Workin' after work and on weekends, an intended two-car garage and workshop materialized as a four-room with bath temporary dwelling. We moved in during '52. A short time later, with the birth of Walter "Bill" Morrison, we became a family of five.

The address of the place was 15838 Harvest Moon Street, San Dimas, California.

25

THE AWESOME FOURSOME

CONSTRUCTION JOBS IN THE L.A. BASIN were abundant. We weren't hurtin' for income, but we could always use a little supplementin'. The 1954 L.A. County Fair at Pomona was coming up. Flyin-Saucers had done very well there when Franscioni and I had worked it back in 1948 and 1949. If Flyin-Saucers were still available it might be worthwhile to give it another shot. A phone call was placed to Ed Kennedy, by then head honcho at SCP. Yes, he had the mold and could supply us Saucers…at twenty-eight cents each…*COD*.
(I couldn't have cared less *who* owned the mold, so I didn't ask. It was enough to know that Saucers could be had.)

Would the Fair Manager sell us space again? "Yes." The Fair Manager was the very same manager who, back in 1948, had compared Flyin-Saucers to boomerangs and said "No"… then changed his mind to "Yes." He remembered the '48 and '49 fairgoers' acceptance of the Saucers. We were given the same space we'd had before; and *Glory Be!*…there warn't no middleman. We could sell Saucers "on the spot" where they were being demonstrated. Saucer buyers wouldn't have to go in search of a Saucer booth in a crowded building. The "nut" (cost of our space) would be the same as the previous years: four hundred dollars.

Chapter 25 — The Awesome Foursome

I went to see Kennedy. He showed me a Saucer that had been molded from a flexible plastic I'd never heard of: polyethylene. The plastic's characteristics were ideal for the abuse Saucers were subjected to. Polyethylene—what a fantastic improvement over the original Flyin-Saucer plastic!

An order was placed for two thousand Saucers. The colors would be bright, primary colors: red, yellow and orange. Kennedy agreed to keep us supplied with Saucers should the need arise during the Fair. When the order was ready, two thousand Flyin Saucers were picked up at Kennedy's plant…at twenty-eight cents apiece…*COD!*

When Franscioni and I had worked fairs in the past, rest breaks and other interruptions took away from our demonstrating. Obviously, continuous demonstrations would have increased our sales.

Enter the Hoornbeeks. Lu's younger sister, Marge, and her husband, Paul, were family members who had been flipping Saucers from their inception. They were the best of the lot of the family's flippers. They hadn't achieved Lu's and my level of expertise (who could ever?)…but they were *GOOD!* We reached a mutually satisfactory money-sharing arrangement. We would work the L.A. County Fair together.

The joining of forces was most fortuitous. Marge and Paul had seen the Saucers demonstrated at the '48 and '49 fairs. They quickly picked up on the "wire" and "pitch" routine. Alternating flippers made it possible to demonstrate almost continuously. We didn't have to interrupt the demonstrating to transact sales. One of us was always available for that rewarding chore. Paul and I always did the "wire" and "pitch."

Marge was a near-duplicate of Lu: same bright smile, always cheerful, fun to be around, and good with customers. She flipped an accurate Saucer, but was uncomfortable makin' the "pitch." She acted mainly as our cashier, but would step in and spell one of us when needed.

Paul & Marge Hoornbeek demonstrating their accuracy with Pluto Platters in 1957

Paul, nicknamed "Wog" (like in polliwog), was one of a kind. He was tall and lean. He had a unique sense of humor, and enjoyed flaunting it. When he was at the business end of the demonstrations doin' the pitchin', he was in his element. His launching of a "crock" was smooth and, at the same time, awkwardly contorted. He was a *HOOT* to watch and listen to…and he was the most accurate disc flipper I've ever flipped with.

Chapter 25 — The Awesome Foursome

Paul was *NOT* a handsome man! I often accused Paul of being *"The Ugliest Man in the World."* I continually kidded him: "Don't die…you'll make me Number One!" His response was always: "Don't tell me what to do! You don't know me well enough to tell me what to do!" He gave up the ghost during the mid-seventies. Paul…if you can, look at what you did to me! *Damn your ever-lovin', disobeying black heart!*

A few days into the L.A. Fair it was obvious we were gonna need more Saucers. I ordered what I thought would be more than enough to last out the Fair. Kennedy provided additional Saucers as promised. The Saucers were the Fair's "hot item." At Fair's end, we were getting close to not having any…and we didn't owe Kennedy a dime.

Everything had worked swimmingly! We laughingly began referring to ourselves as *"The Awesome Foursome."* Never worked another fair without 'em!

The Arizona State Fair was coming up. The Awesome Foursome took a sizable order of Saucers over to Phoenix. We were given the same space that had been so profitable back in '48 and '49…just inside the Fair's main entrance. The Phoenix fairgoers liked what we had to offer. When the Fair ended, our pockets were jingling.

The Saucer income from fairs was most gratifying, but there was a price to pay. Demonstrating all day for days at a time was wearing—especially for the girls. We used over-the-counter ache and painkillers to ease the agony. We joked that cracker-sized aspirins were part of our survival kit. Sleep was *never* a problem.

Pitchmen are always looking for "hot" items to peddle. They keep tabs on everything on a fairground that's making money. They'll plagiarize anything they think will make 'em money!

Pitchmen usually work alone. Our method of "pitching the discs" included four people. Accuracy was vital and there was the rigorous physical element. I'm not aware of any pitchman, or anyone else, ever trying to duplicate the way we went about selling the Saucers.

As long as The Awesome Foursome flipped their lids at fairs they (we) had the "Ex"...fair lingo for *Ex-clusive!*

26

A MOLD OF OUR OWN

*S*UPPLYING US WITH COPIOUS NUMBERS of Saucers at twenty-eight cents each must have had Ed Kennedy dancing in the street! What we'd been paying Kennedy for Saucers wasn't chump change. The expense got the Morrisons to supposin' about creating a flyin' disc mold of their own.

The original idea for a plastic flying disc had been ours. Our interest in the original Flyin-Saucers had been relinquished in 1950. Lu and I weren't bound legally in any way to the Franscionis. Flyin-Saucers weren't patented. No way were we obligated to the past. What would the cost of a disc be if we owned our own mold?

Early in 1955 I went to see the people at Rainbow Plastics in nearby El Monte, California. I asked for a quote on what it would cost to mold something similar to a Flyin Saucer. The management had observed our operation and Saucer sales at the Pomona Fair, and had been impressed. They opined that they would very much like to be the molders of such an item. Their quote was a surprisingly low eleven cents per polyethylene disc. The cost differential between eleven cents and Kennedy's twenty-eight cents got our attention! Eleven cents a copy was too good to be ignored. A mold for a newly-designed disc would be created. Rainbow Plastics would do the molding.

I sat down at the kitchen table, and again, with french curve in hand, set about fashioning what was hoped would be a better-performing piece of "airborne crockery." A Flyin Saucer was used as a point of reference. The diameter would be about the same as the Saucer's. The rim was slightly deepened and thickened. The rim's added mass would supposedly increase a spinning disc's centrifugal force and add stability to the disc in breezy conditions. The disc's top and bottom surfaces would remain unengraved while we pondered what a media-created flying saucer might look like.

The drawings were given to Caco Engineering in Pomona (injection mold-making specialists recommended by Rainbow Plastics). Caco's engineers converted the sketches into working drawings for the tool and die makers. We approved the drawings. Could the mold, complete with engravings, be ready to produce discs in time for the 1955 Pomona Fair? "Yes." Caco was given the go-ahead.

While the mold was being created, Lu and I pondered what to name our new plastic baby, and what a real(?) flying saucer might look like. We speculated that space aliens needed visibility to navigate. To make alien visibility possible, a raised cockpit with little round windows would be engraved on the top, and in the center of the disc. To further suggest "space," the names of the planets would be engraved around the disc's circumference near the outer edge. A name and flippin' instructions would be engraved in the mold after we'd had time to think up something appropriate.

The name "Whirlo-Way" was again given consideration (see Chapter 11). The name didn't fit; we wanted something "spacey." Pluto was the most recently discovered planet.

Chapter 26 — A Mold of Our Own

There were rumors that "Plutonians" had already landed and were blending in with the populace. The configuration of a disc kinda resembled a dish. A platter was a dish. How 'bout "Pluto Platter"?

Pluto Platter was it! Our baby had a name!

It was during this pondering period that Lu came up with her "FLAT FLIP FLIES STRAIGHT" instructions. That would be engraved for posterity in the underside of the mold.

Contemporaries—Model U.F.O. and Pluto Platter

27

PLUTO PLATTERS ENTER DISCDOM

*C*ACO HAD OUR MOLD READY and test run, as promised, in time for the three-weekend L.A. County Fair. Rainbow Plastics would be molding the Pluto Platters. How about their availability? We were assured that the discs had priority molding status. Our initial order was for five thousand Platters. We had five thousand Platters the day the Fair opened...and we'd been extended credit!

The Pluto Platter debut was spectacular. The opening weekend was near overwhelming. Paul and I did the "pitching." The girls were kept busy harvesting the before-inflation 1955 greenbacks. Five thousand Platters weren't going to be enough. More Platters were ordered; more than enough to last out the Fair. Rainbow Plastics considerately delivered each day's moldings to the fairgrounds. We never had it so good!

Each night after closing, the Fair's security cops offered to escort us and the day's "take" out to the parking lot and our cars. Cops have kids. Our protectors didn't hurt for gratis Platters.

The Phoenix Fair followed the L.A. Fair. Platter sales exceeded the Flyin Saucer sales we'd enjoyed the previous year. The Platters were turning out to be a *very* rewarding source of the stuff that's put in banks.

Chapter 27 — Pluto Platters Enter Discdom

After Phoenix we worked a coupla smaller fairs in the Southern California area. The Platters sold very well when there were crowds, but we'd become greedy. We were after large crowds every day of a fair. That was it for the '55 fair season.

The Awesome Foursome kicked back, licked their chops, reviewed the past season's successes and contemplated the future. The really *BIG* money had been made at the really *BIG* fairs. It was decided that during the '56 fair season we'd limit our Platter endeavors to only the really *BIG* fairs.

Paul ("Wog") was also a carpenter. While waiting for the '56 fair season to start, we worked on construction jobs—once in a while together, more often not. The Hoornbeeks had the same predilection for supplemental income as the Morrisons. With the start of the '56 fair season's really *BIG* fairs, we dropped our hammers and the Awesome Foursome went flippin' Platters.

1956 presented new opportunities. We had it on reliable authority that the San Diego County Fair was a *REALLY BIG* two-weekend show that included the Fourth of July. We decided to give it a shot. The Fair was held at the Del Mar Race Track. Our location was fantastic—immediately inside the main gate. Everybody entering and leaving the fairgrounds *HAD* to see us. The weather was perfect. The crowds were fabulous. Rainbow Plastics never stopped molding, and again delivered Platters to the fairgrounds. Many, many people left that Fair carrying colorful plastic discs that had Pluto Platter molded in the top surface. The San Diego County Fair was indeed *BIG!*

Concessionaires who had worked it said the Iowa State Fair in Des Moines was "bigger than Del Mar." Des Moines was a long way from home, but…"Bigger than Del Mar"? The Fair Manager was contacted. He'd seen and liked our operation at Pomona. His response to my "Could we?" inquiry was: "I've got just the spot for you. Come on!"

Our space was a small, triangular-shaped grassy park smack in the middle of the extensive fairgrounds. Foot traffic on all sides of the park would have visibility to what was going on inside the park. Large trees provided shade. Park benches were scattered about. The park was well-lit at night. Location-wise, we'd been granted a place in a Platter flipper's paradise.

One of the tree's limbs got in the way of a curving Platter. With a borrowed ladder a flight path was cut through the tree's branches so a Platter could complete its assigned curve unhindered. Plywood was laid on the grass so the Platters could be made to skip. The park benches were rearranged so the benchsitters would have a better view of the action.

The Fair opened and the whopping crowds seemed to be on a spending spree. We assumed that a recently harvested corn crop was a factor leading to their extravagance. Whatever, they liked what we had to offer and were willing to have their bankrolls shucked. People didn't buy just one Platter, they bought one for everybody in their family. Some hauled 'em away by the carton. We hired a gal to help Marge take the money. It wasn't real. Folks were waiting for us to get to the park in the morning.

We'd brought fifteen thousand Platters to Des Moines anticipating that would be more than enough. The Fair was a ten-day event. We sold out the morning of the last day. The Iowa State Fair exceeded our expectations sales-wise, but we weren't totally surprised. Pluto Platters, once demonstrated, had a way of selling themselves. The Fair's management invited us to come back the next year and do it again. It would have been idiotic not to accept!

CRIME AND PUNISHMENT

Iowa suffered with Blue Laws: no alcohol on Sundays! The Fair ended on a Sunday. With nothing left to sell and feeling the need of refreshment, I entered a nearby tent whose source of income during the fair was Sloppy Joes and *BEER*. The tent's flaps were down, screening the public from what was goin' on inside: the quaffing of the forbidden devil's brew.

The first mug of the illicit brew was approaching my eager lips when the joint was raided by the Fair's gendarmerie—farmers the Fair had employed to "keep peace" and "enforce the law." Their official uniforms: white shirts, pith helmets, and shockless hog prods (wooden canes). I was intimidated by the possibility of being hog-prodded, so no attempt was made to rationalize my criminal misdeed. With quiet acquiescence I was conveyed to the municipality's place of confinement—there to await Monday morning…the earliest date it would be possible to make bail. Most of Sunday and all of Sunday night were spent in the Des Moines escape-proof "repenting center."

Back home, we banked the out-of-state loot and got ready for Pomona. It wasn't uncommon at previous fairs that certain types, walking with their heads down, would unconsciously come between us "lid-flippers." The intrusions disrupted our operations. This year steps were taken to alleviate the problem.

A bright yellow line was painted on the asphalt across the business end of our flippin' space. A fifty-foot-long chicken-wire fence was erected along the outer length of our space, creating a twenty-five-foot-wide corridor. The fence did a lot to solve the problem. Our demonstrations were carried on with considerably less interruption.

Pomona was the same anticipated bonanza as the previous year. Phoenix followed Pomona—with the same results. Phoenix ended the fair season for us. We'd never had it better. The Morrisons went on a spending spree. New curtains were hung in the living room, and the pinching toilet seat was replaced. A new car replaced the used one and a contract was signed for the construction of a house on the front of the lot—a house appropriate for a family of five. The kids were going to have their own bedrooms. We salivated as we anticipated the coming of the 1957 fair season. Del Mar, Des Moines, Pomona, and Phoenix were all scheduled.

It never happened. A total stranger said something that set off a series of events that changed forever the future of the Morrisons…*and their Platters!*

28

WHO WAS THAT GUY...?

*T*O QUOTE McMAHON: "Morrison was demonstrating his Pluto Platter in a Los Angeles parking lot in 1955 when Rich Knerr and Spud Melin spotted the unusual flying object."

POSH!

This same falsification of disc history is repeated in many of the Frisbee articles and places that can be clicked up on the Internet. It's fair to assume that there's been some plagiarizing.

Actually there *WAS* an L.A. parking lot involved in disc history. What occurred there became a landmark Frisbee history event. The following is what transpired that fateful day.

It was a few days before Christmas 1956—*not* 1955. I had prepaid the parking lot operator for adjoining parking spaces alongside a building in a downtown L.A. parking lot. Paul and I figured we could pick up some extra bucks demonstrating the Platters before the pre-Christmas shoppers.

We started flippin' shortly before noon. (We had waited for the downtown foot traffic to develop.) No "wire," no "pitch," just basic flat flips, skips, curves, and friendly selling banter with the "tip." The airborne Platters worked their magic. People accumulated to the extent that they prevented cars from entering the parking lot. The delayed parking caused cars to be backed up in the busy downtown street. Normal street traffic came to a standstill. Impatient drivers began honking their horns. We stopped flippin'. The horn honking stopped. The crowd dissipated. Cars waiting to park got parked. Street traffic returned to normal. When we resumed flippin' the problem was reconstituted.

The traffic problems attracted a cop. The cop was there to solve the traffic problem. He asked to see our business license. Business license? Didn't have one. (Didn't know we needed one?) Things had not been going well…too many delays. Did we want to go through the routine of getting a license? Not really. It wouldn't be worth the bother and expense. We packed up and left. End of story?

Not quite….

During a Platter flippin' interruption, a stranger had emerged from the crowd and offered that the management at Wham-O Manufacturing had been considering marketing a flying disc. "It might be worthwhile to meet with 'The Boys' at Wham-O." Who were "The Boys"?

That stranger's suggestion set off the chain of events that initiated Frisbees. That stranger deserves a noteworthy place in Discdom history…but who the hell was he?

Who *WAS* that guy?

29

THE AMALGAMATION

I WAS AWARE OF WHAM-O through their slingshot mail-order advertising. That's all I knew about Wham-O. Lu didn't know what a slingshot was.

Having some company distribute Pluto Platters for us was not a new idea. An aggressive distributor might be a good thing. On the other hand, we didn't want to get tied up with a company that couldn't provide us with an income at least equal to what we were making with our fair demonstrations.

Financially the Pluto Platters had been treating us kindly. Wham-O didn't have the national recognition that the major sporting goods companies enjoyed. Did we want to jeopardize our current "sure thing" with a company we knew nothing about? If the parking lot stranger's comment was true, and Wham-O was considering adding a flying disc to their line, it couldn't hurt to see if they'd be interested in our disc. A call was made for an appointment.

Lu and I went to Wham-O and met "The Boys," Rich Knerr and Spud Melin. When it was explained that a "parking lot stranger" had initiated the meeting, they knew nothing about a parking lot, and couldn't imagine who the stranger might have been?

When asked where and when they first saw our Pluto Platters, their answer was "At both the 1956 Del Mar and Pomona Fairs." (So much for McMahon's quote about where Rich Knerr and Spud Melin first "spotted the unusual flying object.")

The Boys had been impressed with our Platter demonstrations, had seen the crowds that gathered to watch, and the quantity of Platters being sold. They offered (just like the parking lot stranger had said) they'd been considering adding a flying disc to their product line. They said they were pleased we had wanted to meet with them.

With the preliminaries out of the way, we got down to the reason for the meeting: why was Wham-O interested in the Morrison Pluto Platters? We asked questions; they asked questions. Their questions almost amounted to an inquisition, covering everything Lu and I ever knew about or had experienced regarding flying discs. Nothing was held back! The question-and-answer session ended. We were given a tour of their operation. It was eye-popping to see how many slingshots were being produced to supply just their mail orders. In addition to the mail orders, their slingshots were being sold in sporting-goods stores all over the country. Another product being manufactured was a modern version of medieval crossbows.

We were impressed by The Boys' operation, their straightforwardness and their senses of humor. We liked the guys.

Chapter 29 — The Amalgamation

They seemed like people we could work with if the price was right. As we were leaving, The Boys said they'd get back to us. A coupla days later the phone rang...they wanted to "talk."

The Boys' concept of how they would go about merchandising the Platters made interesting listening: For the discs to sell off store counters in profitable numbers, the populace would have to be exposed to the capabilities of flipped discs. Providing that exposure would be costly. The expenditures would be "humongous." Any contract would have to allow for the "humongousness." "Humongous" has an ominous ring to it.

The discussions to determine the Morrison royalty percentage continually bumped up against the "humongous investment." The Boys held the high cost of promotion over our heads like the Sword of Damocles. We wanted a bigger percentage. They couldn't see it! We went home shaking our heads.

Two more meetings ensued. Wham-O's lawyer, Ken Mallard, was always present at the meetings, keeping the discussions on track, and offering suggestions. Although he represented Wham-O, we believed he was being fair and honestly looking out for the interests of both parties. At the end of each meeting we'd go home fretting and stewing. What were we getting into? How binding was the contract? How would we get the Platter mold back if Wham-O didn't perform? We weren't being represented by a lawyer. Should we get one? Lots and lots of questions.

During the last meeting, our collective minds came together. Wham-O would manufacture, promote, and distribute the Platters. The agreed-to royalty percentage would be paid quarterly. Wham-O had the option to discontinue royalties any time sales dipped below a specified figure. Should that happen the mold would be returned to the Morrisons. The contract further required that everything we had relating to Pluto Platters—cartons, advertising materials, bags, etc. would be given to Wham-O.

The hardest part of the contract to accept: Wham-O would have absolute control of the mold. All decisions regarding the promotion of the Platters would be exclusively Wham-O's. We could only stand by and watch and hope for the best. The Morrisons were gonna be totally cloutless!

The agreement also provided that we could purchase Pluto Platters at Wham-O's cost for public demonstrations (like at fairs). We could continue to feather our nests doing what we did best. The Boys liked that proviso. Demonstrating Platters in public places would be providing free public exposure (advertising).

It wasn't included in the contract, but it was verbally agreed to that the Hoornbeeks could get Platters same as us—at Wham-O's cost—again, for demonstration purposes only. Wham-O kept their word. During the sixties, the Hoornbeeks went back to New York, got a great location, and for an extended period, substantially enhanced their bank account.

Even though the contract and its whereases were agreed to, there remained nagging doubts that we were doing the right thing. We hadn't been represented by our own lawyer. (In a later lawsuit that fact worked to our benefit.) Were we giving too much away? Aw…What the hell. On January 23, 1957, with understandable trepidation, Lu and I took pen in hand and signed the contract.

Chapter 29 — The Amalgamation

Two guys we'd known for hardly a month now had exclusive rights to do with our Pluto Platters whatever they chose to do. Would the results of their merchandising be beneficial? Or would the Morrisons be chasing Pluto Platters into their Golden Years? Only time would tell. The disc was cast!

The contract signing date was memorable. It just happened to be my 37th birthday. Who coulda guessed that "our baby" would grow up and one day become a Frisbee—the most money-makin' sporting-goods item of all time! The decision to go with The Boys has become the best, longest-lasting birthday present I ever got.

I was also left a lasting, perplexing question. The Platters weren't patented. The Boys could have developed a flying disc mold of their own without infringement. They didn't need the Morrisons. So….

Why did they choose to go with us and our Platters??

(See Appendix M)

30

HOOPS AND PLATTERS

*H*OW GOOD A JOB would Wham-O do managing Pluto Platter promotion and sales? We realized that it would take time for Wham-O to get the Platters ready for marketing. After what seemed too long to us, we got wondering why "our baby" wasn't producing royalties. I asked The Boys why? They explained the obvious: "Getting a new item on the market took preparation, time, and money." Actually things had been happening. Packaging had been designed. A TV commercial was being prepared. Selected sporting-goods stores had agreed to sales test the Platters once the packaging was ready. We were given this free advice: "Patience now would have its reward later. Keep the faith!"

Be patient? Keep the faith? Wham-O had complete control of the Platter's future. The only recourse we had was to "be patient." We were forced to exercise forbearance. "Faith" was left to the clergy.

The Morrisons and the Hoornbeeks had given up chasing the Platters at fairs, except for the Pomona Fair. Construction jobs provided income until it was time for the Pomona Fair. Wham-O provided us with Platters. As always, the Platters provided an enhanced income. (We worked that Fair every year up to and including 1960. It was close to home, and, after a day's flippin', we could sleep in our own beds.)

Chapter 30 — Hoops and Platters

After Fred and Lu signed the Wham-O contract they continued to push Pluto Platters on their own. Lu made the spacesuit.

The Pluto Platter's introduction to America was finalized about the same time Wham-O was preparing to market another product. We had already booked into the San Bernardino County Orange Show as usual. Wham-O persuaded us to take a dozen rather primitive-looking wooden hoops with us to demonstrate in front of the people that gathered to watch us peddle our Platters. The Boys wanted to know how the fairgoers reacted to someone waving his or her hips, Elvis-like, to keep a circular piece of wood gyrating about their midriff.

When I tried "hooping" onlookers winked at each other and nodded knowingly...NOT a reaction I cared to encourage! Lu had the technique. When she did the "hooping" the response was totally different! The few hoops that sold were sold while Lu was doing the waggling.

The wooden hoops weren't "pretty." We didn't "hoop" often so we probably didn't do 'em justice. (Only ten of the dozen hoops sold.) I thought the hoops were a waste of time. Back at the plant, The Boys hadn't waited for my negative evaluation of the hoops. They had begun assembling hoops made of plastic tubing while we were demonstrating the wooden ones. A few short months later "Hula Hoops" were inundating the country. The Boys weren't prepared for the sudden, overwhelming success of the Hula Hoops. The crush of Hoop orders exceeded Wham-O's production capabilities. Obviously, The Boys had their hands full meeting the demand. It's understandable now why the Platters weren't getting The Boys' full attention.

There was nothing in the Wham-O contract about when the promotions of the Platters was required to start. So, the press of Hoop production delayed fully marketing the Platters. In retrospect, it's remarkable that Wham-O was able to have the Platters test marketed and on the shelves as early as they did.

....

One undeniable fact has so far withstood the ravages of time. Albeit a minor claim to fame, the Morrisons may have been the first to "expose" themselves waggling Hula Hoops in a public place!

31

PRE-FRISBEE FUN 'N GAMES

*D*URING THE FIRST COUPLA MONTHS of my association with Wham-O, I was made to feel that I'd been included in the Inner Circle (if there was such a thing). I got to laugh and scratch with The Boys, who had great senses of humor, and become friends with the people that were making the place tick—the plant's management. And I got to witness some of what it takes to make a manufacturing and distributing company a goin' concern. It was a most enlightening period.

I got to sit in on a few meetings when other inventors were seeking Wham-O's backing. It was mentioned in an earlier chapter that inventors are reluctant to reveal what it is they've invented for fear that their idea will be stolen. One such seeker of Wham-O's backing got off on the wrong foot by adamantly refusing to reveal his marvelous invention until Wham-O signed a written guarantee that they wouldn't *steal* whatever his terrific(?) idea was. It was a very short meeting. The Boys didn't cotton to having their integrity questioned. Rich Nerr stood up, declared the meeting was over, and suggested to the secret-keeping seeker of Wham-O's backing: "Don't let the door hit you in the butt on your way out!" None of the ideas that I witnessed being presented in those meetings made it to Wham-O's production line.

On several occasions a reassuring phenomenon developed in the street outside Wham-O's front door. The Boys, or somebody, would take visiting businesspersons out in the street to show off the Platters. The airborne Platters worked their magic. People not occupied came out of the plant to join in. The making of the phenomenon was underway. Additional flippers seemed to come out of the woodwork. As the number of perspiring flippers increased, proportionately more Platters were provided for the flippers to flip. Result: the air was literally thick with "Airborne Crockery."

(This book is the *true* history of "flittin' discs." To say that the closeness of the airborne discs *cast a cooling shadow over the perspiring flippers* would have been a *slight* exaggeration.)

Were all those flippin', catching or chasing bodies that were physically undergoing self-induced stress relief and attitudinal readjustment a manifestation that the *Pluto Platters have "possibilities"?* Were those spontaneous "mass flippings" in the street an omen of good things to come? The broadness of the grins on the faces of The Boys suggested that such was the case.

Occasionally after hours, The Boys, assorted friends, and often business-connected associates would gather out in the open spaces of the plant to test their skills with the Platters. One of the tests was how many flips it took a flipper to pick a paper cup off its pedestal from a given distance. Another was how many flips it took to successfully curve a Platter through the roof trusses and be successfully caught by a catcher. Money was known to change hands. The social respite from the daily grind included the consumption of adult beverages. Accuracy, which was always the determining factor during the gaming, seemed to diminish as the evenings wore on.

Chapter 31 —Pre-Frisbee Fun 'n Games

Not always, but there were times when the aforementioned activities were interrupted by a craving to eat. Desiring to continue the camaraderie, the contestants would relocate to a food establishment—a bar being a necessary adjunct to the dining area. Graciously, Wham-O always picked up the tab for those indulgences.

There were downsides to those evenings on the town. Getting home required navigating through the uniformed people that are attracted to errant driving. Another was the morning-afters. Worst of all was the remorse I was made to suffer as Lu vehemently expressed her previous evening's anxiety regarding my whereabouts? Suffering the wrath of my beloved was *never* pleasant.

Eventually the newness and novelty of the association with the people at Wham-O wore off. Less and less time was spent at the Wham-O plant. I had little contact with the The Boys as they finally got around to exploiting the reason behind our association.

The Boys' earlier advice that "patience would have its reward" proved to be good advice. Three months after the deal with Wham-O was signed, the Pluto Platters had been test-marketed with favorable results. Stores were putting 'em on their counters. Early sales started a trickling of royalties.

Help was on the way!

1957 Wham-O in-store display. Note that kids can reach the crossbows but not the Platters!

32

UNEXPECTED HAPPENSTANCES

*T*HE BOYS DIDN'T ALWAYS TELL the Morrisons what was going on. It had to have been fairly early during our relationship that it was decided that the Platters needed a different name (it takes time to rework a mold's engravings). Printed disc history has it that a Frisbie Pie Company had inspired Rich Knerr to appropriate the name "Frisbee" and apply it to the top of the discs? If true, the name of a defunct pie company was engraved in the top of the Pluto Platter. The Pluto Platters had been given a very short run, then had been forced to suffer a renaming. Henceforth, the Platters would be marketed with the name "FRISBEE" emblazoned on their top surfaces— the last "i" in "Frisbie," whether by mistake or designs, having been replaced with an "e."

Thus was the birth of the FRISBEE.

Were the Morrisons asked for permission to alter the mold? No! Was Wham-O obligated to get permission for the alteration? *NO!* The Boys were authorized by contract to do as they chose to do with the mold. Had I been consulted, I'd have vehemently objected.

"Frisbee"?...*GAWD!*

(Earlier I'd been wrong about the future of the Hula Hoops. *This time I sure as hell knew I was right!* Substituting a nondescript name like "Frisbee" to replace our proven "Pluto Platter" was a stupid idea! What perverse minds thought a name like "Frisbee" would add sales appeal to anything? I thought the name stunk! Whadid I know? Today the name "FRISBEE" has entered the public consciousness and is recognized worldwide as referencing plastic flying discs.)

In 1958 Wham-O altered the Pluto Platter mold, creating the FRISBEE brand disc.

Apparently, The Boys believed the Frisbee discs had a future. Early in July '57 we got a phone call from Wham-O: "Bring a check for one hundred, twenty-eight dollars made out to the U.S. Patent Office." Again, unbeknownst to the Morrisons, The Boys had engaged the firm of Christy, Parker and Hale, patent attorneys, to prepare a patent application for the disc. A check and my signature were required to further the process. The application was submitted to the Patent Office on July 30, 1957. Fourteen months later, September 30, 1958, a seven-year design patent was issued for a "Flying Toy." My name was on the patent certificate.

With no previous expectation of ever being one, I'd become a certified *"INVENTOR"!*

(See Appendix Q)

33

THE INVENTOR...?

*T*HE YEARS 'TIL 1961 WERE A MIXED BAG of construction, annual Frisbee demonstrations at the L.A. County Fair, and attempts at somewhat less-than-fruitful creativity.

The Frisbee royalties began creating substantial spendable income. Why not use a portion of the spendable stuff to develop another moneymaker? After all, I was a *Certified Inventor!* On the theory that several brains were better than one (mine), a group of buddies were invited to assemble in our living room for a session of brainstorming (adult beverages were available to lubricate the process). Once assembled, they were requested to focus their thoughts on coming up with some unthunk-of something that might tickle the public's fancy. It was made clear that any benefits resulting from the brainstorming would recur to the Morrisons.

KRAZY EIGHT BOWLING BALLS

The buddies, being sporting types, thought primarily of things that had sporty applications. Once all the different sports had been considered, it was resolved that "bowling balls for kids" had yet to be exploited. Mold makers were then contacted and "Krazy Eight Bowling Balls" rolled off the line.

Krazy Eight Bowling Balls were basically spherical bottles — slightly smaller than the size of real bowling balls. Water could be poured through one of the finger holes to give the ball a desired weight. It was up to the kids to decide how much weight (water) they'd be comfortable with. The finger hole was then sealed with a hollow, wedging plug that left room for a finger. They were meant for "home bowling" only; on driveways and the like; using milk cartons, beer cans(?), or whatever for bowling pins.

The Bowling Balls were introduced at the San Bernardino Orange Show—the same fair at which, a year before, Lu and I had introduced Hula Hoops to the public at Wham-O's request (Chapter 30).

Three plywood bowling alleys were set up. The bowling balls were red, yellow, and black. "Marks" (customers) were charged twenty-five cents and given three chances to knock over three stacked beer cans. Kids were hired to restack the cans and roll the balls back. The gaff was: losers had their twenty-five cents applied to the cost of a Bowling Ball.

The Bowling Balls drew attention and made money, but didn't lend themselves favorably to fair demonstration (finding kids willing to restack the cans was one problem). Howsomever, The Boys thought they were worthy of being added to Wham-O's product line. The Bowling Ball contract provisions were the same as the Pluto Platter contract. The Balls were merchandised in a display carton that included six plastic bowling pins. The public's acceptance of "plastic bowling balls for kids" was less than sensational. The Morrisons benefited only slightly royalty-wise. Wham-O didn't benefit enough to continue their production. The manufacture of Krazy Eight Bowling Balls passed into limbo.

Chapter 33 — The Inventor?

Wham-O briefly carried Fred's Krazy Eight Bowling Ball as part of their eclectic product line. Here it is sold alone, without bowling pins.

POPSICLE MACHINES

Being of fertile mind, another attempt was made at merchandising a moneymaker. A mold was developed that would make eight popsicles in one freezing. A second mold produced ten "Cup 'n Sticks." The Cup 'n Sticks snapped down over a juice filled popsicle cavity creating a seal. When a popsicle was removed from the "Machine" it was frozen to the "Stick." The "Cup," having a larger diameter than the cavity, served to catch popsicle drippings for slurping. The popsicle tray was colorless and opaque. The Cup 'n Sticks were molded in bright colors. The product was packaged and sold as a "Popsicle Machine." Popsicle Machine? "Machine" was a deliberate misuse of the word. Machines have moving parts. Popsicle molds are inert!

Popsicle Machines were demonstrated at fairs and home shows. Home shows were the best. The day before a show opened we'd fill a horizontal-type freezer with Hawaiian Punch-filled Popsicle Machines. Dry ice had to assist the freezing (the equivalent of a bathtub full of water won't freeze overnight without it). The Hawaiian Punch company furnished—at no cost—their canned punch to make the popsicles. All that was required of us was that we mention that the popsicles were made of frozen Hawaiian Punch. No problem there...Hawaiian Punch made tasty popsicles.

A later product similar to the "Popsicle Mach

Our method of merchandising the Machines had a "hook." One person in a group of people passing our booth was handed a popsicle—preferably a kid. That stopped that group and got the attention of other passing people. This created the opportunity to verbally extol the merits of the Popsicle Machine.

It was a fun pitch! The pitch included suggestions that Martini-sicles, or Frozen Daiquiri-sicles would be a novel way to entertain guests (overlooking the fact that such alcoholic beverages won't freeze). Serutan-sicles would make one a "regular fellow." (Serutan is "natures" spelled backwards and is an over-the-counter laxative!) The pitch ended with the invaluable counsel: "Fruit juice-sicles are healthier than sugar water-sicles." Popsicles were then handed to everyone that raised a hand. The off-the-wall pitch and the magnanimous generosity sold a lot of Popsicle Machines! (At day's end the freezer was restocked with refilled popsicle molds so that the frozen confections would be available for the next day's influencing benevolence.)

The Boys looked at the Popsicle Machine's home show sales, liked what they saw, and added the item to their product line… again using the Pluto Platter contract provisions. Everything was going swimmingly. The Machines were producing a worthwhile income as long as virgin plastic granules were used to mold the product.

Without warning, the Hula Hoop craze crashed overnight. Wham-O accumulated a warehouse-full of returned Hula Hoops. The Boys decided that ground-up Hula Hoop plastic could be used to mold the colorful Cup 'n Sticks. The staples and the wooden dowels that held the ends of the Hoops together hadn't been removed when the Hoops were reduced to granules. Staples and splinters of wood clogged the Cup 'n Stick mold's orifice where the hot plastic is injected. It took days to remove the hardened plastic from the mold and clear the orifice. After a couple of contaminated plastic cloggings, The Boys gave up on the Popsicle Machines. The reason given: "Unreliable production." Really…? Using virgin plastic would have solved the problem. The discontinuance didn't sit well with the Morrisons.

Both the Krazy Eight Bowling Ball and Popsicle Machine molds remained with Wham-O. Where are they today? Who knows?

THE BUILDER'S BUDDY

A "Builder's Buddy" was a 4″ x 5″ plastic slide-rule-type calculator that would fit comfortably in a construction worker's shirt pocket. It could be used to calculate how much concrete to order. There were conversion tables, math formulas, and rafter tables printed on both sides of slidable inserts. They were meant to be a hardware store and lumber yard advertising giveaway. A business's name and address could be printed on the back. Contractors, carpenters, and do-it-yourselfers liked 'em. The Buddies were a good idea that ran afoul of production costs. We couldn't produce 'em cheap enough for hardware stores and lumberyards to buy, then give away... and the retail cost wasn't realistic. The Builder's Buddy's life span was short-lived.

OH...WHAT MIGHT HAVE BEEN!

Was this a good idea, or what? I took some pencil sketches of what I thought had possibilities over to The Boys at Wham-O. The sketches depicted a different kind of roller skate. What made the skates different? My skates could be used like ice skates. Four lined-up wheels would be round, like a handball (possibly pneumatic) and permanently attached to hi-top shoes. The ball-like wheels would supposedly provide greater traction on smooth surfaces and roll more smoothly over rough surfaces. It was hoped Wham-O would foot the costs of designing and engineering the skates. Wham-O would then exercise their manufacturing and merchandising skills. We even were willing to have the cost of developing the skates deducted from future Frisbee royalties. The Boys couldn't see it!

Oh...what could have been. Because The Boys didn't go along and we didn't pursue the development of the skates on our own, both parties blew a golden opportunity in the making.

Today...the world has enthusiastically embraced "in-line" skates!

34

THE MORRISONS TAKE A HIT

*B*Y 1961 THE SIZE OF THE FRISBEE ROYALTIES had escalated to the extent that the Morrisons could forgo relying on past sources of income. An opportunity presented itself to eat at the public trough. In 1961 I went to work for the City of Los Angeles as a Building Inspector. Civil service ended—for all time—our public demonstrations of plastic discs that "amazingly flew on Invisible Wire!"

Lu (center) and the kids in 1958

(A pox upon all the purveyors of erroneous Frisbee history: Plastic flying discs were conceived by a former Air Force pilot [me] during 1946, became a reality during 1948 [with the molding of the Flyin-Saucers], and were patented by a carpenter [me again] in 1958. *Frisbees were NOT invented by a Building Inspector!*)

Soon the Morrisons were living quite comfortably on Frisbee royalties and the supplementing Building Inspector's salary. Then one day during 1965, Lu and I were called to meet with The Boys. Subject: Reduction of our royalty percentage?!

The stated reasons for the reduction were twofold: increasing freight cost had significantly reduced the Frisbee profit margin (probably true), and Frisbee promotions were soon to be initiated on a much larger scale. The expanded promotions were going to be "humongous." (There, *again*, was that dreadful word that The Boys used during the contract negotiations back in early 1957.) The justification for the reduction: the greatly increased sales created by the promotions would more than offset the percentage reduction.

The largest the royalties had been providing was in jeopardy! The very thought of a percentage reduction was repugnant. The percentage reduction was, in fact, brutal, and we vehemently and vociferously argued against it. There was *no way* that future Frisbee royalties, figured at the lower percentage, *could possibly* amount to the income we had been receiving and enjoying!

Rich Knerr, finally tiring of our resistance, put it bluntly: "The lower percentage is the way it's going to be! *Live with it!* Wham-O doesn't need your approval. Go along *with* us… or we're going ahead *without* ya!"

End of discussion!

Knerr's declaration had teeth. The Morrisons had agreed to an earlier contract amendment that gave Wham-O the right to determine royalty percentages after the seven-year patent expired. Seven years had passed…the patent had expired. The Boys were merely exercising their legal prerogative. Without recourse, a revised contract was agreed to. It was "go along" or lose out. A life without royalties was far too unpleasant to contemplate.

Chapter 34 — The Morrisons Take a Hit

(Remember…Wham-O hadn't been obligated to sign the *original* 1957 contract with the Morrisons. Wham-O *could* have made a disc mold of its own—and the Morrisons would have been left on the outside looking in. Again in 1965, The Boys *could* have written off the Morrisons. That they *chose* to give us the option to stay in the game speaks volumes as to their integrity.)

35

THE MAN WHO MADE IT HAPPEN

NOT LONG AFTER the percentage reduction, we got a preposterous phone call. I took the call. The caller said he was Wham-O's new General Manager and Vice President in Charge of Marketing, and "Would we allow seventy-five thousand dollars to be deducted from our future royalties?" The purpose: to have Sandy Koufax (a prominent Dodger pitcher at the time) endorse the Frisbee.

Who WAS this guy? What an outlandish request! The caller said his name was Ed Headrick. Never heard of 'im. The call had to be a con. The guy got an emphatic and impolite "GET LOST!" I then called The Boys and related the incident.

Ed Headrick, GM & VP...
Frisbee Promoter Extraordinaire!

The Boys verified that Headrick was all he said he was and that the request to deduct future royalties for Koufax's endorsement had their approval. Headrick would be managing Wham-O's expanded Frisbee promotions. Headrick's phone call was the beginning of his "Market Managing." That call was

Chapter 35 — The Man Who Made It Happen

our introduction to the man who was to become The Man behind the Frisbee's phenomenal success.

Had I only known. It would have been prudent for me to have called The Boys first before so abruptly dismissing the unknown caller. (On the other hand, maybe something good came out of my abruptness. We were never again asked to contribute to Frisbee promotions.)

Headrick was convinced that the Pluto Platter Frisbee needed a more "adulty," more "sporty" look if the expanded Frisbee promotions were to succeed. He had all semblance of the Platter's image as a spacecraft removed. Gone forever was our beloved, dreamt-up (admittedly adolescent) appearance of a flying saucer.

Ed Headrick had the Pluto Platter mold retooled in 1964 to create the Official Pro Model

Headrick had an eye for product design. The new top surface had the words "WHAM-O FRISBEE" and "OFFICIAL PRO MODEL" raised high in bold block letters encircled by a wide, printed black ring that looked like a racing stripe. There were also a series of low-profile rings molded around the disc's outer circumference. A sticker sported Olympic rings. The "NEW LOOK" provided the "adulty, sporty" appearance that would make the disc more appealing to a wider market.

The "NEW LOOK" contributed mightily to its phenomenal success.

Once the Frisbee promotions were underway, the sums on the royalty checks began increasing. The increased sales were reflected in the length of the numbers to the left of the decimal on the royalty checks. The royalties were paid quarterly. The amounts were subject to the time of year. Mid-year checks were always the largest. Lu and I played a little game on the day we received the checks. We'd slowly slide the check out of the opened end of its envelope...sweating each number, one by one...until the total was exposed. We never experienced disappointment. It got to the point it wasn't real!

How sweet it was, and there was no end in sight! The Boys had been right that the reduced royalty percentage would be offset by greater income for the Morrisons.

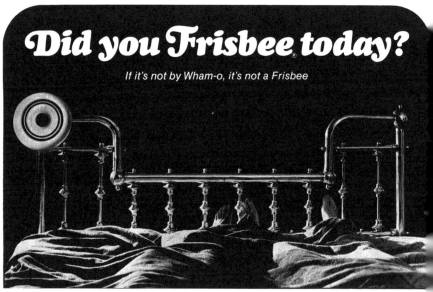

Headrick's aggressive marketing to young adults made Frisbee sales soar!

Chapter 35 — The Man Who Made It Happen

I've never known what financial arrangements Headrick had with Wham-O. It would have been interesting to know, but knowing wouldn't have changed anything. It was enough to know that under Headrick's guidance our increasing bank account was due to what he was doing.

By 1968 royalties had significantly fattened our bank account; we were pretty well fixed. The Building Inspector job had never been a necessity. The time had come to contemplate how we might further supplement the royalties. Investing in and operating a (hopefully) nest-feathering enterprise would require our full-time attention.

I turned in my Building Inspector badge.

Before getting involved in whatever it was we decided would be the additional contributing factor to our future, we decided to finally have a real honeymoon. (In 1939 we had stayed in Lu's folks' house while they went off and enjoyed what would have been *our* honeymoon. See Chapter 7.)

Arrangements were made with my folks to care for the kids while we'd be gone and off we went. We sightsaw all the way to Cripple Creek, Colorado where it was decided that the hardness of motel beds wasn't going to soften. We took the most direct route home; a business was waiting to be created.

Thank you Ed Headrick for the fabulous lifestyle you created for the Morrisons!

36

SPECULATION

*I*N 1968 FRISBEE ROYALTIES were providing sums of money far in excess of our needs. The stock market had no appeal. What could Lu and I invest in that would provide additional return?

I had a working knowledge of construction and the tools it takes to get things done. Why not put that knowledge to good use? Housing construction was booming in the surrounding area. Hardware stores sold construction and home improvement stuff. A hardware store seemed like a logical way to go. We went looking for a location for a hardware store.

Location, location, location.... We found what we thought would be a pretty good location in the city of La Verne (pop. 28,000) on Foothill Boulevard, a main road leading from L.A. into Pomona. The area was surrounded by orange groves. The price of the property was acceptable; a fairly large building was constructed and stocked with a wide variety of hardware store merchandise.

WALT'Z HARDWARE opened its doors during 1969.

Chapter 36 — Speculation

Unlike peddling Frisbees at fairs there was more to operating a multi-product business than just ringing the cash registers. It soon became evident that I was an "on-the-job trainee" once again. I had a lot to learn about how to deal with the complexities of operating a hardware store. I had a theory that if I kept the prices up it would keep the bums out. (Arrogant? *Yes*…but I stuck to the theory.) During the years of the store's operation nothing was ever discounted and not one "STOREWIDE SALE" was conducted to move merchandise. A coupla years after the store's opening the earthwork for a large mobile home park adjacent to the store property brought about a different name for the store. Untold numbers of displaced gophers moved (tunneled) under the asphalted parking area in front of the store. Traffic sunk the paved area. New paving had to be provided.

WALT'Z changed to GO-FER HARDWARE, INC.

The off ramp of the newly-finished construction of the San Bernardino Freeway led onto Foothill Boulevard. To handle the increased traffic coming from L.A., Foothill Boulevard was widened and paved with concrete. A median planted with trees separated opposing traffic. Foothill Boulevard became a major artery passing in front of the store.

The La Verne City Council then toughened up the zoning laws. Getting a building permit became an expensive, complicated, restrictive procedure. Result: only the nicest of commercial buildings could be constructed along the Boulevard.

With time, the area surrounding the hardware store was transformed by modern business centers and multiple apartment building complexes. Nearby super home stores with their cut-rate products began siphoning away our Go-Fer customers. Go-Fer Hardware needed every dime it could generate just to keep up with its overhead and pay the taxes. Operating a business without an appreciable bottom line was a waste of time. Things weren't going to get better....

Ta hell with it!

A company specializing in store closures was contracted to get rid of the merchandise and store fixtures. During 1979, the store's doors were closed for the last time.

Property values in the area had escalated to the point of incredulity. The store property was right in the middle of where a developer was acquiring land for a large shopping mall. He *HAD* to have my property. My asking price for the property was, I thought, overly excessive. The developer paid the whopping price without a whimper.

(Had I asked too little?!)

37

GETTING PERSONAL

*O*VER THE YEARS I'd become alcoholic. My addiction finally exceeded Lu's level of toleration. She filed for a divorce during 1970. I straightened out briefly…long enough to get Lu to take me back. We remarried. The second marriage didn't last two months. My addiction to alcohol was more demanding than our relationship. We redivorced. The judge split the Frisbee royalties evenly. Lu wanted me to have the store. Lu retained everything else, and deserved more.

The final divorce worked out well for Lu. She invested in escalating real-estate properties, and did very well for herself. I turned myself in to a V.A. hospital, and underwent the government's cure for alcoholism. The cure took! The devil's concoctions became a thing of the past. Our original marriage had lasted thirty-two years. We remained the closest friends. I always believed that, somehow, someday, we'd get back together. Cancer ended that hope during 1987.

Once released from the V.A. rehab program, and single, I was approached by an attractive real-estate broker. She avowed as how I was a handsome specimen—suitable for providing the compatibility she'd been seeking. (She knew about the Frisbee royalties.) I succumbed to her seductive wiles. We married Christmas Eve 1972. Eight years later I had served her purpose; I was handed divorce papers.

1982—I was single again. My half of the Frisbee royalties, plus the recent sale of the hardware store property was available. Ecologists were pronouncing that global warming was melting the polar ice caps, and the rising ocean was going to inundate the L.A. basin. Until that happened, freeway traffic, California taxes, and smog were impeding a pleasurable lifestyle.

A change of habit was in order! It was decision time…what to do? I could afford to evacuate. The pristine place of my birth and ancestry beckoned.

The City of Richfield in central Utah would be my new home!

38

ALL DID NOT GO WELL

*R*ICHFIELD IS OVER A MILE HIGH, located in the middle of central Utah, and has a population slightly surpassing seven thousand. In 1982 the prodigal son (me) returned to the place of his gestation. (The family had moved to L.A. when I was eleven.)

Back in the seventies, reminiscing about my Air Force days had got me back into flying. Did a lot of it. Flying was something I knew something about and enjoyed. The Richfield Municipal Airport's lease could be had for a price. I bought the airport's lease.

Fred (left) piloting his air racer in the 1970s.

A major financial dilemma accompanied my move to the Beehive State. The Infernal Revenue people were gonna deduct forty percent of the recently-acquired hardware store sale money if it wasn't invested within ninety days! The airport purchase solved part of the financial problem. Another major investment was vital if the IRS was to be deprived of its hijacking requirement. Richfield's newest, nicest, fifty-room motel (with coffee shop, dining room, large convention room, and pool) was in bankruptcy. My CPA, having examined the motel's books, believed the motel had potential, so I bought its mortgage. The Airport and Motel expenditures fell within the IRA's ninety-day investment requirement. Circumstances evolved that paying the IRA its forty percent would have been the more prudent way to go.

(Another McMahon misstatement: "The motel was in Monroe, Utah." WRONG! Monroe is a few miles south of Richfield. It's a relatively small town that has been bypassed by major highways. Monroe would NOT be the ideal place to own a large motel!)

THE "WAITRESS" DEBACLE(S)

1984—Having again assumed that I symbolized the epitome of what a husband should be, I thought it would be nice to once more have a female companion with whom to share the good life...someone who would respond to requests such as "FETCH" and respectfully address me as "YES, MA LORD AND MASTER." A waitress acquaintance from the L.A. area agreed to a proposal of marriage. (My somewhat perverse expectations regarding the relationship were not discussed prior to the marriage.) The union was the beginning of what can be best described as "The Waitress Debacles."

The union was short-lived. The newlywed spouse couldn't be restrained from continually commuting to southern California to subsidize that area's swap meets, and visit her borderline-delinquent kids. She never once graciously reacted to the word "FETCH," and couldn't bring herself to refer to me as her "LORD AND MASTER." It was *not* a happy relationship! We divorced after only four months.

The following year—1985—I went back for seconds. (To this day, I can't comprehend how I could have been *SO* stupid!) The second excursion into conjugality with The Waitress was endured until 1987. An unforeseen disruption of income forced me to apply for Food Stamps. Being unable to deliver the lifestyle to which she'd become accustomed additionally strained our uncomfortable marital status. Things got nasty!

In the mornings she'd descend from her web, crank up her Lincoln Continental, and set about publicly making disparaging remarks regarding my business acumen and the tightness of my wallet. The marriage was not without turmoil, and once again the relationship became intolerable. Add another divorce. The divorce went uncontested.

The court's decree was final. I had been awarded the mobile home we'd purchased, and all the stuff within its walls. I was away at the time when The Waitress looted the household of everything that might sell at a swap meet, including my personal valuables and the portable electric generator. I was later informed by a friend that her car's rear end was streaming sparks as she headed south outta town.

So ended that less-than-torrid relationship? The Waitress Debacles were over? *WRONG!* Periodically I'd get phone calls that oozed remorse, apologies and lovelornliness: "I LOVE YOU and miss you *SO* MUCH. Please…Can I come back?" "Sure," I'd respond. "Leave the parakeet and bring back the generator." It took awhile, but eventually she got the message.

Recapping my marital commitments: There's been three wives and five divorces. The marriage to Lu was the only one with meaning and substance. Lu was incomparable. The ill-chosen and unsuccessful relationships with the other two wives would seem to indicate that I had developed a diminished capacity to differentiate between "The Good, The Bad, and The Ugly"? Not so!

None of the wives was UGLY!

39

THE BOMBSHELL

MY MARITAL PROBLEMS ASIDE, the airport and motel acquisitions had been paying their way, and everything was moving along satisfactorily. Came 1986, a recession, and things started to unravel. Aviation fuel prices, aircraft insurance, and aircraft maintenance costs soared. The area's aircraft owners opted not to indulge themselves with their expensive toys, and expensive transportation. Many of the owners sold their planes. Fueling the few transient planes wasn't providing enough income to sustain the airport's operation. The Airport lease was literally "given" back to the City. I was out of the small-airplane and general-aviation business.

The sagging economy was also affecting the motel's operation. Meeting the motel's overhead was exceeding its ability to show a profit. On occasion royalty money was being used to help keep the place afloat.

During the early eighties, a company named Kransco had acquired Wham-O along with our Frisbee contract. Kransco continued to make royalty payments as before. Then one day in May 1986, outta the blue, the worst thing that could possibly have happened…*HAPPENED*. A letter from Kransco arrived stating that the royalties were being *terminated*.

It was a shocker! Woe was us…me and Lu.

STUART B. SCHNECK
General Counsel

May 15, 1986

Ms. Lucille Morrison
830 E. 25th Street
Upland, CA 91786

Mr. Walter F. Morrison
Sunlight Aviation, Inc.
Box 572
Richfield, Utah 84701

Re: Morrison/Wham-O Agreement

Dear Mr. and Ms. Morrison:

It has just been brought to Kransco Manufacturing, Inc.'s attention that it has been paying you royalties under an agreement between Wham-O and Morrison based on U.S. Des. Patent 183,626. That patent expired on September 30, 1965, and all royalty payments should have stopped on that date.

No further royalties will be paid under that expired patent, and consideration is being given as to what should be done about the previously paid royalties you were not entitled to.

Sincerely,

Stuart B. Schneck
Gen. Counsel

SBS:lf

The Kransco Bombshell

Chapter 39 — The Bombshell

The absence of royalties plus the minimal room rentals made retaining the motel's ownership a losing proposition. The motel was repossessed during 1987.

The airport was history…the motel had been repossessed… Kransco had stopped royalty payments. Food Stamps and the State Food Bank were providing a welcome but limited diet. This sixty-seven-year-old inventor of the Frisbee was just about flat on his ass.

Things were not all bad. Social Security checks were a monthly source of income that kept the mortgage-free homestead's lights on and bought gas for a debt-free pickup. Friends who were aware of my circumstances often asked me to eat out with 'em or invited me to their homes for dinner.

Homelessness and starvation were never a concern…

40

EXCEPTIONAL REPRESENTATION

*A*S RELATED BACK IN CHAPTER 38, during the early eighties, I needed investments to avoid paying the IRS their forty-percent assessment on the recent bonanza from the sale of the hardware store property. Part of that windfall was put towards acquiring a bankrupt motel. A local attorney was engaged to take care of the legalities.

The retrieval of the motel from its bankruptcy turned out to be a surprisingly complicated procedure. I sat through the negotiations and hearings and was impressed with the attorney's skills. In the end, the motel was purchased for considerably less than the mortgage holder's lawyer was asking. I sure liked that attorney! The guy's name was/is Kay L. McIff.

The 1986 Kransco letter not only put an end to the royalties, it also threatened to sue the Morrisons for reimbursement of the royalties dating back to 1965. The Morrisons needed a *really good* attorney!!!

I contacted Lu and recommended McIff. Lu said okay. Under a contingency-fee agreement, McIff agreed to take the case. He then filed a suit against Kransco that would, hopefully, restore the royalties and obviate Kransco's threat to recover the back royalties. (That would have really been a ton of money!) The suit was filed in a federal court in Salt Lake City. Kransco responded, claiming the case didn't have jurisdiction in the federal system. That was fine with us.

Chapter 40 — Exceptional Representation

Our boy was already ahead of the game. He wanted to litigate the case in Utah courts. While the federal case in S.L.C. was pending, he had prepared Papers for filing an action in the Sixth District Court in Richfield, Utah.

A process server in San Francisco (Kransco's headquarters) was given copies of The Papers. McIff then voluntarily dismissed the S.L.C. federal court action. He was waiting outside the S.L.C. Courthouse when the federal court dismissed the suit. He immediately and simultaneously had Kransco served with the necessary Papers, notifying them of the S.L.C. action and the filing of an action in the local court.

It had been critical that The Papers be filed in Utah before Kransco could get their papers filed in the L.A. County Superior Court. Kransco's attorneys wanted the case heard in California. McIff's anticipatory actions had beaten Kransco to the punch, and given us a leg up! Kransco would have to find a way to defeat the case being heard in Utah. Undeterred, Kransco filed an action with the L.A. County Superior Court that challenged jurisdiction of the Utah courts, to have the Wham-O contract declared null and void, and force repayment of past royalties dating back over two decades. The fight was on!

The wheels of jurisprudence ground along at a snail's pace. Originally Kransco had been represented by a large law firm with offices in Portland, Oregon and Palo Alto, California. Then prestigious law firms in Los Angeles and Salt Lake City were added to their legal team. McIff was up against a powerful array of legal beagles.

There ensued a series of hearings held in California and Utah. After the federal jurisdiction issue was resolved, the major dispute centered on whether Kransco's business activities in Utah were sufficient to bring it under Utah's "Long-Arm Statute." McIff had to court-order the submission of Kransco documents regarding its operations in Utah over the relevant years. (Kransco had denied having done sufficient Frisbee business in Utah!) The submitted documents overwhelmingly proved otherwise. Both the Utah Court and the L.A. County Superior Court ruled in our favor.

McIff had Kransco's attorneys eating their shorts!

There were prolonged delays in the actions. At one point one of Kransco's lawyers fell ill. Correspondence with and from Kransco was held up pending the lawyer's extended recovery. On another occasion McIff's horse nearly killed him. His full recovery was a miracle…and lengthy. For months on end nothing was being accomplished. The lawsuit dragged on interminably.

Once back on track, on two separate occasions, different Kransco lawyers were flown to Utah to take my depositions. (A Richfield lawyer whom I considered to be a friend? allowed himself to be engaged by Kransco to participate in the last deposition.)

Lu died during 1987. Her will designated our younger daughter as her Executrix. The daughter didn't share her mother's confidence in our attorney. Conference calls with her were, at times, difficult and embarrassing. McIff never lost his cool during the calls (on the other hand, I could have wrung her neck!). Her resistance to listen to reason further delayed things.

Chapter 40 — Exceptional Representation

Then in 1989 Kransco's lead attorney made a fatal mistake. He called me personally on the phone. He complained about how much the lawsuit was costing Kransco, and suggested we bypass McIff and settle the case outta court. McIff was incredulous when I informed him of the call. Kransco's leading attorney had placed his license to practice law in jeopardy when he personally contacted me. Lawyers are supposed to work through opposing lawyers and not personally contact the other party. McIff informed the guy that he was aware of the legal boo-boo. I don't know what effect McIff's call had on the case, but the errant lawyer must have been uncomfortable knowing that McIff was aware of his chicanery.

Kransco petitioned the Utah Supreme Court to overrule the previous decision that would allow the case to go forward in Utah courts. If we lost that on appeal, the case would be heard in California. McIff was loaded for bear, and his presentation before the District Court had been magnificent! That Court had ruled for the Morrisons in a thirty-six page written opinion. The Supreme Court was impressed and declined to overturn. The case would be heard in a Utah Court—the *LAST* thing Kransco had wanted!

The trial was to start during November 1991. The issues would be complex, involving contract, patent, and copyright law. McIff, having done his homework, was ready. At the last minute, Kransco sought a continuance. The case was postponed until February 1992.

Guess what? During December '91, an emissary representing Kransco appeared at McIff's office with a directive to settle the case; to wit: "What'll it take?" McIff's answer was equally succinct: "Pay any delinquent royalties going back to 1965 and continue to pay Mr. Morrison royalties until he dies."

Kransco caved in. The Contract War was over. McIff had prevailed. Kransco came up with the owed "ton of money."

There aren't words enough to express my appreciation, respect, and admiration for Kay L. McIff, Attorney at Law. He had out-thunk and bested a battery of high-powered attorneys in a lawsuit that had lasted over five years. His superior lawyering skills had become manifest as he outmaneuvered the opposition, and thereby restored the means which allowed me to resume the lifestyle to which I'd become accustomed.

Thank you, Kay.

One of the first expenditures the restored largess financed was an appreciative "steak-of-your-choice" dinner. The friends who had helped me through the half-a-decade of financial drought were served the best meal the area had to offer. Missing was Lu. Lu wasn't there to celebrate our victory!

After the lawsuit Mattel acquired the royalty contract from Kransco. For a short period, Mattel sold Frisbees under their own name (the "Wham-O" name having been discontinued) and paid royalties. Mattel then sold the business to another company that restored the name "Wham-O." The current Wham-O Company has honorably continued to pay the Frisbee royalties.

I have a lot to be grateful for!

41

HORSIN' AROUND

*A*BOUT FOUR MONTHS before the royalty cancellation in 1986, I was gabbing with a financially hurtin' horseman in the motel's coffee shop. The horseman asked me to make him an offer on a couple of (he said) "very well-bred" quarter horses. I made him an offer I was surprised he didn't refuse.

The newly-acquired horses were given to a trainer to get 'em conditioned for the racetrack. After the requisite training, the mare won her first out (race). The same day, at the same track, the gelding placed a close second in his first out. What a remarkably easy and fun way to make money. I was hooked!

The horses were gonna need a permanent home. Eighty acres seven miles out in the boonies south of Richfield were purchased for that purpose. The site is located on the western slopes of "Mt. Manure" (actually Cove Mountain, elevation 11,000 feet). The sagebrush-covered acreage has a terrific view of the Sevier Valley to recommend it. A doublewide mobile home was moved on the site and occupied. Corrals were erected to contain the two beasts. "Crooked Arrow Horse Ranch" emerged from the sagebrush. I had become a rancher—the name on the checks said so.

Then came the cancellation of royalties and the motel's repossession. Racing horses was unsupportable. The horses were sold.

BACK IN THE SADDLE AGAIN

The Kransco settlement made it possible to get serious about racing horses. Jerry Cropper, the trainer that had trained my original two horses was/is an exceptionally knowledgeable horseman with an eye when it comes to judging horseflesh. Cropper had connections with trainers all over Utah and the big tracks in California. Through those connections, new horses were acquired that had "talent" (another word for being a runner). Cropper did the training. The horses that proved themselves on Utah's bush tracks went on to run and win races at the major tracks in Wyoming and Colorado, as well as Utah.

Additional horses were purchased at horse auctions—all on the advice of Cropper. (Only those with outstanding pedigrees and conformation were considered.) Breeding, raising, racing, and selling quarter horses was what we were all about.

The most successful horses, when they were retired from racing, became part of our breeding stock. Getting a horse from foaling to the starting gate takes three years. It's costly and a gamble. There's no way of knowing if even the best-of-bred horses can "run" until the race is run.

The Ranch's horses won more than their share of races, but none of the really big money races...like those at Los Alamos in California. Purses (winnings) are used to justify a racehorse's ongoing training and associated expenses: veterinarians, jockeys, entry fees, and alfalfa—horses never stop eating!

Racing and winning purses on Utah's bush tracks can't support a racehorse, let alone a herd. There was one redeeming factor that kept me entering horses in those bush track races: winning a race gave me "braggin' rights" until the next race. Bottom line—I got to brag a lot, but paid dearly for the privilege. *Oh, but it was fun...!*

2001—I was 81. Time and its associated infirmities had crept up on me. A life devoted to sedentarianism had greater appeal than operating a horse ranch. A married couple, Charlotte and Ray Reiter, had handled the chores and cared for the horses almost from the Ranch's inception. Together we had shared the exhilaration of victory—and the agony of defeat—when our horses didn't get to the finish line first. Telling them that the horses were going to be dispersed and their services no longer needed was an exceedingly dismal message to relate.

Crooked Arrow Ranch horses had developed a reputation for being "runners." The thirty well-bred, beautifully conformed quarter horses were not hard to sell. Cropper handled the sales and got top prices. I was outta the racehorse business.

THAT'S ALL FOLKS

Everything worth remembering that had to do with the history of discs—from a popcorn lid, cake pans and Flyin-Saucers to Pluto Platters and Frisbees…and the effect the Frisbee's success had on the Morrisons—has been told.

(Unfortunately, my predilection to excise my Internet character assassin, Jeff McMahon, remained undiminished. The final solution to that problem had yet to be decided.)

SURPRISE, SURPRISE!

Lord O' Mercy! Life is full of surprises. Into my life there materialized a Frisbee collector whose knowledge of disc history and disc minutia is unsurpassed. His contributions to this History of Discdom doubled the thickness of this book.

He's the reason there's a Part II...

Part II

The Yellow Pages

"The debunking of canonical legends ranks as a favorite intellectual sport for all the usual and ever-so-human reasons of one-upmanship, aggressivity within a community that denies itself the old-fashioned expression of genuine fisticuffs, and the simple pleasure of getting details right."

Stephen Jay Gould, *I Have Landed*, page 55

42

MR. EYE-OPENER

*J*UNE 2002—I was sittin' in my favorite beanery, gagging on a bowl of purée of liver soup. A large, brown manila envelope, fresh from the post office, lay on the table beside the slowly corroding bowl.

I noted the name of the sender: Phil Kennedy?... Never heard of 'im. Having slid the butter knife under and across the flap, I withdrew the envelope's contents. What emerged was an assortment of the most brilliantly-colored glossy pictures of antique Frisbees I'd ever seen. A letter explained who the guy was, where he was, and what he does. He was a graphic imager living in Connecticut and a collector of Frisbees.

There was also a questionnaire....

Except for occasional requests from aspiring student authors, I had long before given up answering letters requesting Frisbee history (usually from media types that, when given the facts, had proceeded to get 'em wrong). This package was different. The quality and presentation of its contents deserved attention. Responding to Mr. Kennedy's letter and answering his questionnaire has led to unexpected beneficial consequences.

Chapter 42 — Mr. Eye-Opener

I looked him up on his web site. He runs an electronic graphic imaging business. His web site, www.GoGraphicImages.com, was impressive and entertaining, and well worth a look! We started trading emails. Things got friendlier. On a road trip from Connecticut to California he stopped by my place. We sat and exchanged pleasantries. I gave him a rough draft of my first attempt at setting the record straight.

He became energized….

Phil doesn't just collect Frisbees (he has over a thousand in his collection by now), he collects Frisbee minutia...*in depth!* He politely noted discrepancies in my draft, and offered, gratis, to lend his wealth of information and graphic talents in furtherance of the cause of this book: a totally factual history of plastic "flittin' discs." (For a guy with a college education he seemed like a pretty smart guy!?) When he further offered to edit and handle the complexities of getting the book marketed, I jumped at the opportunity to have him aboard. Further discussion ensued. I wasn't happy with his offer to work for nothing, so he agreed to accept a stipend. Our joint literary efforts were solemnized with a simple one-page agreement. (Later as the project flourished, a more comprehensive contract was signed which defined Phil Kennedy, deservedly so, as this book's co-author.)

My getting hooked up with Phil was a stroke of remarkable good luck. Phil's corrective contributions to my not-always-accurate recollections of the distant past made Book One's history of the disc truly factual.

Phil is not a procrastinator. The original draft shown to him during our first meeting was titled: "The True History of

Plastic Flying Discs." The ink was hardly dry on the simple contract when I got an email with a suggested color layout for the book's cover depicting a hand-held Flyin-Saucer with a proposed new book title: *"Flat Flip Flies Straight!"* My so-so title was summarily junked! *Flat Flip Flies Straight!* was a title Frisbee flippers could relate to. The book had a name!

Our collaborating began with Phil questioning some of my recollections and correcting others. (At times I felt he was testing my recollective honesty?) [Editor's note: Recollections? Yes. Honesty? *NEVER!*] Email by email, plastic disc data began arriving that I had forgotten or was totally unaware of. Then, once the working draft of Book One was completed, he sprung a startling surprise.

There came in the mail a professionally put-together binder he'd assembled and named *"The Yellow Pages."* In it was disc history that left me flabbergasted.

The Yellow Pages is the reason there's now a Part II.

43

DISTORTION AND UNHAPPINESS

*A*FTER THE MORRISONS' DISASSOCIATION with Franscioni in 1950, he had complete control of what would become of the Flyin-Saucer mold, and the discs that it produced. Franscioni had indicated he might reenlist in the Air Force (which I only recently found out he did). I had assumed that as far as Franscioni was concerned, Flying-Saucers were a thing of the past…dead on the vine. A half-century later, thanks to Phil Kennedy, I learned, to my astonishment, that such was not the case. Franscioni had *NOT* been idle. A committed effort had been made to make the Saucers a success.

It was mentioned earlier that Phil is not only a Frisbee collector, he collects everything and anything even remotely relating to Frisbees. Phil had obtained copies of Warren Franscioni's business records, plus other related documents and letters. The documents provided a detailed, extensive history of Franscioni's continued efforts to make something of the Flyin-Saucers.

Phil had assembled those documents with other information from his collection into a booklet titled *The Yellow Pages*. What a revelation! The letters and business records revealed more than the sources for some of Jeff McMahon's derogatory Internet references that characterize me as a charlatan. Franscioni had not been totally honest with the people he worked with. Disclosed were subterfuges and misrepresentations he had used in his business dealings.

The original source of many of the documents was one of Franscioni's daughters, Coszette Eneix. McMahon had reported: "Eneix keeps folders full of yellowing letters and old business records to document what happened next."

Coszette not only shared the information in Franscioni's records, she expressed her unhappiness with the way the success of the Frisbees had upset the tranquility of her life.

Here are excerpts from McMahon's article quoting Coszette:

> "Every time I see a Frisbee I want to cringe," she said. "I get angry inside. It shouldn't be called Frisbee. It isn't Frisbee. How come they're calling it Frisbee? That's not right. It's Flyin' Saucer [sic]."
>
> "When you read about the history of the Frisbee, you always hear Fred Morrison. Fred Morrison did this. Fred Morrison did that. Bullshit. Excuse my language. Bullshit. It was Warren Franscioni and Fred Morrison. It was a partnership. I think they should have equal billing."
>
> "I want it in the history books, as it comes down, that my father was there, not Fred Morrison alone."

And finally, McMahon says:

> Eneix hasn't decided whether to use her files of yellowing papers in a lawsuit or in a book, but she wants justice for her father.

Stay tuned....

44

AN OPEN LETTER TO COSZETTE ENEIX
(Daughter of Warren Franscioni)

*D*EAR(?) COSZETTE,

Remember back...several years ago now. You called me here in Utah...three times, as I remember. The first time I was actually pleased when you introduced yourself. You had to remind me that you were Warren Franscioni's daughter. Then I remembered. You and your sister were the little girls who watched me lay up a concrete block wall along the side of your dad's house on Conejo Drive in San Luis Obispo. That must have been back in 1947.

To this day the purpose of your calls remains a blur. Each call lapsed into a one-sided harangue. All I got out of the verbal abuse was: I had done a bad thing when I developed the Pluto Platters, that you were proud of your dad, and that I was *not* one of your favorite people. During the last call you threatened to sic a lawyer on me. I offered to give you my lawyer's name and number. You hung up....

End of phone calls.

I was clickin' around the Internet some time ago and came across Jeff McMahon's "Where the Frisbee First Flew."
I expected to be enlightened; "Where the Frisbee First Flew" would make interesting reading.

I wasn't prepared for McMahon's version of disc history. I couldn't believe what I was reading. McMahon had pieced together a history of the Flyin-Saucers totally alien to what it really was. He not only corrupted disc history, he speciously assaulted my integrity and character. That I was profoundly shaken hardly describes my feelings of frustration and anger. My afterburner ignited and I went orbital. I was so incensed by McMahon's Internet crap that I was driven to write the true history of plastic discs and, in the process, take McMahon to task for scandalizing my good name.

Surprise, surprise! One of McMahon's revelations was "Eneix keeps folders full of yellowing letters and old records to document what happened next."

Those yellowing documents are your dad's records of his attempts to continue promoting the Saucers after I was out of the picture. *YOU*, Coszette, were the source of McMahon's subject matter!

Here's two extracts from McMahon's piece that are particularly interesting, since he presumably was quoting you:

> In 1957, the Frisbee had not yet made its millions. The rights to the toy hardly seemed worth the cost of a lawsuit.

> ...Eneix hasn't decided whether to use her files of yellowing papers in a lawsuit or in a book, but she wants justice for her father.

Added together, those two quotes suggest more than "justice for your father" was behind your considering filing suit against me. 1957 would have been the "proper" time for a Franscioni to file a lawsuit. Why the years of delay? Could the "Frisbee millions" be an influencing factor…?

McMahon's libelous "quotes" and noxious misinformation provided the grist that initiated the writing of Part I of this book. I had considered the feasibility of filing a suit against you and McMahon for the slanderings, but there was a problem: I didn't have concrete facts to substantiate a suit.

Now I do.

In the course of writing this history of the discs, I came into possession of some of your "yellowing letters and old records to document what happened next." The "what happened nexts" would easily justify my filing a suit.

Instead, I opted to set the record straight!

There's an unfortunate consequence of your collaboration with McMahon. An unsavory chapter has been added to the discs' otherwise unsullied history.

In the following chapters I've critiqued your dad's "yellowing papers," including those that didn't find their way into McMahon's poorly-conceived account of plastic disc history.

Have a nice day.

Fred

45

DWINDLING INTERESTS

*E*ARLY IN THE MORRISON/FRANSCIONI RELATIONSHIP there had been discussions about the formation of a corporation. Franscioni, his mother and mother-in-law, and the Morrisons would be the stock holders; fifty percent for the Franscionis and fifty percent for the Morrisons.

Lo and behold, in *The Yellow Pages* appeared a reproduction of a handwritten letter I had written to a lawyer named "Harry" (last name long forgotten). I don't recall engaging a lawyer. We may have been using a lawyer familiar to the Franscionis.

I'd always assumed that while Franscioni and I were out demonstrating the Saucers, we were fifty/fifty partners. My letter suggests that the Morrisons were willing, at some point, to have their percentage reduced to forty percent.

The letter's existence confirms that at one time there had been discussions with the Franscionis regarding the formation of a Flyin-Saucer Corporation. I don't remember why the formation of a corporation was never finalized. I don't recall ever signing Papers of Incorporation, nor being notified in any form that Papers of Incorporation had been filed with the State of California. Since there's no references to a Flyin-Saucer Corporation prior to the time Franscioni and I split, one has to conclude that the Morrisons and the Franscionis were never corporate CO-ANYTHINGS.

Chapter 45 — Dwindling Interests

...eople with the correct % of share (60%)
however the shares are 25-25-5 and 5.
I assume there are equal amounts of
Preferred and Common stocks.
    Warren and myself show a total of
47% of both with Mrs. Francioni and
Mrs. Brown 6%.
    In other words — I believe it should

70; Warren   — 1850   not   1350
     Fred   — 1250   "   1350
     Mrs. Francioni — 250   "   150
     Mrs. Brown   — 250   "   150

the way its written now — Warren + I
are getting more than should be and the
two mothers are being left short.
    If I'm wrong on ~~the~~ these counts,
ship 'em back and I'll put the ink...
Meantime, look them over close,
maybe there are some things I missed
    Regards to all
                        Fred

46

A DATE TO REMEMBER

THE SEPARATION FROM FRANSCIONI and his family was absolute, and unfettered with untidy, dangling entanglements. As stated previously, the date of the "PIPCO Separation" was the last time the Morrisons ever had *any* contact—of *any* kind—with *any* Franscioni family member, or *anyone* even remotely connected with the Franscionis.

Why is the date of the Morrison/Franscioni "last goodbye" important? *The Yellow Pages* documents yielded brow-raising activities that Franscioni had engaged in after our split. A "last goodbye" date is pertinent to what Franscioni was doing with Flyin-Saucers after, and possibly before, the finalizing adioses.

There aren't any *Yellow Pages* documents that specify the date the relationship actually ended, so an exact date can't be pinpointed. However, there's a copy of a California State Department of Employment Registration Form which bears my signature…the last time it appears anywhere in *The Yellow Pages* on anything relating to Franscioni. The date it was filled out is February 4, 1950 and it is stamped "received" by the Auditing Section on February 5, 1950.

Chapter 46 — A Date to Remember

DEPARTMENT OF EMPLOYMENT
REGISTRATION FORM

FOR DEPARTMENTAL USE ONLY

Predecessor A/C: None
Subject Under Section: 11S 9
E.W: MS 10-1-49

TYPE OF ORGANIZATION: copartnership

RECEIPT NUMBER: G-28362

OWNER(S):
- Warren R. Franscioni — Partner
- Walter F. Morrison — "

DBA: Pipco

TERM BOND ADM: On file

LOCATION: 1767 Conejo Dr., San Luis Obispo, S.L.O.

MAILING ADDRESS: same

DATE STARTED AT THIS ADDRESS: 10-1-49
OTHER PLACES OF BUSINESS: none

NATURE OF BUSINESS: Manufacture and wholesale distribution plastic toys

PERMIT NO.: G-41331
ADDRESS: 1305 Flower St., Los Angeles
DATE CLOSED: moved

RECEIVED
AUDITING SECTION
FEB 5 1950
DEPT. OF EMPLOYMENT
SAN LUIS OBISPO

NAME: Change of business address from
DBA: Los Angeles District

not applicable

(a) No. of Employees: 0   (b) Approximate date first wages paid: 0   (c) Approximate date on which quarterly payroll will be (or was) over $100: 0

[SIGNED] Warren R. Franscioni — Title: Partner
[SIGNED] Walter F. Morrison — Title:

Application taken at San Luis Obispo, California, Feb. 4, 1950.

The next pertinent date is found in a March 15, 1950 Franscioni letter responding to a request for Flyin-Saucer specifics. Part of the letter (paraphrased) says: "For additional information you can contact Franz and Rothrock, our representatives in your city."

Sometime between February 5th and March 15 (six weeks) Franscioni is back in the Flyin-Saucer business with heretofore unmentioned business associates.

February 5th is on the last document that has me officially tied to Franscioni. If that isn't the exact date of our split, it had to have been within a few days after. For convenience, February 5, 1950 will be used as the "last goodbye" date in following chapters.

47

LYING IN A FIELD OF DREAMS

Now we get to Robert Burandt's March 13, 1950 letter to Franscioni and Franscioni's *SCANDALOUS* response!!

Manager
Pipco Products
"Official Flying Saucer" Mfrs.
Glendale, Calif.

Dear Sir:

A few days ago I saw one of your "Official Flying Saucers" on sale at a local sporting goods store. It seemed to me to have the makings of a good feature story for King Features, to be distributed nationally to daily newspapers.

So—if you have no objection to my writing such an article—I would appreciate greatly if you could send me as much general information as possible about your Official Flying Saucers: how you thought of the idea... and any other details which you may deem to be of interest.

I sincerely hope that this request will merit your consideration.

Very truly yours,

Robert J. Burandt
359 San Benito Way
San Francisco, 27, Calif.

COMMENT: The day our hands were wrung, and the last good-byes were said, was the last time I *ever* had *any* kind of contact with Warren Franscioni. Franscioni had indicated to me that he might re-enlist in the Air Force. I thought PIPCO and the Flyin-Saucers were dead on the vine.

Burandt's letter was written March 13, 1950, over a month after the "last good-byes."

Following are extracts from Franscioni's letter of response. The entire original letter is reproduced in Appendix E. Keep in mind that this letter was written for Brandt's "makings of a good feature story for King Features, to be distributed nationally to daily newspapers." It's *UNBELIEVABLE!*

EXTRACT:

> March 20, 1950
>
> Robert J. Burandt
> 359 San Benito Way
> San Francisco, 27, Calif.
>
> Dear Mr. Burandt:
>
> We have received your letter, dated March 13, 1950, in which you request information concerning our "FLYIN-SAUCER" operation in it's [*sic*] entirety.
>
> Enclosed you will find copies of our advertising matter, which should do for some of the information requested. Also included are a few copies of the glossy prints. These are not the best, but seemed to be the only ones available at the moment. Most of our photo work has been in connection with the development of a 16MM color film with sound. We came up with 250´ of pretty good stuff however the film is in the East right now. Further assistance on the photo or demonstrational angle could be supplied by contacting FRANZ & ROTHROCK, our representatives in your city [San Francisco]. Or you can call

Chapter 47 — Lying in a Field of Dreams

Mr. C. J. "Chuck" Franz…who I am certain will be happy to assist in any way possible.

COMMENT: Who are "we" and "ours"?

Franscioni and I did in fact make the referred-to 16mm film shortly after getting molded Saucers. It was produced by professionals, in color, complete with narration, sound, and music (deserving of an Oscar!). Franscioni and I were the entire cast; we did all the flipping. In theory it was meant to demonstrate the capabilities of a Saucer to those "buyers" who were reluctant to come out from behind their desks and witness a Saucer's capabilities firsthand. The film failed miserably in what it was meant to do: no stuck-behind-their-desk "buyers" did any buying.

As for "Franz & Rothrock"? Didn't know 'em! Never knew 'em! Who in hell were they? Earlier I told about flying up to Sacramento, California just prior to our split, to meet with three potential Flyin-Saucer investors. The names of those people hadn't stuck because nothing in the way of investment commitments had resulted from the meeting…nothing that I was made aware of anyway. Were Franz & Rothrock two of those three people we'd met in Sacramento? And *when* did Franscioni first start playing footsie with Franz & Rothrock?

EXTRACT:

> Now for the general information, if I can do so with out [sic] becoming too wordy and involved. Mr. Walter F. Morrison and myself, are the sole owners and developers of the item [Flyin-Saucers]. The idea originated from the practice of sailing ordinary domestic cake tins. Cutting high school one spring day, we found ourselves at the beach thoroughly enjoying our illegal holiday; someone

suggested that we do something other than just lay in the sun. Fred, as Morrison is called, picked up a cake tin we happened to have brought along, and started to sail it. It seemed he had been swiping his mother's cake tins and practicing for some time. Before long we were all being instructed by him in the rare art of sailing cake tins. This went on for several seasons, including the experience of earning extra funds by commerciallizing [sic], in a minor way, on our unique abilities. We would buy a couple dozen of the tins, find a spot where things seemed to be quiet, start playing, work up interest, then start peddling the tins. We didn't do too badly either.

COMMENT: Developers of the Saucers? Yes! Owner? Can't be…Franscioni's on his own! The Morrisons renounced all interest in the Saucers six weeks earlier than the date of this letter. Franscioni has propagated a falsehood.

We cut high school for a day at the beach? My high school was in southern California (L.A.) and I graduated in early 1938. Franscioni lived up in central California, the Paso Robles area (nearly two hundred miles north of L.A.), and was three years my senior. Like astronauts have been known to say: "We have a problem!" We lived two hundred miles apart, went to high school at different times, and met for the first time during 1947…nine years *after* our allegedly-shared high school days!

When was all this stuff that never happened going on? Had I been available to "play hooky" during the fictional high school period, it certainly couldn't, and wouldn't have been to "flip" with Franscioni. In reality, I had a beautiful pan-flipping, future wife for a beach companion during the period Franscioni is lying about.

As for "swiping my mother's cake tins" to flip with Franscioni? *That hurts!* Cake tins cost only a nickel then. I would have *bought* the cake tins with the small change I filched from my mom's purse!

"This went on for several seasons earning extra funds with our unique abilities." That reads like a page out of Chapter 7. As such, it's just more of Franscioni's horse droppings!

EXTRACT:

> Nothing was done to really push the idea at that time; and as time passed we merely grew up and more or less went on our seperate [sic] ways. Then came the war. I had been flying, and working as a Primary Army Air Corps Flight Instructor, so-- went the full time as a member of the Air Transport Command; spent two years in the C.B.I., working the HUMP deal, and wound up with nothing more serious than one Bail-out to my credit.
>
> Fred too wound up as [a] "Fly-boy." After his training here in the States he wound up in a Fighter Group in Italy. Just 45 or 50 days before V-E Day, and on his 58th mission, as he puts it, he was shot down in flames. He to [sic] used the Nylon Pack, and hitting the ground was the most serious part of his inglorious end. However he was taken prisoner, and spent the time up to V-E Day as a guest of the Gerry visiting such places as Nuhrenburg [sic] and the like.
>
> Came the Post-war adjustments and in the course of events Fred went to work for me in the little business that I had started, peddling Bottled Gas. In talking over old times as we went from one job to the next, our cake tin experiences came back into focus. After that things moved pretty fast. More than one [person], while watching us flip the thing back and forth would exclaim, ["]Where'd you get the Flying Saucer?".

COMMENT: The first paragraph tells it basically like it was except for "growing up and going our separate ways. Then came the war." Hell, Franscioni didn't exist to me before the war! The third paragraph's "talking over old times and cake tin flipping experiences," was supposed to have been vocalized after I was working for Franscioni. It's just more of the "same-old, same-old" best described as Fairy Tales.

EXTRACT:

> With the flight experience and what little book learning we could remember our cake tin took on a streamlined appearance. The metal, which was noisy, would eventually break and cause cuts, became a tough flexible brightly colored plastic [Flyin-Saucer]. All this, after hours of redesigning and test, working on lift, gyroscopic balance and the like.

COMMENT: "Hours of redesigning and tests...lift...gyroscopic balance"? Neither Franscioni nor I had any formal aeronautical engineering smarts. The aerodynamic design of the Flyin-Saucers was left to me. The eight original prototype designs were designed specifically by ME. All the prototypes were developed using applications of "Morrison's Modulus"—my self-developed, very complicated, aeronautical formulae that were later stolen by NASA and used to engineer the Space Shuttle..... (Wanna know the truth? Read Chapters 11 through 16.)

EXTRACT:

> Plastic dies, and all that goes with it soon went right through our meager savings. So as a last effort, the little business went by the board, and all our coconuts gathered in one basket. It has been almost two years now and things have just begun to really roll.
>
> We have learned the hard way. Personal demonstration, knocking around at Fairs and what have you. Gradual progression has brought us up through a group of direct representatives, such as Franz & Rothrock, now

Chapter 47 — Lying in a Field of Dreams

Manufacturer's Representatives, and finally Jobbers, Dealers and a flow of orders which is so essential to the success of any venture.

Present manufacturing equipment is capable of a monthly output of 75,000 units. At the present rate, this output will be reached by early summer.

COMMENT: "…the little business went by the board, and all our coconuts gathered in one basket." Trying to run and fund two emerging, struggling businesses at once proved too much for Franscioni. His "little (butane) business" had to go, and all of his funds were "gathered in one basket"…PIPCO.

Then Franscioni adds: "It has been almost two years now and things have just begun to really roll." This letter was written March 20, 1950, only a little over a month since the Morrisons threw in the towel and kissed Franscioni good-bye. Actually the dearth of orders and the lack of any foreseeable "we're on a roll" was the reason for the Morrisons' departure. What happened in a month to suddenly get things "rolling"?

EXTRACT:

> The reprint from PACIFIC PLASTICS runs pretty true to form. The shot of the young fellow gives about as good an idea as any on how to launch the thing. By running through the instructions, etc., you will see that we repeatedly point out that an easy smooth snap of the wrist is all that is necessary. From your own observations you should have learned that a lot of "beef" is a hindrance rather than a help.
>
> Once the SAUCER is properly launched, with a good fast spin, it is guided by use of regular Aeroplane Flight characteristics; ie. bank it, and it will turn, sail it level and it will go straight.
>
> I trust my dissertation has been of assistance. And I most certainly want you to know that your interest in our little gadget is gratefully accepted.

Thank you, I am

Very truly yours,

PIPCO

Warren Franscioni
Co-partner and Sales Manager

COMMENT: "Co-partner and Sales Manager"? Who's the other partner, or partners? I'm a Non-Partner! Have Franz & Rothrock become Franscioni's partners? If so, the recurring questions is: "When?" Nowhere in this letter, or any other letters(?) have the Morrisons ever been definitely discarded. In fact they've been included!

The first time I read this letter its duplicity was mind-boggling! Why would Franscioni descend into such a dismal abyss of prevarication and corrupt facts to the extent he has in this letter? I've had three years now to recover from the initial shock, so my comments have been somewhat tempered. But really...*this letter was meant for national publication!!!*

This whole letter is a *CON*-undrum to me!

(See Appendix E)

48

LI'L ABNER FALLACY

*S*HORTLY BEFORE THE MORRISON RELATIONSHIP with Franscioni came to a close, Franscioni had suggested having a colorful product insert printed that would better describe how to flip a Saucer and, hopefully, influence store managers to put 'em in their stores. The Flyin-Saucer display bags hadn't accomplished what they were meant to do; the Saucers hadn't wound up on store counters. I'd become convinced that the only thing that was going to sell Saucers in any kind of quantity was to demonstrate 'em in front of people! (We had quit using the display bags at fairs even though Saucers sold well in 'em. Stuffing Saucers in bags was a time-consuming nuisance.)

Our business understanding was for the Morrisons to repay half the Saucer promotional costs when the business showed a profit. The Flyin-Saucers hadn't been the overwhelming success we'd anticipated; *there hadn't been any profit!*

It was late in our relationship that Franscioni brought up the insert idea. The cost of having inserts designed and printed would have been excessive. Digging the Morrisons' financial obligation hole deeper didn't seem like a good idea. I argued against it, and the subject was never mentioned again. A very short time later the Morrison interest in the Flyin-Saucers was relinquished to the Franscionis.

Nevertheless, Franscioni proceeded with his insert idea. The following excerpts were selected from McMahon's version of Franscioni's association with the famous cartoonist Al Capp and his nationally-syndicated "Li'l Abner" cartoon strip.

> Then Morrison and Franscioni struck a deal with Al Capp, who agreed to include the Flyin' Saucer in his "Li'l Abner" cartoon strip. That strip appeared in national newspapers sometime around 1950. [Editor's note: around April 15, 1950] Franscioni and Morrison printed "Li'l Abner" inserts and packaged them with their Flyin' Saucers to capitalize on the publicity.

COMMENT: That quote, when I read it in McMahon's claptrap, was the first I learned that I was part of an agreement that Franscioni had signed with Al Capp. There's not a word of truth in that!

> The inserts infuriated Capp, who felt they had exceeded the terms of their agreement.

COMMENT: How could the inserts have infuriated Capp? *He created 'em!*

Capp felt they [PIPCO] had exceeded the terms of their contract.

COMMENT: The letters from Capp are contradictory on the use of Saucer labels. Without seeing the actual document, it is impossible to tell if Franscioni operated within the terms of the contract he'd signed with the cartoonist.

Did the contract specifically forbid the use of Capp's artwork on product decals?

Capp threatened to sue and demanded $5,000 in compensation.

Franscioni borrowed $2,500 from his mother and $2,500 from his mother-in-law.

COMMENT: Apparently Capp's threat to sue Franscioni got his bill paid.

"How could Li'l Abner do this to my daddy?" Eneix said. "That was a hunk of change that put them down. That was quite a bit of money back then."

COMMENT: "...put them down." *THEM* is the revealing word in that quote. Franscioni had acquired business associates by the time he signed with Al Capp. I wasn't one of 'em. (There's more about his business associates in following chapters.)

The Capp payoff devastated Pipco.

...and the demise of the Flyin' Saucer began.

COMMENT: "Demise" and "devastated" don't mean terminated. Nothing in McMahon's whole article specifically puts an end to PIPCO.

The Saucers must have got their inserts inserted sometime in May or June 1950. To have indulged myself in such an activity after February 1950 would have been an impossibility.

I never had the pleasure of wedging a "Li'l Abner" insert up a Flyin-Saucer's underside!

"Li'l Abner" cartoon strip dated 4/15/50 — Two months AFTER Fred left Franscioni. (Note that because this strip was drawn months BEFORE Capp and Franscioni first had contact, Al Capp's saucer bears little resemblance to a PIPCO Flyin-Saucer...it's even upside down!)

Apparently Capp must have approved of the Saucers... his organization promoted them through national ads!

49

PIPCO RECONSTITUTED

*I*T'S NO SECRET FLYIN-SAUCERS SURVIVED* the February '50 Franscioni/Morrison split. What is harder to decipher from the surviving documents in *The Yellow Pages* covering that period is exactly how Saucer business was conducted by Franscioni and his new business associates.

In an April 18, 1950 letter from Capp Enterprises to Franscioni is the statement:

> Enclosed are four copies of your advertising agreement.
>
> We have assumed that your organization is a California corporation. If this is not the case, please make whatever correction is required and initial the correction.

In Franscioni's follow-up letter dated April 27, 1950 he writes:

> We are going ahead full speed. Formation of a corporation is being rapidly brought to a close; in order that we might have the ability to fully justify the expectations of the job to be down from this end.

There follows an undated Rothrock letter addressed simply "Dear Doc." (Who's Doc?) The lengthy letter suggests possible stock options available to Doc with the formation of a corporation. Following are pertinent excerpts from the letter:

> Chuck has been here since Thursday and I came down on the week end on the strength of what Warren had told us on the phone about the Capp deal and his plans.
>
> Warren needs dough to buy...one new double impression die...
>
> He's going to incorporate, which I think is certainly wise, and the only way to handle the deal properly. 50 grand capitalization, of which 60% will be his and Morrisons and Warren's mother-in-law. They are contributing the present die, the 2500 to Capp and the contract.
>
> Because of our early association with him he's giving us first crack. You and Walt [not Morrison] for 10 and Chuck and I for 10 or any part of it.

COMMENT: 60 percent of the stock will be Franscioni's, his mother-in-law's...*and Morrison's?* Why had Franscioni lied to his future corporate partners? If the Morrisons ever had a legitimate legal "interest" in the Flyin-Saucers it was relinquished to Franscioni on February 5, 1950! He knew that.

Then, *The Yellow Pages* coughed up this sign-off on a June 8, 1950 letter having to do with another Saucer promotion:

> Very truly yours,
>
> Warren R. Franscioni
> PIPCO PRODUCTS, INC.

COMMENT: PIPCO PRODUCTS, *INC.* Franscioni had arranged for investment money to promote the Saucers and produce a new higher production double-die mold. His corporate associates were Franz and Rothrock (possibly more?).

The PIPCO name which I thought had become defunct had evolved.

After 1950, there's a lapse of approximately three years in *The Yellow Pages* until this next letter from Ed Kennedy, by then President of Southern California Plastic Company (original molders of the Saucers), picks up the story of the Flyin-Saucers. Meanwhile, Franscioni had returned to the Air Force, been promoted to Major and was stationed in remote South Dakota.

Kennedy to Franscioni — July 13, 1953

> It has been a long time since we have heard anything from you or from Fred. We wonder what happened to the promotion on the "Flyin' [sic] Saucer."

COMMENTS: After three years of no orders from PIPCO to mold Saucers, Kennedy got curious where the business went. Also, it's obvious nobody had bothered to tell Kennedy I had left Franscioni back in February 1950. Franscioni's response is not in *The Yellow Pages*, but Kennedy's next letter is.

Kennedy to Franscioni — August 26, 1953

> Thanks a lot for your interesting letter of August 16, giving us the painful details in regard to the Flyin' [sic] Saucer and bringing us up to date on your own activities. It certainly looks like the Capp organization let you down on the promotion, as their original correspondence showed a terrific potential.
>
> We are still receiving calls here for the Flyin' Saucer. We believe we could handle some over-the-counter sales here, provided the Saucers are made out of Polyethylene. Do you still have the single cavity die, or was it incorporated into your dual cavity Flyin-Saucer? ...we would like to run a few Saucers on it and pay you some kind of a royalty on the ones sold.

COMMENTS: Depending on Franscioni's business relations with his corporate buddies, agreeing to a royalty deal would be kinda enticing. (Life is good when it includes royalties.)

Franscioni to Kennedy — September 18, 1953 (unsigned)

> I have heard from my many business associates in the Saucer venture. I have proposed that you deal direct with all of the power up San Francisco way. For the sake of business on our part I will let Rothrock get the dope to you on the agreement.
>
> For my money Ed, I am willing to drop the die in your plant and say here it is. If you can do something with it we will all make a little dough.
>
> I would like to see…some of those new poly [polyethylene] jobs when you get them run.

COMMENTS: "Deal direct with all of the power up San Francisco way (Rothrock?)." Had Franscioni lost controlling interest in the Saucer mold? Or did he feel he was too busy, or too far away from the action…or too tired of it to get actively involved?

Rothrock to Franscioni — Undated follow-up letter

> Chuck [Franz] has your letter—looks o.k. to me—nothing for us to lose. We'd have to circulate some simple form of agreement among ourselves agreeing to split the proceeds in the same percentage as our original investment because the die was written off…when the corporation was liquidated.

COMMENTS: The PIPCO, Inc. corporation is no more. There's no reference to when it went belly up. It seems to have had a rather short life!

All of the original corporate investors (including Franscioni) have to agree on who gets how much if the mold goes back to molding Saucers. I wonder what percentage of the profits Franscioni is in for if and when the Saucers start producing revenue?

Franscioni to a James S. Bower in Rodondo Beach, CA — September 18, 1953
(Bower is a former Saucer seller who wants to do it again.)

> I do not have sole say so for the welfare of any future commitments; however, we are in the process of placing our die with [SCP]. The arrangements… with Mr. Kennedy will include…sales through his company. I am certain…that you will be able to work out arrangements to increase sales.

COMMENT: "I do not have sole say so…" It's official! Franscioni has lost full control of the Saucer mold. Kennedy is going to be running the store. Bower, and the like, will have to buy their Saucers from Kennedy directly.

FACT: In February 1950 the Morrisons gave up all interests in PIPCO's assets (the Flyin-Saucer mold) and forsook, forever, our relationship with the Franscioni clan. Three years later… try to figure this out:

Franscioni to Rothrock — September 18, 1953

> I am going to write Ed Kennedy…that all future agreements be made…direct through you. Both Fred and I can assure you that So Cal pl [sic] is not a hard outfit to get along with.

COMMENT: That my name popped up again (in the present tense) was an eye popper! Is Franscioni still referring to me as a part owner of the saucer mold…a silent partner in a now defunct corporation I never knew existed? Or is Rothrock supposed to look me up in the phone book and have me verify that SCP is easy to work with? Who is this guy Rothrock?

What'n hell was goin' on?

(See Appendices I & J)

50

INTRODUCTION TO FRUSTRATION

A LOT OF PAPER GOT PASSED AROUND regarding a patent for the Flyin-Saucers. It all started way back in the book, Chapters 11 through 14, to be specific. To save the reader the inconvenience of reviewing those back chapters, a summary of those chapters relating to obtaining a patent for the Flyin-Saucers is presented here as an introduction to the following chapter.

Aside from the cake pan period (1937 to 1947), it all started with the 1946 design drawing of the Whirlo-Way which I mailed to myself to establish a "date of conception." After I went to work for Franscioni he was shown the Whirlo-Way drawing to help convince 'im that a molded plastic disc could be financially beneficial. He agreed and we proceeded to develop what became the Flyin-Saucers. Franscioni financed the mold, and the molding of the discs. An attempt was then initiated to obtain a patent for the Saucers.

The Whirlo-Way drawing was given to a San Luis Obispo, California attorney to conduct a patent search. Did the attorney actually conduct the search? I don't know. Whatever, Franscioni informed me that the attorney had said that the discs weren't patentable. So the discs weren't patentable? Okay…so be it! Gettin' a patent for the discs was a dead issue.

Apparently Franscioni wasn't convinced. Some time later, shortly before we ended our relationship, he mentioned that he had given some Saucers to the engineering students at a San Luis Obispo college to "evaluate." What Franscioni didn't tell me was that he had contacted another attorney: a Patent Attorney. The attorney needed "application engineering data" for a patent application. Franscioni was acting on the advice of the Patent Attorney when he gave the Saucers to the students. I didn't know about that! The attorney then filed an application for a patent with the Patent Office using the students' "engineering data" to support the application. Fifty-two years later, in *The Yellow Pages* provided by Phil Kennedy, I learned of Franscioni's renewed attempt to obtain a patent for the Saucers.

The attorney had also included the Whirlo-Way drawing in the patent application. "A devise [sic] designed by Walter Frederick Morrison Sept. 10th, 1946" was on file in the Patent Office for all eternity. Warren R. Franscioni's name was missing on the drawing. I was the sole originator of the flying disc concept. There's more.

The patent was applied for under both Warren R. Franscioni *AND* Walter F. Morrison. Applications for patents require signatures. Since I wasn't there to sign the application, my

Chapter 50 — Introduction to Frustration

written signature was missing. The Patent Office couldn't issue a patent without it!

My missing signature on the patent application, and later documents, and the absence of Franscioni's name on the Whirlo-Way drawings, caused Franscioni's attorneys to write lots of letters to Franscioni re: Gettin' the Flyin-Saucers a patent.

For Franscioni, obtaining a patent for the plastic discs is a saga of persistence over time. The attorneys' letters to Franscioni tell a story of what must have been a prolonged source of frustration and heartburn for Franscioni and finally, unrequited satisfaction (other than financial) for the attorneys.

The story, in its entirety, is related through the attorneys' letters to Franscioni in the following chapter.

EDITOR'S NOTE: Current speculation is that Franscioni's original attorney (1948) felt the Flyin-Saucer would not qualify for a "Utility" Patent—the most common type—which judges whether a device's claimed functionality critically relies on its unique, patentable structures. Franscioni's first patent application (1950) describes the function of the vanes (to increase lift) as being important (but not critical) to the flight of the Saucer. A much later application (1956) was submitted for a "Design" Patent (see Chapter 51).

51

THE PATENT LETTERS

WHILE THERE IS NO RECORD in *The Yellow Pages* that gives the date when Franscioni actually filed for a Saucer patent, there is ample evidence that he did, starting in 1950. There exists an impressive paper trail left by Franscioni, the patent attorney A.V. Muller in San Luis Obispo, California, and the patent attorney firm of O'Brien & Jacobson in Washington, DC. From just a few of the letters it's possible to piece together a fairly complete picture of Franscioni's attempts to acquire a patent for the Flyin-Saucers.

(Attorneys use a lotta words to get their points across. In the interest of brevity excerpts have been used to separate the wheat from the chaff.)

The first evidence that Franscioni had filed an application is in a letter between the two law firms.

Chapter 51 — The Patent Letters

Muller to O'Brien & Jacobson—November 8, 1950

> Clarence A. O'Brien and Harvey B. Jacobson
> Patent Attorneys
> District National Building
> 1406 G Street, Northwest
> Washington 5, D.C.
>
> Gentlemen: Re: Walter F. Morrison and
> Warren R. Franscioni
> Toy, Serial Number 24,346.
>
> In answer to your communication of September 15th, 1950, the following is a general discussion of the item our client had submitted for patent. Certain of the data or findings referred to have been ascertained by actual experiment and even though we are unable to state by actual degree or amounts the variances stated, all claims or findings are nevertheless positive and accurate to the best of our facilities and ability.

COMMENTS: "Re: Walter F. Morrison...1950." Franscioni has "graciously" included my name on a patent application filed prior to September 15, 1950 which was assigned Serial Number 24,346.

There then follow three pages of single-spaced legalese describing the Flyin-Saucer's aerodynamic performance. *The Yellow Pages* contain five pages of undated, unaddressed, single-spaced engineering data including some drawings resembling hen tracks. The pages end with:

> Results of all tests compiled by:
> Warren R. Franscioni
> Co-Inventor

COMMENT: The complexity of Muller's evaluation of the data, the uncriticality of the performance of the vanes, the absence of Franscioni's name on the Whirlo-Way drawing (see Chapter 11), and the necessity of having my written signature on a patent application and later documents put Franscioni in a world of hurt...patent-wise!

Fast forward to 1956 and the next Saucer patent communiqué. Remember that Pluto Platters had come on the scene in 1955.

O'Brien & Jacobson to Franscioni—March 19, 1956

Major Warren R. Franscioni
205 Frank Avenue
Ellsworth AFB, South Dakota

In re: Walter F. Morrison and Warren R. Franscioni
Toy, Serial Number 24,346 — Abandoned

Dear Major Franscioni:

This will acknowledge receipt of your communication of March 10 from which it appears that you are now interested in again attempting to obtain patent protection for your above invention.

As you are aware, the above application was finally rejected by the Patent Office on September 12, 1951. Inasmuch as no appeal was taken to the Patent Office Board of Appeals by March 12, 1952 the application automatically became abandoned in the Patent Office.

The only procedure that can be followed at this late date is to file a new application. However, in view of the considerable lapse of time since the original application was rejected and the possibility that... additional pertinent patents...may have been issued... it is our suggestion that a new...search be conducted... to determine the probable patentability. This is especially so, if any changes have been made in the invention since the original application was filed.

Harvey B. Jacobson

Chapter 51 — The Patent Letters

COMMENTS: Note the confirmation that there was a previous patent application submitted during 1950, rejected in 1951 and abandoned in 1952. Why was it rejected by the Patent Office?...Wanna guess!

Franscioni to O'Brien & Jacobson—March 27, 1956

Gentlemen:

I have received your letter of 19 March 1956; and am enclosing my check in the amount of $15.00 to cover the patentability search and report fee.

However since there have been no changes made in the invention since the original application was filed, I do feel that you should be able to make a fairly accurate estimate of the action that will follow when this matter again comes before the examiner.

Also, in view of previous action and rulings [by the Patent Office], would you recommend a reappraisal of the descriptive material relative to the explanation of the principles embodied in the basic invention?

COMMENTS: So Franscioni agreed to go ahead with the new patent search. He declares that the Saucer design has remained unchanged since the original application, but expresses his concern that the support materials (the engineering data?) may need additional examination. (Something to do with the Saucer's aerodynamics?)

O'Brien & Jacobson to Franscioni—April 9, 1956

We have completed our preliminary patentability search...

The enclosed patent copies were...taken from your file relating to the previous application. The prior art fails to show a device which is similar in construction and func-

> tion to yours. Should a new application be...filed in the same Patent Office it would be examined by the same Examiner and would probably be finally rejected by him on the same grounds. Therefore it would be necessary for us to [make] an appeal...to obtain a reversal of the Examiner's position.
>
> ...we agree with you that the descriptive materials should be changed to point out the criticality of the arrangement [of the ribs or vanes]. With such alterations we believe that the Examiner would be more favorably disposed toward the proposed application. In the final analysis, though, we feel that it will be necessary to appeal...before the question of patentability is determined.

COMMENTS: Apparently Franscioni suspected, or realized there were discrepancies in the original patent application that should be corrected.

(But if emphasizing the aeronautical function of the Saucer's vanes was meant to influence the Examiner, it should be noted, as it was in an earlier chapter, that the vanes were molded in the Saucers as one of my guess-work afterthoughts. Turned out the vanes were merely cosmetic...and *hazardous* to fingernails! They weren't aerodynamically engineered to be critical to anything!)

> We suggest that you consider the possibility of instructing us to proceed with a design application covering your invention. The design patent law is intended to cover the external ornamentation and configuration. If the ribs on your toy are reasonably critical as to their location and arrangement...design protection may serve your purpose.
>
> The proposed design application for patent would be examined from a different point of view. The functioning of the toy in the air would have no bearing on the question of patentability. However, the shape and general appearance of the device would be the important factor.

COMMENTS: *Hello*... After all of the enlightening verbiage, we get to the bottom line: "The shape and general appearance... would be the important factor." But how much protection does a Design Patent really offer? Change the shape or size or design frills just enough and the look-alike qualifies for its own patent protection.

Franscioni to O'Brien & Jacobson—April 12, 1956

> It is my decision that you proceed with the necessary action for application of design coverage for our item.
>
> The decision...for a design paten [sic] coverage at this time was based upon my belief that it would afford the most expeditious means of obtaining a degree of protection.

COMMENT: In a subsequent letter Franscioni asks about the option of securing the "easier-to-obtain" design patent first and then working on obtaining the fuller protection of the previously denied utility patent only to be told that it was a one-or-the-other deal with the Patent Office.

This next letter has an interesting postscript which introduces another potential roadblock.

O'Brien & Jacobson to Franscioni—May 10, 1956

> P.S. Kindly advise us as to the residence and Post Office address of Mr. Morrison, in order that it may be inserted in the application papers.

COMMENTS: Why does the attorney want my address? Because it's *required* to have my name and address on the new patent application. Because of the original 1950 patent application, I'm on file in the Patent Office as a Co-Inventor of the Saucers.

O'Brien & Jacobson to Franscioni—June 11, 1956

> We are now proceeding to complete the official drawings in ink after which the application papers will be placed on file in the Patent Office.

COMMENTS: The application is about to be submitted for review. Franscioni had been advised that it would take five weeks for the filing action and, since the Patent Office was backlogged, another six to twelve months for the application to be reviewed.

Now we jump ahead almost a year. The next communication has some good news and some bad news.

O'Brien & Jacobson to Franscioni—April 2, 1957

> In re: Walter F. Morrison and Warren R. Franscioni
> Design for an aerial sounding toy or similar article
> U.S. Ser. No. D-42,045
>
> The Examiner has indicated that the application contains patentable subject matter and that the application will be allowed as soon as certain informalities are corrected.
>
> First of all, it is necessary for you and Mr. Morrison to file a new oath, since there were informalities in the original oath. Accordingly, we have prepared an oath which should be signed by you and Mr. Morrison in the presence of a notary public.
>
> In view of the foregoing, we await the return of the executed oath.

COMMENTS: The *GOOD* news is "The application will be allowed..." Franscioni is going to get his patent. Hooray!

The *BAD* news: "It is necessary for you and Mr. Morrison to file a new oath, since there were informalities in the original oath."

I've told ya...I've told ya! The Patent Office couldn't approve the patent application without my written signature! Only if Franscioni can get me to sign the oath can the Examiner grant Franscioni (and me!) the patent. (This was the first I ever knew that I was required to take an oath when applying for a patent?)

There followed several more letters from the patent attorneys asking Franscioni to return the signed oath and instructions on how Franscioni wants the attorneys to proceed.

And finally this:

O'Brien & Jacobson to Franscioni—June 25, 1957

> We note that you have experienced difficulty in obtaining the cooperation of Mr. Morrison in executing the new oath.
>
> In the event the new oath is not signed by you and Mr. Morrison and filed in the Patent Office by September 8, 1957, the application will automatically become abandoned.
>
> An application for patent must be filed in the name of and signed by the inventors. Since you and Mr. Morrison are coinventors of this toy, it will not be possible for you to obtain valid patent protection...in your name alone.

COMMENTS: I wish I could have been there to commiserate with Franscioni and share in his grief when he finally got the word that all his attempts to patent the Saucers had been exercises in futility. I'd have happily shared with him how excruciatingly devastating my anguish had been when my pet crawdad drowned....

McMahon quotes Coszette that some members of the Franscioni family were deeply hurt by occurrences in the 1950s and have been painfully upset all these years. Upset with whom? It seems to me that the lack of a patent number embedded in the bottom of a Flyin-Saucer was the direct consequence of Warren Franscioni's inability to finish what he had started; to seek out what was needed to get the job done. Franscioni alone was the one who dealt with the attorneys, even long after our split. Documents show he was kept fully informed as to what was required to complete the patent process...most notably my signature.

WHY didn't Franscioni, even once, contact me regarding his attempts to patent the Flyin-Saucers, especially when he knew an oath needed my signature or the patent application would lapse?

What if Franscioni *HAD* called me? What would my reaction have been had I been asked to sign an oath?

An oath for the original 1948 patent consideration? *No sweat!*

Had I known about and been asked to sign the 1950 patent application after Franscioni formed his PIPCO Corporation? I'd have wanted to know, "Why?"

After Pluto Platters? *Not likely.*

After Wham-O? *NEVER!*

(See Appendix L)

52

EDWARD L. KENNEDY, EXPOSED!

I WAS CONSTRAINED TO REWRITE THIS CHAPTER because my first draft had a strange and discordant effect on the Book's Editor and Co-Author, Phil Kennedy. (Phil vehemently denies *any* relationship to the Kennedy that's about to be exposed.)

According to his wife, Pat, Phil was perusing the first draft when he violently quivered, began mumbling, then slumped in his chair. A doctor was called. Suddenly, he jumped to his feet, crashed through the French doors leading out onto his estate's Disc Golf course, and ran stumbling into the night, raving incoherently about stupid authors (presumably me). When the search party finally located Phil, he was found lying unconscious next to a badly bent Disc Golf PoleHole (which it's assumed got in his way).

Actual photo simulation!

The sanitarium has since released Phil into the care of his wife who graciously agreed to provide emergency editing. Phil has been showing some improvement. It's hoped he'll recover sufficiently to resume his editing chores in time to finish this book. I swear I had no idea my authoring was such a terrible drain on an editor's faculties!

My initial reading of Ed Kennedy's letters in *The Yellow Pages* was similarly traumatic. The lies and deceptions were beyond the pale. I was stressed. Fortunately, my mental state has become sufficiently adjusted to carry on.

Ed Kennedy, as you'll remember, was Vice President of Southern California Plastic Company when they molded the original Flyin-Saucers starting back in 1948. There's nothing in *The Yellow Pages* that relates specifically to what happened to the mold after the Morrison/Franscioni partnership split on February 5, 1950, but it's known the mold was removed from Kennedy's plant, and at some point, may have been converted to a dual-cavity mold. Be that as it may, in 1953 Franscioni persuaded his former corporate associates to return the mold to Kennedy, who was by then President of SCP. Kennedy would mold and merchandise the Saucers for somebodies...it's not clear who those somebodies were.

Kennedy's early letters to Franscioni were informative, but of no significance until we jump ahead to 1957. These two letters were shockers. I had to read 'em twice, then read 'em again to even begin to comprehend their content!

Kennedy to Franscioni — March 21, 1957

> I called Chuck Franz approximately a month ago and told him that we had just found out that Fred Morrison had had another die built on the Flying [sic] Saucer and was merchandising the product under the name of "Pluto's [sic] Platter".

COMMENTS: Did Kennedy and all the people who worked for him have their heads up somewhere unpleasant? Pluto Platters were first demonstrated at the 1955 L.A. County Fair

Chapter 52 — Edward L. Kennedy Exposed!

(just across town, Ed) two years before this letter was writ. For almost two years, Ed, Platters were being demonstrated and sold at major fairs (and very successfully, thank you) as far south as San Diego, and as far east as Des Moines, Iowa. Surely, somebody must have called your attention to the fact that Pluto Platters were your major competition? Pluto Platters were NOT being kept a secret.

Fact is, Pluto Platters had attracted so much attention that Wham-O Manufacturing had just signed us Morrisons to a contract on January 23, 1957 to merchandise the Platters... big time!

I have to admire Kennedy. Ed Kennedy was just the sort of aggressive, plan-ahead executive that the big, mega-buck corporations are looking for!

Try this next contradiction on for size.

> I knew nothing about the fact that he was having the Saucer built until the time he started demonstrating it in the various fairs and he was also calling on our accounts.

COMMENTS: Ed Kennedy, you would have flunked "Lying 101." Your time associations are atrocious. You said in the previous paragraph you didn't find out about Pluto Platters until about a month before this March 21, 1957 letter. Now in this paragraph, you state you knew that the Platters were being sold at various fairs.

Ed, when you wrote this letter winter had just ended. There weren't ANY major fairs going on at that time of the year. Small fairs, IF there even were any, weren't worth the effort. So the last worthwhile fairs were over with back in the fall of 1956. Were the nonexistent fairs you refer to before or after you found out about the Platters (about February, by your account)? The fairs *AFTER* you found out about the Platters hadn't even happened yet. Jeez…!

And Ed…*HAD* I known you had Flyin Saucer accounts, I may have damn well called on 'em. In the competitive business world, isn't calling on the competition's accounts the name of the game…an accepted procedure?

Here's a doozy.

> During the time that he was having the Saucer [Pluto Platter] made, he was also accepting sales commissions from the company here.

COMMENTS: An astounding prevarication! While I was developing Pluto Platters I was "accepting sales commissions"? For what? The only Saucers I ever knew about were the ones I bought from Kennedy for the 1954 Pomona Fair. None before, none after! And I certainly wasn't buying saucers to sell to myself for any "commissions." That road only leads to the poor house!

The "Big Lie" continues:

> I promptly told him [Morrison] that he had to bring his account up to date with us as, at one time, it ran over three thousand dollars. He has now sent in a check to clear up the account and we are mailing you a commission check which brings us up to date on the Saucers sold.

COMMENTS: *What* account? *What* check? I never had an account with SCP! The Saucers I bought for the 1954 Pomona Fair were paid for, in full, at the time of pickup. That's no account: *that's COD!*

Chapter 52 — Edward L. Kennedy Exposed!

Here's an interesting thought: (Coszette, have you been keeping up with this crap?) Did Franscioni have to wait almost *THREE YEARS* to get his commission on the Saucers I bought from Kennedy while Kennedy was waiting for me to pay a nonexistent bill? Kinda makes one wonder if other commission checks for Franscioni were held up for the same baseless reason?

And Ed…if I truly *WAS* supposed to be getting a commission on Flyin Saucer sales, I'm *STILL* waiting for my commission on the Saucers I bought from you in 1954. Let's have it… *WITH INTEREST!*

Get this one:

> Only this morning, I found out that Fred had also been out there [Disneyland] in order to try to get the account away from us. However, we lowered the wholesale price from forty-five cents to thirty-five cents per Saucer and I believe that Fred will find, before he gets through, that he is working on a very slim margin.

COMMENTS: Don't cha just love it? I gotta laugh. I hope the reader enjoys this excerpt as much as I do.

I wallow in the afterglow of the unintended financial consequences Kennedy created with his strategic merchandising. I'm sure the Disneyland people appreciated Kennedy's reduced Saucer price. Were Franscioni and his buddies enthralled with Kennedy's clever sales techniques? All it cost 'em was money!

After our January 1957 contract signing Wham-O *might* have sent a Pluto Platter salesman to call on Disneyland, but I wasn't privy to Wham-O's day-to-day sales strategy. What I do know is I have *never* been to Disneyland. *EVER!* Not even to take the kids. Honest!

This last letter was particularly hard to take.

Kennedy to Franscioni — August 7, 1957

> I have a copy of the letter to you from Dr. Walter F. Morrison [my dad] which is entirely misleading.
>
> Mr. [Dr.] Morrison called me to change the construction of the die along the lines he suggested in his letter to you.

COMMENTS: Dad called Kennedy and suggested he (Kennedy) reconfigure the Flyin Saucer mold???

We, the Morrisons, had signed a contract with Wham-O to promote the Pluto Platters earlier the same year this letter was written. My dad was fully aware of our business association with Wham-O. What in hell's name would he hope to accomplish by sticking his nose in our affairs? Why wouldn't he tell me what he was hoping to accomplish?

At first, I didn't want to believe what I was reading. But, if Kennedy did in fact(?) have a copy of a letter Dad had sent to Franscioni, then such a letter had(?) to exist.

Had my dad confided in me and shown me what changes he was suggesting to Franscioni on how the mold or the Saucers could be improved, it might have made for an interesting dialogue. Dad was a pretty creative guy, but he knew even less than I did about the mechanics of how an injection mold operates. If his ideas would have improved the flight charac-

Chapter 52 — Edward L. Kennedy Exposed!

teristics of a Flyin Saucer, *why* would he give the idea to Franscioni and Kennedy? *WHY* would he even consider associating with the known Pluto Platter competition?

Our father/son relationship had been close and friendly after he recovered from the shock he experienced when I told him of my '39 marriage to Lu. He'd had 18 years to get over it.

(See Appendix N)

....

Well, that's it for *The Yellow Pages*. They've proved to be an amazing revelation for me. A lot of Flyin Saucer stuff was going on while I was busy beatin' on the heads of nails. No one can fault Warren Franscioni for continuing to promote the Flyin Saucers. The Saucers had a lot going for 'em.

Had I been aware of Franscioni's attempts to promote the Saucers, I frankly don't know what I would have done. Had I known what was goin' on at the time, the Pluto Platters and their transformation into the Frisbee might never have happened. As it's turned out, ignorance was bliss!

I'm still plenty disturbed by the allegation in the "yellowing letters and old business records" released by Coszette, and later quoted by McMahon in the Media. I can understand why, as a family member, she would *want* to believe her dad's records regarding his efforts to promote the Flyin-Saucers.

Coszette's trust in her dad was/is admirable but sorely misplaced. That the Franscionis would be bitter about me and the Pluto Platters is understandable…and unfortunate. Was envy of the Frisbee's success combined with an ingrained dislike of my guts the reason Coszette chose to give out her dad's phonied-up records, to be exploited by Malafronte and McMahon? Whatever…She shouldn't a done it!

Even if I so desired, at this late date, there's no one left to hassle. Franscioni died in 1974 and Kennedy's Southern California Plastic Company is long kaput.

Part III

Frisbee Folks Remembered

53

STANCIL JOHNSON
'Super Shrink'

STANCIL JOHNSON was a fun guy to be around. How he got involved with flying discs and what his connection with Wham-O was (if any), remains a mystery. He always seemed to be present at the major competitive Frisbee events I attended, offering outlandish verbal twists to whatever was going on. When Stancil talked, people listened.

Stancil Johnson was/is a psychiatrist unlike what one would expect a professional psychiatrist to be like. What normal psychiatrist would appoint himself:

"Official Psychiatrist for the International Frisbee Association"
"Mind Mender for the Frisbee Afflicted"

It was usual for early Frisbee "characters" to assign themselves nicknames such as 'Stork' Roddick, 'Sky King' Richardson, 'Friz Whiz' Kirkland and 'Steady Ed' Headrick. Stancil let it be known that he was 'Super Shrink'…how appropriate!

Chapter 53 — Stancil Johnson

One day during 1973 he stopped by my hardware store. Frisbees had been making history. He said he was writing the history of Frisbees, and wanted my input. We sat down and spent the bulk of the afternoon going over my experiences

Fred & Stancil Johnson in 1973 outside Walt'z Hardware.

with plastic discs. I had nothing to hide. His voluminous questions were answered with my best recollections. The interview ended; Stancil had scribbled a notebook full of notes. We had our picture taken together. It had been a pleasant afternoon complete with laughs. Stancil left. The interview and his plans for a book were forgotten.

We met occasionally after the interview, but it was at the 1982 Houghton, Michigan Hall of Fame Installations that I had the pleasure of spending some extended time with him.

Ed Headrick, Fred, and Stancil Johnson at the Hall of Fame in 1982

During the event Stancil let it be known to all that he had been dealt what he considered to be a grave injustice, and he was incensed. Seems, while standing next to the pagoda in the center of the Eagle Harbor, Michigan City Park, he had launched (he said "unleashed") "a Frisbee that was still soaring when it hit the steeple of the Catholic church more than two blocks away. The distance the disc had covered was well beyond the then-recognized distance record for Frisbees and the distance would have been even greater if the steeple hadn't gotten in the way."

Stancil was determined that the new distance be recorded. Record-setting achievements require witnesses. No one had

Chapter 53 — Stancil Johnson

witnessed his record-setting accomplishment. Nevertheless, Stancil argued his case before the Frisbee Records Committee… *RECORD DENIED!*

Caricature of Stancil Johnson for the Hall of Fame disc

Stancil was the first to admit he wasn't handling the rejection well; the rejection was disturbing him mentally, and he needed psychiatric help. Our "shrink" being the 'Super Shrink' vehemently opposed seeking outside psychiatric help: *the shrink didn't exist who was capable of shrinking a shrink of his stature and preeminence.* Stancil had placed himself under his own personal care, and begun shrinking himself.

The 1982 Hall of Fame event ended my contact with the man…never saw him again.

BETRAYED BY THE YELLOW PAGES

The years evaporated. Came *The Yellow Pages*. Within *The Pages* were copies of Franscioni's replies to correspondence Stancil had initiated with him around the time Stancil had interviewed me in 1973. Stancil wanted Franscioni's version of disc history for his book. Curious, I looked up Stancil Johnson on the Net. There is was. Stancil Johnson had published his book: *FRISBEES: A Practitioner's Manual and Definitive Treatise.* (I found the title to be typically Stancilistic!)

Our '73 interview had gone along swimmingly. The entire interview had been carried out in English. He had scribbled copious notes in his notebook as I related my history of the discs. There was no reason not to believe that Stancil's book, when published, would reflect *my* disc history.

According to McMahon, Stancil learned about Franscioni from Ed Kennedy, President of Southern California Plastic. Stancil then contacted Franscioni, who was stationed in Oslo, Norway, and asked him to provide disc history for his book.

Apparently Stancil preferred Franscioni's version of disc history over the in-depth account I'd provided Stancil during our interview. Franscioni's responses add to the deception that's become so typical of his perverse litany of disc history.

Franscioni's Reply to Stancil — August 14, 1973

> Dear Dr. Johnson:
>
> In response to your letter of 24 July 1973.
>
> I have had time to evaluate my initial concern about whether your book might interfere in any future legal

proceedings about the subject. I have come to the conclusion that your book, if based upon the facts, would not.

COMMENTS: "Future legal proceedings"? McMahon mentioned that Franscioni was considering bringing a lawsuit at the time of his death (in 1974): "[Franscioni died] unknown, just as he began to fight for a share of the credit and millions in royalties the Frisbee generated."

Had Franscioni filed a lawsuit, who would have been the defendants? The Morrisons? Wham-O? Both?

"Your book, if based on facts…"? Whose facts? Franscioni's facts would have created a terrible embarrassment for the Franscioni family in a courtroom.

EXTRACT:

> I tackled the job of working up a design that would transform the pie tin shape into the best configuration of an injection molded plastic Flyin' Saucer.

COMMENT: That's a fallacious statement! The actual designing of the Whirlo-Way disc (pre-Franscioni) and its offspring, the first Flyin-Saucer, is related in Chapters 5 through 13.

EXTRACTS:

> Your research should have also revealed much about our attempt to exploit the association with Al Capp and his Li'l Abner; also, the demise of PIPCO INC following this abortive and mismanaged venture.
>
> Shortly after all of this, in the Fall of 1951, I was recalled to active military duty. From here on Fred and I began to drift further and further apart.

COMMENTS: "Our attempt…"? I don't know who "our" refers to. Is Franscioni still trying to include me in his involvement with Al Capp and the "Li'l Abner" cartoon? As stated previously, I was NEVER involved in any of Franscioni's dealings with Al Capp or the "Li'l Abner" cartoon.

"In the Fall of 1951, I was recalled to active military duty. Fred and I began to drift apart." Interesting misstatement. I was long gone, out of the Flyin-Saucer business after February 1950. Franscioni goes into the military and gets assigned to some faraway post. I haven't heard from the guy since February 1950, and after 1951 "we drifted apart"? It doesn't compute!

EXTRACT:

> I do want to see what Fred has stated for your interview.

COMMENT: Smart guy! What plaintiff (Franscioni) wouldn't like to know what the defendant's (Morrisons) defense would be?

Also in *The Yellow Pages* are three typed, undated pages of what appears to be a Franscioni rough draft for a later letter to Stancil. If the finished letter got mailed, there's no copy of it.

Some of what Franscioni was writing was factual. Two excerpts caught my attention.

EXTRACT:

> I "like" the way you have Morrison scrapping [sic] up enough money for the mold.

> There was only one signature on the check that paid for that mold, mine, against my personal bank account.

COMMENTS: I've *always* given Franscioni credit for paying for the mold. I was working for Franscioni when I had suggested to him that a plastic flyin' disc (based on the Whirlo-Way) might have marketable possibilities. Franscioni and the Franscioni Family were the financiers of the Flyin-Saucers during the entire period the Morrisons were associated with the Franscionis.

Why would Stancil tell Franscioni that I said I had scraped up the money for the mold? I had given Stancil the facts about my relationship with Franscioni—in total—during our '73 interview. He had been told that the Franscionis were financing the deal. It just doesn't add up! If I had had the money to pay for a mold, the Morrisons might not have needed Franscioni….

I was somewhat perturbed that Stancil would turn to a falsifier (Franscioni) of disc history rather than use the factual disc history I'd provided him. I suppose I should have purchased and read Stancil's book. Does his book contribute to all the media nonsense that's been regurgitated about "Flittin' Discs"? I think I'm happier not knowing. Stancil Johnson is something of a respected icon in the world of Discdom. It's fair to assume much of his book is factual.

I liked him then and I like him now! The hope burns eternal that his "self-shrinking" hasn't diminished his sense of humor.

(See Appendices U and V)

54

'THE BOYS'

*F*LYIN-SAUCERS were the first "flip-to-fly" *plastic* discs. They were a good idea that should have set the world on fire (moneywise)…and didn't! The people that introduced 'em didn't have the means, nor know-how, to successfully merchandise 'em.

Pluto Platters evolved from the Saucers. The Platters were an improvement over the Saucers. Like the Saucers, the people that developed the Platters didn't have the means, nor the know-how, to mass merchandise the Platters either. But the developers of the Pluto Platter got lucky. They connected with a couple of guys that were in the process of gaining big-time merchandising experience promoting other good ideas. The lucky developers of the Pluto Platters were the Morrisons.

'The Boys' were the two guys I had the privilege of getting to associate with as they went about making the Frisbees a phenomenal success.

Chapter 54 — 'The Boys'

'THE BOYS'...RICH KNERR AND 'SPUD' MELIN

'The Boys' were Wham-O Manufacturing's President and Vice President. To this day, I still don't know who was which.

Both guys were USC graduates. Their first endeavor together was to open a used car lot on L.A.'s "used car row" (success unknown). From there they moved to San Gabriel, California, opened a small shop, called themselves "Wamo" and started manufacturing a modern version of a medieval, hand-held weapon that had instant recognition by a large segment of the country's male population. The weapon was the foundation of Wham-O Manufacturing, Inc.

Hail the Lowly Slingshot

Slingshots have been around forever. When I was a kid in Utah we called 'em "flippers." Flippers were made from the crotched branch of a fairly large bush, two rubber bands cut from an old inner tube, and a "pocket"— usually the tongue from

Slingshot from a 1957 Wham-O Sales Brochure

a leather shoe. Flippers were used to launch rocks or marbles. Flippers went wherever the kids that made 'em went, often hanging out of a back pocket. Anyone that doesn't know what a slingshot is should just ask any male person who grew up in a rural area.

Initially, mail orders for the slingshots were the source of the small company's business. Eventually the slingshots found their way onto the counters of sporting-goods stores. Additional products were added to the Wham-O line such as crossbows and realistic BB guns. (In an in-house "fast-draw" competition reminiscent of the Old West, a Wham-O employee ineptly shot himself in the foot!) The company remained relatively small…but that was about to change.

The change began the day someone dropped a circular thing made of wood in The Boys' laps. The Boys thought the circular thing had possibilities. They started producing the circular thing out of colorful plastic tubing. The plastic tubing thing caught the public's fancy and sold like crazy. The Boys had to learn quickly how to merchandise a fantastically desirable product. That they managed to merchandise the product to its fullest is apparent. One would be hard-pressed to find anyone in the civilized world who doesn't know what a Hula Hoop is and what it takes to make it work.

The Boys took on the Morrison Pluto Platters just prior to the introduction of the Hula Hoops. The Platters were still in their infancy when they were put on the back burner while The Boys were getting the incredible demand for Hoops under control.

While the Morrisons waited for The Boys to get around to promoting the Platters, I got to spend time at the Wham-O plant socializing and becoming friends with The Boys and their employees. These are my lasting impressions and reflections of The Boys.

Chapter 54 — 'The Boys'

RICH KNERR

Rich Knerr was a big guy, fun to be around, easy to talk to, easily likable. He wore colorful short sleeve shirts and cotton twill chinos. I don't recall ever seeing him in a suit (he obviously suited up at least once for this photo).

Rich Knerr

When it was "lid-flippin' time" out in the street in front of the plant (which was often) he was likely to be the first guy out the door. It was Rich who came up with the name "Frisbee."

When discussing business matters Rich did most of the talking. His nature was generally friendly, but he didn't hesitate to use feistiness to stress a point he was trying to make. On one occasion, which I'll never forget, Lu and I had been arguing against a reduction in the royalty percentage. Rich, finally tiring of our resistance, resorted to bluntness: "Take the deal or we'll go on without you!" End of arguments. Since we really hadn't had a choice, we decided to "take the deal."

Later, after the plant was enlarged, Rich's new office pretty much reflected his personality. The room's decor, while not lavish, suggested money hadn't been a problem. On the walls hung photographs taken of Rich on hunting trips with people of influence. There were pictures of Rich and the victims of his marksmanship taken on African safaris. From the most prominent location in the office hung a large, autographed photograph of then governor of Texas, John Connally.

At the big events, like the Rose Bowl Tournaments, Rich's dress and decorum fit the occasion. He was the "Greeter"… the "Glad-Hander." He saw to it that the visiting dignitaries were made "comfortable," and that everybody met everybody. And he was good at it! I heard him observe more than once: "I like having friends in high places."

The last time I saw Rich was at the 1974 Rose Bowl International Frisbee Tournament. By then he sported a full-faced, well-groomed, white beard. In pleated shorts and expensive sport shirt tastefully advertising Wham-O, he was a very impressive figure. His demeanor fit the occasion. He had spent the day doing his "thing": hobnobbing and obviously enjoying himself.

The day's activities were coming to a close. We were in the process of saying "see ya later." I remember his parting words: "Great isn't it! I told you we'd make you a millionaire!" (Not exactly a correct statement…but close enough.) Actually, I don't recall his ever previously saying anything about "making me a millionaire."

I *DO* remember his *"Take the deal, or we'll go on without ya!"*

Chapter 54 — 'The Boys'

'SPUD' MELIN

Spud was the more conservative of the two. He was quiet, dressed tastefully, and at times effected a long-stemmed pipe (I never saw it lit). He was soft-spoken and wasn't much for small talk.

Arthur 'Spud' Melin

During serious discussions Spud's input was minimal. He'd listen until the subject matter had been covered then dissect and comment on what he'd been listening to. He was a pretty sharp cookie. That was during office hours.

When not concerned with business, Spud became "one of the gang." He came alive when we were flippin' Frisbees out in the street. He laughed and scratched with the rest of us when we were imbibing and gambling on Frisbee games in the plant after hours or socializing with the guys in some local bistro.

He was not without a sense of humor.

One event Spud initiated is memorable. Both Boys and I, along with some others, were enjoying the horse races at Santa Anita. Spud had set it up (for laughs?) to have someone at the plant call the racetrack and have it announced over the public address system: "Dr. Melin, call your office. You have an emergency." The announcement was *not* made! The track security people were *NOT* amused! (Such announcements are a no-no…NObody can make a phone call from a racetrack while the races are being run. It's the law, strictly enforced to frustrate bookies.) The phone call was traced. Two very serious security men from the track were waiting for Melin when we arrived back at the plant. It took Ken Mallard, Wham-O's in-house attorney, to explain away Spud's frivolous malfeasance.

Like with Rich, the 1974 Rose Bowl tournament was the last time we got together. Spud Melin died during 2002. Typically, the news media got Spud's obituary wrong. It was printed that Spud was the "Inventor of the Frisbee." My phone started to ring the day he made the obits. Friends were calling to express their concern that credit for inventing the Frisbees had been bestowed on someone they'd never heard of.

....

The Boys were gamblers. They risked capital on all kinds of quirky products. Some were spin-offs of items that had been played with when they were kids. (For instance: "Water Wiggles." Remember the water fights on the lawn with the water coming out of the hose while flippin' the hose around?) Not all of their products were blockbusters, but a lot of "different" ideas were given a shot.

Chapter 54 — 'The Boys'

Rich Knerr, Fred Morrison & Spud Melin at the Rose Bowl (IFT 1968).

Starting a used car lot on "used car lot row" in Los Angeles, The Boys made it to being listed on the New York Stock Exchange in a relatively short period of time. During their tenure they provided sources of recreation for millions of people. They improved the lifestyles of a lot of the people who had the good fortune to have been associated with 'em—like the Morrisons.

They even got a patent in my name making me a CERTIFIED INVENTOR. In poker parlance: The Boys really were "a pair to draw to"…and for that I'm eternally grateful.

(See Appendices Q & S)

55

ED 'STEADY ED' HEADRICK
Vice President in Charge of Marketing and General Manager of Wham-O

Ed Headrick...Frisbee promoter extraordinaire! (Character sketch for the 1982 Hall of Fame Disc)

Illustration by Ann Goldstein

*E*D HEADRICK WENT TO WORK for Wham-O during 1964. I haven't the foggiest where Ed came from nor what qualifications he had for the job Wham-O's brass assigned him. Ed turned out to be a superbly aggressive, superbly successful advocate for Wham-O's products. Under his guidance Wham-O became a major manufacturing entity. His accomplishments were many. His most resounding success has to have been the Frisbees.

Gawd...what a number he did with those!

Chapter 55 — Ed 'Steady Ed' Headrick

The Morrisons' introduction to Ed Headrick has been related earlier in Chapter 35. Briefly, he was an unknown person soliciting, over the phone, seventy-five thousand dollars that would be deducted from future Morrison royalties and given to a prominent Dodger baseball player, who would then endorse the Frisbees. Who in hell was this guy? We'd never heard of him! I presumed we were being conned. I had emphatically told him to "Get lost!" I called The Boys at Wham-O to relate the incident and was told the guy was legit. Not an auspicious beginning with the man that was commencing the process of creating record Frisbee sales. An instant apology was made at our first handshake.

Up until the time Ed went to work for Wham-O, The Boys were doing a fairly good job of marketing the Frisbee. Then Ed came on the scene. One of his first moves was to get rid of the Platter's "kiddish, spacey" look. He redesigned the mold, giving the new design a "sporty," more "adulty" look, more likely to attract mature customers; and it did! The new disc was designated the "Professional Model Frisbee."

Once Wham-O was producing respectable royalties, my visits to the plant were minimal. We—Lu and I—became involved in other pursuits. There were only brief associations with Ed. We were on a friendly, small-talk, first-name basis, but that was about it. There wasn't any serious socializing.

By 1968 the Frisbees had become a big-time, national item. That year's International Frisbee Tournament at the Rose Bowl was a really big promotion. As the "Inventor," Ed invited me to attend, I suppose, to lend atmosphere(?). That tournament was my first such event. Ed was a very busy boy running the show. Still, he found time to introduce me to the visiting

FLAT FLIP FLIES STRAIGHT! — Book One, Part III

Ed posed Fred with a young model for this famous publicity photo around 1967.

Chapter 55 — Ed 'Steady Ed' Headrick

Ed often teamed Fred with sports and entertainment stars. (IFT 1968)

Fred with Actress Tatum O'Neal at the 1974 Rose Bowl Tournament

dignitaries, the "flipping participants," and the beautiful models he'd hired to enhance the festive atmosphere. My regard for the man soared.

I got the same treatment all over again at the 1974 Rose Bowl Tournament where I got to admonish the forty thousand attendees to "Beware of cheap imitations." The attention Ed directed at me on those days gave this guy's ego a hell of a boost! (Those were the only two Rose Bowl events I was invited to attend.)

One day in 1982 I was asked (I don't remember by whom) to participate in the upcoming Frisbee Hall of Fame installations. On the flight out to Michigan, other than Vic Malafronte, I didn't know any of the people who would be participating in the installation festivities (and there was a plane-load of 'em). I didn't even know who was sponsoring the trip and the festivities. I was a fish out of water.

Ed and his gracious lady met the plane when it landed. They immediately took me under their wings and made me one of their group. I think Ed kinda liked flaunting me. After all… I was the "Inventor." I never had it so good. I even got to be a team member and play Guts Frisbee for the first time.

Ed checks to see if Fred has sufficient "intestinal fortitude" to play Guts Frisbee at the 1982 Hall of Fame Installation festivities

On the last night, following the Installation Dinner, and before a packed room, each of the Installees had someone extol the Installee's accomplishments. I was the subject of Ed's discourse. His scenario of my past Frisbee history was blown all out of proportion to what was real. I reveled in his every misrepresented articulation. The whole event was a blast! In my mind Ed Headrick had become a god!

Chapter 55 — Ed 'Steady Ed' Headrick

During the period I was on Food Stamps (thanks to the Kransco lawsuit), CBS called me here in Utah. Would I be a participant on the "3rd Degree" TV show... all expenses paid?
(The show was a spin-off of "What's My Line?".)

The prize was two thousand dollars, to be split with a mandatory partner. Ed agreed to be my partner. To get the money we had to outlast their panel's questions for three minutes.

ED & FRED getting the "3rd Degree"

The panel's task was to try to uncover that we were "The Inventors of the Frisbee." They didn't!

After the show we got the kudos of the backstage personnel. According to them, our bit on the show was the best they'd ever had. Ed had gotten to display and demonstrate his Disc Golf PoleHole on national TV. My share of the winnings, a thousand bucks, couldn't have come at a better time (it supplemented the Food Stamps). The time Ed and I spent together getting reacquainted and preparing for the show had been a laugh-filled, totally enjoyable reunion.

We had finished our contribution to TV posterity and were walking out to the parking lot, making plans for a later dinner. I was looking forward to an evening of friendly gab, reminiscing about what had been. We shook hands: "See ya later...." We missed connections. "Later" became "never."

Ed died about two weeks after Spud's death. Ed had requested in his will that his ashes be included in the molding of a limited edition of Frisbees. Disc Golf discs contaminated with Ed Headrick's historic ashes have been available on the Internet.

(Sudden thought: Headrick's cremation produced only a limited amount of ashes. Future collectors take heed: *Beware of cheap imitations!*)

(See Appendix T)

Ed promoting Disc Golf in 1979

56

GOLDY NORTON
PR Man

GOLDY WAS WHAM-O'S PUBLIC RELATIONS GUY. It was part of his job description to plug Wham-O's products by arranging for interviews and appearances on TV and radio shows.

I first met Goldy shortly after Ed Headrick arrived at Wham-O to take over the Frisbee promotions. Goldy had arranged for me to address the Southern California Sports Writers' Association in the posh and spacious Los Angeles Dodger Stadium's Convention Room. The subject of my presentation: "Why a Frisbee event should be included in the Olympic Games." I'd been asked to expound on a subject I didn't believe had a

Goldy manning the mike at an indoor disc event in Ann Arbor, Michigan

hope of ever happening. But, desiring to be a team player, and being a bold soul, I agreed to give it a shot.

Regarding public appearances, Goldy acted as the "advance man"—to be at the event site before the event and make the introductions. Introductions are more than just meeting the people running the show. That's when the interviewer or MC announces who the guest is, what the guest has done to deserve being the subject of the event, and what the guest is gonna be talking about.

For the Dodger Stadium appearance Goldy had provided me with some helpful "talking points." The people I'd be talking to weren't kids at some outdoor Frisbee tournament. The people I'd be addressing were sophisticated sports journalists and announcers. I was outta my league and knew it!

Once introduced, I got to talkin'. Not long into my "dissertation" the assemblage began fidgeting and squirming. It was obvious I wasn't making any "points." What to do? Get it over with fast and go to Q&As! The first question was heaven-sent: "How did you come up with the idea for the Frisbee?" The Origin of the Frisbee was something I knew about. I had intelligent answers for Saucer-birthin' questions!

Goldy may have anticipated that the "sports sophisticates" weren't going to be overly awed by the Olympic crap! He had thoughtfully provided me with a "Plan B." He'd left a boxful of Frisbees under the lectern. When the Frisbee questions began running down, I held up a Frisbee and asked, "Can anybody in here throw one of these things back?" The Frisbee was flipped to the first raised hand. The hand flipped

Chapter 56 — Goldy Norton

While workin' a room for Wham-O... Fred switches to "Plan B."

it back. In quick order, a dozen Frisbees were being flipped around the room. The more adroit flippers migrated away from the room's interfering tables and chairs out into a wide, uncluttered hallway. The Olympic Games nonsense had been replaced with the flippin' of "airborne crockery." A good time was being had by all. It would have been suicidal to ask that discs be returned. Goldy's foresight had saved the day!

Goldy's forward thinking that day ingrained a lasting essential. I never went to a guest-speaking engagement without a ready supply of Frisbees to engage the audience in an appearance-ending spontaneous "gang flipping." That kinda conclusion and the donation of Frisbees afterwards, left the gathering with smiles on their faces and an experience to share with their friends. The furtherance of the Frisbee cause had been served!

I didn't get to know Goldy socially; we only got together before and after the events he had arranged.

I wanted to know more about Goldy and relate herein some of his public relations experiences. So I asked Phil Kennedy, the Super Frisbee Memorabilia Collector, if he had anything on Goldy that might be useful. Phil offered to send me his copy of Goldy's book, *The Official FRISBEE Handbook*.

"Not *another* book about Frisbees," I groaned. "Is there *ANYBODY* that ever worked for Wham-O that hasn't written a book about Frisbees?"

"Well...yes," Phil affirmed. "The janitor who swabbed Wham-O's restroom floors was in the process of writing such a book, but he slipped on a wet spot and fatally impaled himself on the mop handle...."

Goldy as sketched for the Hall of Fame disc

I don't have a copy of Goldy's book as of this writing, so there isn't anything to relate regarding his experiences promoting the Frisbees. That's too bad. His experiences would have made interesting reading and contributed substantially to disc history. Goldy, your involvement and contributions to disc history remain an enigma.

Thank you, Goldy Norton, for those times you were there smoothing the way prior to my appearances, and giving me those encouraging pats on the head. And thanks for the hell of a job you did gettin' the Frisbees to be what they've become: a phenomenally financially rewarding success!

Chapter 56 — Goldy Norton

FOOTNOTE: That last paragraph was meant to be the end of this chapter. Then, surprisingly, Goldy contacted me. I mentioned I was writing the history of plastic discs…did he have a copy of his book he could spare? He did, and mailed it. The book is interesting, but, alas, there's nothing in the book about Goldy!

During our conversation, Goldy reminded me that he was Wham-O's Western States PR representative. Goldy asked me to please give credit to and include Wham-O's Eastern States PR representative in this book. Goldy described him as the man responsible for the success of the Frisbees in the eastern part of the country. The man's name is Tony Furman.

I called Mr. Furman. He said we had met more than once. I was embarrassed and apologetic for not remembering. Our conversation was most interesting.

After having made a go of Frisbees in the East, he had produced a TV documentary about the Frisbee for the *Wide World of Sports* program. The documentary, titled *Floating Free,* was a finalist in the 1978 TV Awards. Tony Furman's success story is appreciable. He has represented major business concerns country-wide and has been involved in all types of sports (Furmansports.com).

Goldy Norton and Tony Furman…the Frisbee PR guys that got the job done. The Morrisons can't thank you enough!

57

OTHER MAJOR PLAYERS
Deservers of Recognition & Appreciation

*T*HE PROLONGED SUCCESS of the Frisbees has to be attributed to a multitude of people. Some of the early contributors have become legendary in the field of "Discdom." At the 1982 Hall of Fame Installation Ceremony in Houghton, Michigan, Wham-O introduced a special-issue, limited-run "Dedication Disc." Imprinted on its top surface were the likenesses and names of those individuals deemed worthy of becoming Charter Members in the Frisbee Hall of Fame.

During the ceremonies I got to meet many of those "inductees," and hear of their accomplishments. But besides Ed Headrick, Goldy Norton, and Stancil Johnson (each of whom I've just talked about in separate chapters), I've never had the opportunity to get to know the others up close and personal.

So I went to the Internet and found there was a Hall of Fame web site (www.sas.it.mtu.edu/~dkwalika/frisbee/Hall.html) extolling the "whys and wherefores" for each of us "Famers." Here's what I learned about the "chosen ones":

Chapter 57 —Other Major Players

Limited edition "Dedication Disc" created by Wham-O for the 1982 Frisbee Hall of Fame Induction Ceremonies in Houghton, Michigan.

Depicted (clockwise from bottom) are: The four Healy Brothers, Dan 'Stork' Roddick, John 'Friz Whiz' Kirkland, Fred Morrison, Goldy Norton, Ed 'Steady Ed' Headrick, Victor Malafronte, Paul 'Sky King' Richardson, Jon Davis, Stancil 'Super Shrink' Johnson, and Jo Cahow. Original art was created by Ann Goldstein.

Dan 'Stork' Roddick

Stork was/is a Frisbee champion of great renown. When he wasn't winning Frisbee championships, he was supervising many of Wham-O's competitive events. For many years he orchestrated the World Junior Frisbee Championships...a stellar program which introduced millions of youngsters to the fun of disc sports. In 1975 he became the Director of the International Frisbee Association (IFA). Stork edited *Frisbee World*—a superb magazine that covered Frisbee news during the '70s and early '80s. Stork is also a Disc Golf Hall of Famer.

A young 'Stork' catching his Flyin Saucer around 1956

Well-respected for his thoughtful, considerate manner, broad knowledge and vast experience, Dan's roots in Discdom pre-date the Pluto Platter: a picture in his family album shows the young Stork receiving a Flyin-Saucer as a Christmas present in 1952.

The Healy Brothers

There were/are four Healy Brothers: Bob, Jake, Tim, and Pete. Their claim to fame: back in 1958, at Eagle Harbor, Michigan, they founded the first International Frisbee Tournament...the longest still-running disc competition. Their team retained the fabled and cherished "Julius T. Nachazel Cup" for the first nine years of the event.

Jon Davis
Under Jon's direction, starting in 1970, the International Frisbee Tournaments became truly international events. Jon supervised the 1982 International Frisbee Tournament and Frisbee Hall of Fame Installation festivities at Houghton, Michigan.

Jo Cahow
Before becoming the 1974–75 Women's World Champion, Jo was a member of the renowned powerhouse Guts Frisbee team, "The Humbly Magnificent Champions of the Universe." She also introduced many expressive, dance-like moves to Freestyle Frisbee in the mid-1970s. Jo served as a valued Assistant to the Executive Director of the International Frisbee Association.

Jo's art for the Hall of Fame disc

John 'Friz Whiz' Kirkland
John has been called the "ultimate all-round tournament competitor," and voted "Disc Athlete of the Seventies." He won the Men's Overall World Championship in 1977 and numerous other titles. Over the years, he has amassed the largest collection of flying discs in the world.

Victor 'Macho Sidewinder' Malafronte
Vic was the first World Frisbee Disc Champion in 1974. In 1981, at the age of 35, he earned the World Senior title. He authored *The Complete Book of Frisbee*.

Paul 'Sky King' Richardson
Paul's association with disc sports began with the advent of the Frisbee. He was a constant tournament competitor. Paul personified the spirit of disc sports.

Fred Morrison
(Me of course) Fred designed and got manufactured the first plastic flying disc. He is credited as being the "Inventor of the Frisbee." He may have been the first person to ever "flip" or "catch" a plastic flying disc.

NOT TO GO UNRECOGNIZED

Irv Lander
Irv organized Wham-O's early Frisbee tournaments, one of the foundations of the Frisbee's success. Irv was the motivating leader of the International Frisbee Association. His contributions in the furtherance of the Frisbee cause are many. His accomplishments include the formation of the incredible number of world-wide Frisbee clubs in the early days.

Jay Shelton
Jay set many of the throwing technique standards for others to emulate during early disc competitions.

Jim Palmeri
Jim was instrumental, in the early 1970s, in the development and launching of Frisbee Disc Golf as a competitive sport, as well as promoting and building the popularity of other events such as Double Disc Court and Freestyle. He organized the 1974 American Flying Disc Open Tournament and arranged for a sponsor to offer a car as first prize! (Won by Stork.)

In 1980, he published three issues of the beautifully produced *Flying Disc Magazine*. Jim directed many legendary tournaments including the 1984 Professional Disc Golf Association World Championships in his home town of Rochester, NY. He has been inducted into the Disc Golf Hall of Fame.

Dan Mangone
Dan was one of Disc Golf's earliest promoters and continues to serve the flying disc community worldwide through his Discovering The World disc products business.

Ashley Whippet
Ashley's spectacular leaping catches before huge crowds at sporting events (almost single-pawedly) launched the immensely popular Canine Frisbee competitions and doggie disc market.

IN CONCLUSION

To all of those that have in the past, and all of those that continue to involve themselves with "The Mystical Attraction" of Flittin' Discs…you've provided this guy with a lifestyle that could never have been contemplated in the beginning. It's been one hell of a ride. You have my sincerest appreciation.

Thank you all!

Fred Morrison

EPILOGUE

THE CREATION OF THIS BOOK was motivated by an impassioned desire to fulfill two goals:

First—to correct past misrepresentations of the history of flyin' discs, and in the process, provide a true account of the events that led to the development of Frisbees. That's been done.

Second—to forcefully discipline Jeff McMahon, the author that so slanderously misrepresented me.

It's understandable why, as Warren Franscioni's daughter, Coszette Eneix would want to believe that her dad's records regarding his efforts to promote the Flyin-Saucers were completely factual. It's also understandable that the Franscioni Family would be bitter about the failure of the Flyin-Saucers and the phenomenal success of the Frisbees.

Coszette expressed her bitterness regarding me to McMahon and showed her dad's records to him. McMahon used those documents to write a flying disc history which was inaccurate and painted me in an extremely unfavorable light. He then allowed his published article to be posted on the Internet for the whole world to see. His article so enraged me that it stimulated the writing of this book!

I swore that vengeance would be mine!

To have voiced my total revulsion of the man would not have served my all-consuming desire to drastically punish my defamer. I was loath to express aloud: (to paraphrase "Where's a cop when you need one?") "Where's an assassin when you want one?"

....

Not long ago I had the pleasure of dining with the Gambeanos, recently relocated from Chicago to the nearby little town of Elsinore. The Gambeanos are a close-knit bunch that keep in touch with their Windy City "Family" (the kind of people that make "offers that can't be refused").

*Don*ald Gambeano says they relocated to this area to escape Chicago's wind and cold!? (Folks around here have long suspected that Elsinore is a locale used by the Federal Witness Protection Program.)

The after-dinner small talk was accompanied by the consumption of adult beverages. As the evening wore on, an overly imbibed nephew let it slip that a cousin was a "hit man"....

There's this quaint little out-of-the-way place I know of down Ol' Mexico way. Federales are few and far between. It's remote enough to make "inquisitive tourists" distrusted.

Book writing's been kinda addictive. Such an isolated area would be the ideal place for a guy named "Crisco Gringo" to write a book about *The Joys of Impotence* (a subject of which I'm intimately knowledgeable).

Arrangements were made. A flight was booked…

I MISSED THE FLIGHT!

While waiting for the next scheduled flight, it was discovered I needed the installation of a Pacemaker. During recuperation, I turned introspective, then retrospective, became speculative, and reevaluated my circumstances.

The fact that the other author of this book, Phil Kennedy, had recently received Jeff McMahon's permission to include his copyrighted article in our book had a lot to do with my reconsidering. Maybe Jeff McMahon isn't such a bad guy after all....

This Book is about to be published. I'm 85. I feel great. I have a comfortable income. I've got a roof, a nice car, and GREAT FRIENDS! I've been one of the luckiest guys that ever lived.

The itch that was impossible to reach and scratch has been scratched. It would be remiss of me not to be forgiving:

JEFF McMAHON...*YOU'RE OFF THE HOOK!*

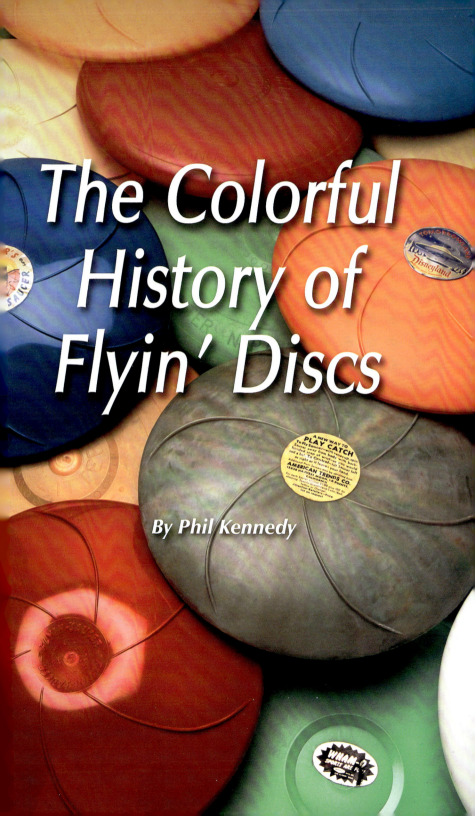

The Colorful History of Flyin' Discs

By Phil Kennedy

It all Began in 1937...with a Humble Popcorn Can Lid!

1— The inspiration for Fred's idea! Popcorn, cookies and candy came in a variety of sizes and shapes of metal tins whose lids fly quite well...and were often flipped!

2— Cake pan similar to the type which Fred Morrison flipped with Lu and sold on CA beaches beginning 1938.

3— Pie tins from the Frisbie Pie Co. were flipped no earlier, nor more often, nor are better flyers than other brands. At the very *most*, "Frisbee" may have indirectly inspired Wham-O's use of the *NAME* "Frisbee" in 1957. They are *NOT* the origin of plastic flying discs!

4— California Pies tin. This shallow, rounded design might actually fly nicely.

Cake Pans & Pie Tins

(PIPCO) Flyin-Saucer, 1st Style, First Mold Run – FS1

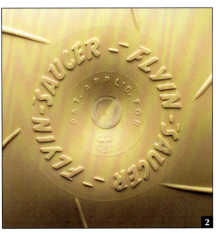

1— **THE FIRST PLASTIC FLYING DISC.**
Based on Fred Morrison's 1946 Whirlo-W
design and produced by PIPCO in 1948
First mold run was 1,000 powder blue
(shown above is the World's Oldest Plas
Flying Disc) and black. Subsequently,
brighter colors were used. Each disc took
28 seconds to mold. This disk was nicknamed the "Rotary Fingernail Clipper"
due to the catching hazards from its
spinning vanes—the term was *never*
used in public! Only a handful of FS1s
are known to collectors to date.

2— The only style of Flyin-Saucer with large
raised letters. Note where extra plastic
(sprue) was clipped off after molding. Th
Saucer was owned by the Franscionis.

(PIPCO) Flyin-Saucer, 1st Style – FS1

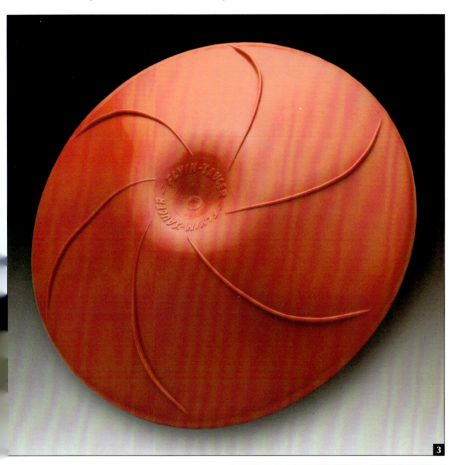

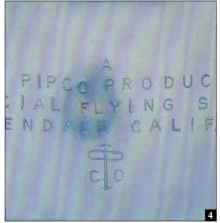

3— Originally the Saucers did not have either raised or sunken centers, nor the overall "volcano" shape they all have today—the hard, brittle plastic has distorted over time (see side views, page 276 and a digital reconstruction of the original shape on the cover). Made of a form of ethylcellulose plastic which some have called "butyrate." This mint red example is the actual disc sent to Al Capp by Warren Franscioni (Fred's former PIPCO partner) as a prototype for the ill-fated Li'l Abner promotion (see FS2).

4— The PIPCO name and logo first appeared on the original Flyin-Saucer and long outlived the business partnership.

FS1s are a collector's "Holy Grail"

(PIPCO) Flyin-Saucer, 2nd & 3rd Styles/Li'l Abner – FS2/LA & FS3/LA

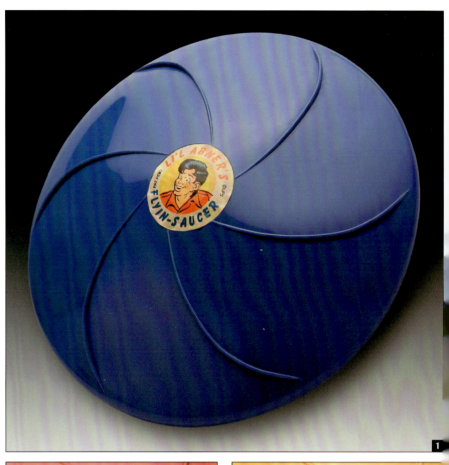

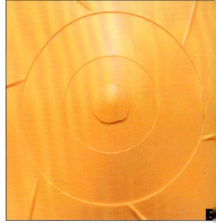

Capp Enterprises—Insert for FS2/LA & FS3/LA

1— In 1950 Franscioni produced 5,000 discs to tie in with Al Capp's cartoon series. Few were sold due to a threatened lawsuit, possibly over unauthorized label. 1,600 mint Saucers were found in 1977.

2— The Flyin-Saucer name was tooled off to accommodate the label.

3— FS3: PIPCO logo and "Pat. Applied For" removed from top; info on back identical to FS2. This disc has signs of a lost label.

4— Heavy paper inserts were produced by Brian Specialties from artwork supplied by Capp Enterprises (*not* PIPCO).

5— Backside illustrates throwing instructions. This particular insert shown came from Al Capp and was never inserted.

(SCP) Flyin Saucer, 4th & 5th Styles – FS4 & FS5

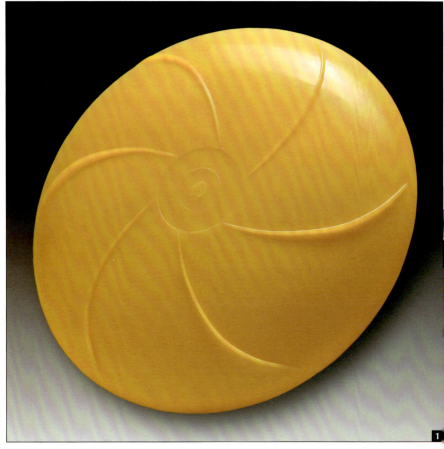

1— In late 1953 SCP reobtained the mold from Warren Franscioni and made Saucers out of polyethylene plastic to sell directly to their own customers, giving Franscioni and his partners (but not Fred) a percentage of all sales. This rare mint FS4 example (above) is identified by its recessed center area.

2— The center of the FS5 (at right and next page) is flush with the top of the rest of the disc (like the FS7). Like the FS4, there are no graphics…the name Flyin Saucer was not restored until the FS6. Both the FS4 & FS5 retain the inner ring from the FS2 & FS3 and the same PIPCO information on the back.

(SCP) Flyin Saucer, 5th Style / American Trends – FS5/AT

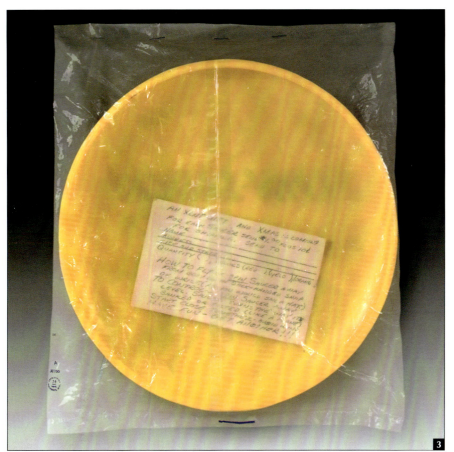

3— In the late summer of 1954 Fred Morrison bought two orders of Saucers (about 4000 total) from SCP at wholesale cost. While most were sold at fairs and were FS7 Style with adhesive labels (see page 255), this (so far) unique FS5 example was sent in a stapled bag with a duplicated, hand-lettered (by Fred) mail-order card prior to Xmas 1954. The presence of the card is the *only* way to identify this FS5/AT. (See page 370)

4— These packages were first made to market the FS1. Many FS7 Saucers were also sold in these bags by SCP.

(SCP) Flyin Saucer, 6th & 7th Styles – FS6 & FS7

1— FS6: "FLYIN SAUCER" was restored to the top with a new spelling—no hyphen. Note RAISED circular center area.

2— FS7: Center area retooled FLUSH with top of disc. Thousands sold by SCP beginning in 1954; many in FS1 bags.

3— Variegated discs like this one result when colors are switched during a nonstop molding run and the plastic pellets mix. (Fred refers to these as "vomit" models.)

4— Labels gave throwing instructions and encouraged mail orders. Labels were later applied underneath to minimize damage.

5— Text changes on label reprints created a second style. Both types appeared later on American Trends Pluto Platters.

(SCP) Flyin Saucer, 7th Style / American Trends – FS7/AT

(SCP) Flyin Saucer, 7th Style / Disneyland – FS7/D

1— In 1956 Southern California Plastic signed a contract directly with Disneyland (which had opened the year before).

2— Special Tomorrowland foil labels were printed for the front of the Saucers. (Some of the FS7 discs used early on came in bags, but without the foil labels.)

3— Saucers were packaged in bags (first open, later heat-sealed) without a header card. Graphics were developed and provided by Disney. The earliest bags were printed in blue, while later versions, such as this mint example, are in black.

(SCP) Flyin Saucer, 8th Style / Disneyland – FS8/D

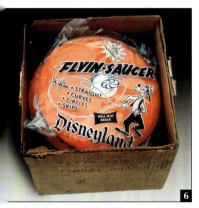

4— Back of the packaging illustrates throwing instructions.

5— FS8: At some point the mold was lightly sandblasted, creating the matte (dull) finished FS8 discs. The PIPCO name and logo remained on the back and were protected during sandblasting leaving that area of the disc shinier.

6— This example was found still in its original shipping carton at a flea market in 1996. (Dan Goodsell)

(SCP & RKI) Flyin Saucers – FS9, FS10 & FS11

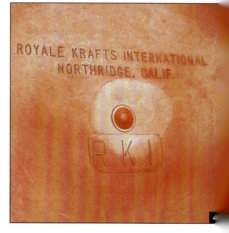

(Unknown) Flyin Saucers, 12th & 13th Styles – FS12 & FS13

6

5

1— FS9: In the 60s SCP had Republic Tool And Die Corp. revise the mold: "Flyin Saucer" was removed; the vanes were shortened to allow space for imprints.

2— FS9: SCP logo & Republic Tool name replaced PIPCO logo & info on back.

3— FS10: Republic Tool name removed.

4— FS11: Royale Krafts International got the mold before SCP's demise about 1970.

5— FS12: RKI logo was crudely removed by an unidentified company in the 1970s. The front is still identical to the FS9.

6— FS13: Finally, three rings were added by an unknown company. Back has faint remnants of the FS12 tooling.

Where is this legendary mold now?

Other "Flying Discs" from the late 1940s & early 1950s

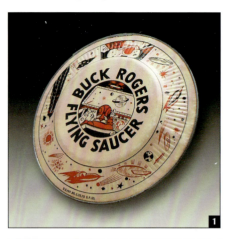

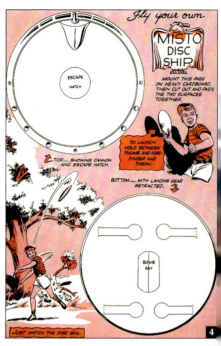

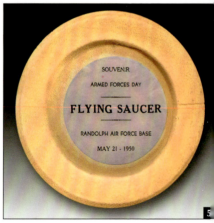

1— Buck Rogers Flying Saucer (BRFS1) 194{ Two identical 6″ paper plates joined by wire ring. Likely not meant to be tossed.

2— Buck Rogers Flying Saucer (BRFS2). Pressed plastic top sheet glued to a fla bottom. Plastic propellers with rivet. Decal. Produced after 1948 and likely not intended to be tossed.

The Space Saucer – 1953 to 1962

3— The Sky Pie, introduced in 1949 by Hall Mfg., used a wire catching device. Patented in 1954. Reissued 1979.

4— Misto Disc Ship. 1948. Dell Comics #190: Buck Rogers—Adventures of the Flying Saucers. ©King Features Syndicate. "Mount page on heavy cardboard. Cut out & paste two surfaces together."

5— Flying Saucer souvenir. Paper plate with label: Armed Forces Day, May 21, 1950.

6— Space Saucer. Many Styles were sold by Bill Robes of NH primarily at Dartmouth and Yale Co-ops. It was never patented.

7— The thinness of the plastic required rim buttresses to prevent cracking.

(American Trends) Pluto Platter – ATPP

Known ATPP colors

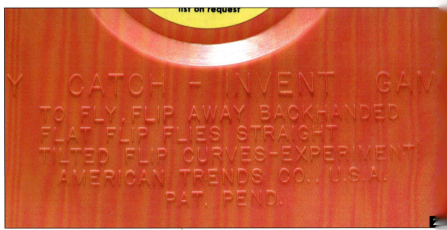

(American Trends) Pluto Platter – Packaging

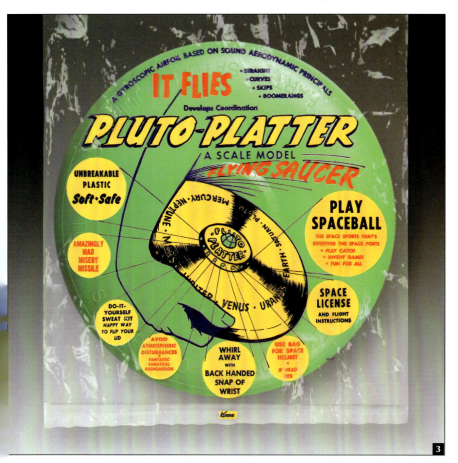

1— **THE PLUTO PLATTER** is the archetype of the modern flying disc. Designed in 1955 by Fred Morrison, thousands were sold at fairs in 1955 and 1956. This mint example with sticker, bag, & return card was found in a Utah barn in 2003!

2—The American Trends address is on the bottom along with Lu Morrison's famous instructions and usually either of the two label variations originally used on the polyethylene Flyin Saucers (FS7/AT).

3— Bags were printed to aid store sales—which never happened. The few mail orders fulfilled were sent bagged with reordering cards.

ATPPs are a collector's dream!

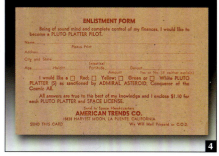

4— Mail order cards were cleverly designed as a Pluto Platter Pilot Enlistment Form. While available colors listed are red, yellow, green, and white, ATPPs were also made in blue. (See page 370)

(Wham-O) Pluto Platter, 1st Style – WPP1

Known WPP1 colors

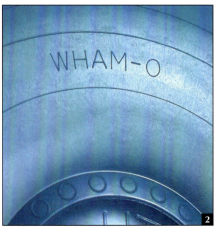

(Wham-O) Pluto Platter – WPP1 Early Packaging

1— On January 23, 1957 Fred and Lu Morrison signed over all manufacturing and promotional rights for the Pluto Platter to Wamo Mfg. Co. including the mold, and all American Trends labels and packaging as part of the deal. Soon after, the first Wham-O Pluto Platters were produced in red, yellow, blue, green, and this very rare and beautiful milky white version.

2— The new Wham-O spelling appears only once (small) on the front of the disc.

3— The "Observation Dome" on top of the "Portholed Cockpit" retained Fred's original "12-paned window" design.

4— Sold loose in test store bins at first, then open bags without the "Frisbee" name.

5— Back of the unsealed plastic bag.

6— The American Trends address was replaced with Wham-O information by engraving into the mold, creating an "esker" (raised bar) on the disc.

7— Foil label on back. Note "wamo" logo.

WPP1 – Later Packaging, WPP1/AT, & Horseshoe Set

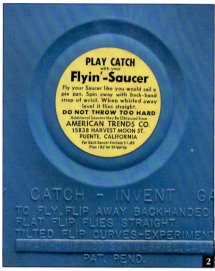

1— "Frisbee" added to bag after June 17, 19[..]
2— Wham-O's contract allowed Fred to se[..] WPPs. Label identifies a WPP1/AT.
3— First Horseshoe Game. "wamo" on bo[..]
4— Four WPP1 discs in various color comb[..] nations. Mimeographed instructions. "wamo" labels on wooden stakes. Two sturdy measuring cords. (See Appendix [..])
5— WPP2 Observation Dome turned *sligh[..]* counter-clockwise compared to WPP1[..]
6— Large "Wham-O" added to the front.
7— "Frisbee" and a second small "Wham[..] added to front. Rare brown (latté?) Plat[..]

The first disc to carry the name Frisbe[..]

(Wham-O) Pluto Platter, 2nd Style – WPP2

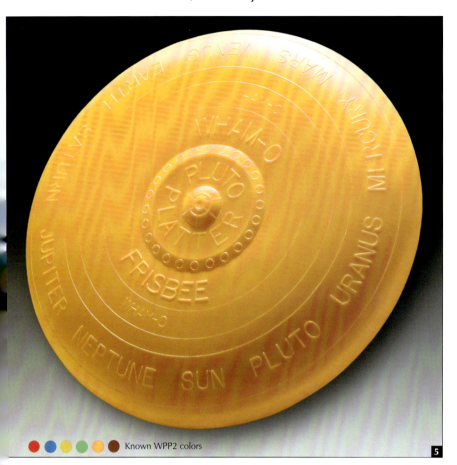

Known WPP2 colors

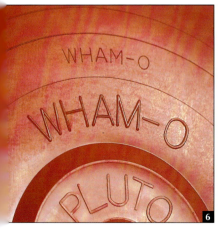

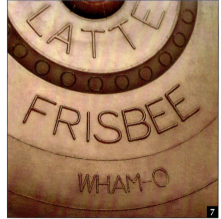

(Wham-O) Pluto Platter, 3rd Style – WPP3

Known WPP3 colors

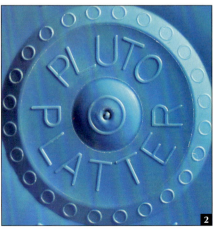

(Wham-O) Pluto Platter, 4th Style – WPP4

Known WPP4 colors

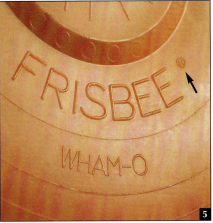

1— The WPP3 is very similar to the WPP2.

2— Both center components of the four-part mold, which formed the top and bottom areas at the injection point, were retooled or replaced giving the WPP3 a smooth Observation Dome (nipple) with no Window Panes or "spokes" and a crater-like "puddle." (See WPP7)

3— Later bags were sealed with a header: both white & yellow headers are known.

4— On May 26, 1959 Wham-O received Registered Trademark #679186 for the name Frisbee. The WPP4 has the ® symbol. A small mold flaw first appeared as a nick in the puddle. (See WPP7)

5— Detail showing the ® after Frisbee.

(Wham-O) Pluto Platter, 5th & 6th Styles – WPP5 & WPP6

Known WPP5 colors   Known WPP6 colors

1— The tops of the WPP5 and WPP6 are identical to the WPP4.

2— The Design Patent Wham-O received on September 30, 1958 was inscribed on the back of the WPP5 on a second esker. Since only a handful of "Double Esker" discs have been found (one apricot, about 15 red and mostly from the upper Mid-West) it has been suggested that the WPP5 mold was run for only a day or two, potentially making it the rarest WPP.

3— Both eskers were removed creating the WPP6. This short-lived, very rare WPP7 "precursor" has been found only in red so far.

(Wham-O) Pluto Platter, 7th Style – WPP7 & WPP7R

Known WPP7 colors   WPP7R

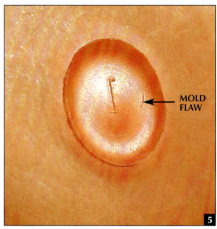

MOLD FLAW

4— The top of the WPP7 is identical to the WPP4–6. Besides being run in red, apricot, and the normal blue plastic, this style was also produced using an experimental blue plastic with a more rubbery consistency…the rare WPP7R.

5— A (so-called "mold number") 1 was added to the ejector pin. It appears backwards in the "puddle" along with the nick (flaw) introduced on the WPP4. On each of the seven WPP7s in the Kennedy Collection the digit (and flaw) is rotated differently…a sure sign that this part of the mold (the ejector pin) was separate. Note crater-shaped puddle, first appearing on the WPP3.

6— In 1964, soon before the mold was retooled to make the Pro Model, "Pluto Platter" was removed from the bag leaving only the brand name FRISBEE.

7— Pluto Platters were demonstrated in the Better Living Pavilion at the 1964 World's Fair in NYC, and sold in Wham-O's newly developed packaging (shrink-wrapped disc on a printed card) with a specially printed paper insert.

The WPP7 was the last Pluto Platter.

Pro Frisbee (Re-tooled PP) and Variations – Wham-O

Early Wham-O Variations on the Pluto Platter Design

1— In 1964 the Pluto Platter mold was forever altered to create the Mold #1 Official Pro Model. This historic mold was reportedly eventually sent to Wham-O's Canadian affiliate, Irwin Toys.

2— Moonlighter Pro (1969)

3— All-American Pro (1971)

4— Sailing Satellite, the first *completely new* disc design by Wham-O (late-1957)

5— Flying Saucer, many styles (1958)

6— Master Model, serialized label (1967)

7— Horseshoe model (late-1960s)

8— Regular model, many styles (1966)

Knock-Offs of the Pluto Platter – Various Manufacturers

1— Mars Platter, Premier Products (1958) After winning a copyright infringement suit, Wham-O acquired the mold and produced its own Mars Platters (1960s).

2— Zo-lar, Empire Plastics (1958)

3— Junior Mystery-Y (possibly from retooled Zo-lar mold), Empire Plastics (1959)

4— Giant Mystery-Y, Empire Plastics (1959) Wham-O acquired all of the Empire molds after winning a copyright infringement suit. Reissued in 1979.

5— Jumping Jupiter, Irwin Corp. (late-1950s)

6— C.P.I. Saucer Tosser (1970s)

7— ChemToy Super Zinger (1970s)

8— Wiffle Flying Saucer (1970s)

Knock-Offs of the Pluto Platter – Various Manufacturers

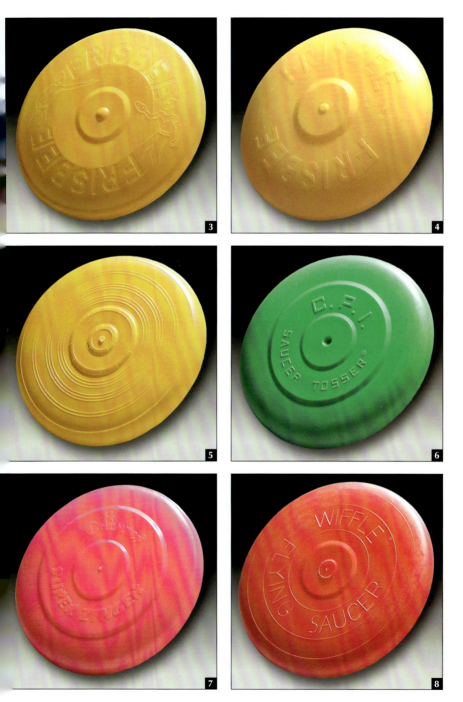

Profile, Cross-Section and Diameter Comparisons

Flyin-Saucer (PIPCO) 1st–3rd Styles (FS1–FS3) (with *sunken* center*)		9–1/8″
Flyin-Saucer (PIPCO) 1st–3rd Styles (FS1–FS3) (with *raised* center*)		9–1/8″
Flyin Saucer (SCP) 4th–8th Styles (FS4–FS8) (orig. shape of *all* FS1–FS8)		9–5/16″
Flyin Saucer (SCP & Others) 9th–12th Styles (FS9–FS12)		9–5/16″
Space Saucer (Robes)		9–11/16″
Pluto Platter, All Styles		9–5/16″
Professional Frisbee® (Retooled Pluto Platter)		9–3/8″
Sailing Satellite		11–7/16″
Flying Saucer (Wham-O)		8–13/16″
Mars Platter, All Styles		8–7/8″
Zo-lar		9–1/8″
Mystery Y, Regular		9–5/16″
Mystery Y, Giant		11–1/4″
Regular Frisbee		8–13/16″

*The shapes of FS1–FS3 Saucers have distorted over time possibly due to stresses on the plastic created by the stiff ribs & lettering. The original molded shapes were identical to the FS4 above. (See pgs. 248–9 & cover image

Book Two

The Essential Guide to Collecting Flyin' Discs

So Many Discs…
So Little Time…
So Little Room!

By Phil Kennedy

FOREWORD

*E*VER SINCE THAT EARLY SPRING DAY in 1957 when I plunked down a full week's allowance on the counter of our neighborhood five-and-dime for a bright yellow, round hunk of plastic (which promised it could do wondrous feats), my Pluto Platter has never been far from my reach. We grew up together. We went to college together. After Pat and I were married we would connect with it. It was in my Navy seabag. I shared it with my toddling son.

By the mid-seventies I had been playing with my Platter for almost twenty years. I knew it was considered a mere toy to toss in the backyard, but it never felt like a toy to me. Cloistered in remote, conservative Connecticut, how was I to know what had been stirring out there.

But the Frisbee-craze was spreading far and wide…even to sleepy little Hartford. Warm, sunny days found the airspace over city parks filled with newer-looking, better-flying plastic. Obviously there were others who didn't view them as simple toys either.

In 1976 I met a local player who had bigwig friends in NYC. I got connected!

One of my first serious introductions into the Frisbee scene was Stancil Johnson's recently published book: *FRISBEE: A Practitioner's Manual and Definitive Treatise.* It was a mind-opener. I couldn't believe what was happening out there. I read the book from cover to cover…again and again.

It was the bible!

Foreword to Book Two

1976...time to get serious. Yikes!

Realizing that I had been one of the "chosen" who was there for the "coming" of Frisbee, I was further surprised and fascinated to learn that a hazy history preceded my "sacred" Pluto Platter.

What was this Arcuate Vane model? Pipco crab? Invisible wire? A Li'l Abner model? Morrison's Flyin' Saucer? Sky Pie? Space Saucer? I had to know!

For the last thirty years, I've had fun solving those puzzles. I discovered what was happening out there in Discdom. I became a serious competitor: PDGA #190; was at the $50K in 1979; won a bunch of East Coast titles; coached my son, Shawn, who was crowned 1988 World Junior Frisbee Champion; became a Master, then Grand Master; collected over 1,000 discs including a powder blue 1948 PIPCO Flyin-Saucer from the very first mold run of the very first plastic flying disc; the actual Saucer that Warren Franscioni sent to Al Capp; the only known apricot "double-esker"; two mint American Trends Pluto Platters; and many, many other historical treasures.

But one mystery remained...who's Fred Morrison? Nobody could tell me much of anything. He was an enigma.

So, one day, I decided to offer my hand to Fred. I figured... what's the very *worst* that can happen...a *snub?* As it turned out, the very best happened: We became great friends...and working together on this book has been a thrilling adventure!

Phil Kennedy

58

THE THRILLS OF DISC COLLECTING

BOOK ONE IS ALL ABOUT correcting the early history of flying discs…as lived and related by Fred Morrison. Therefore, most of the discs discussed and displayed on the following pages represent the discs Fred designed…the earliest, most influential, rarest of all flyin' plastic…also the ones most sought-after by knowledgeable disc collectors.

But because the early history of flying discs has often been misrepresented in the past, published descriptions of the discs from that era have also been sketchy at best or, more commonly, just plain wrong. Limited available resources, gap-filling guesses, incomplete research, and erroneous conclusions by recognized experts have painted a blurred composite of what was produced, when, and by whom. Accepting these accountings at face value, collectors are searching in vain for discs which never existed, while not recognizing the significance of rare items passing under their very noses. As with many pursuits, maintaining a roving mind and a skeptical attitude can reap tremendous benefits.

There's no way to overestimate the influence which the Internet has had on both the joy and also the business of collecting things. All sorts of things…including flying discs.

On-line auctions such as eBay® have folks flocking to musty closets and creepy, dank basements in search of suddenly valuable "junk." Many a plastic saucer, tossed a few times at a long-forgotten family picnic, has been quietly snoozing away for the past fifty years at the bottom of a trunk in grandma's spooky attic. More and more frequently an estate-seller, called in to auction off the crates of worldly possessions of a recently-deceased relation, unearths a buried treasure without realizing its true value or significance. With the vast reach of the Internet at their disposal, general-interest dealers have discovered that simply tossing an old flying disc onto an auction site can occasionally reap monetary rewards beyond their wildest imaginations.

It is my intent in this section to correct and extend the knowledge base for collectors and dealers alike…fully aware that new data await our discovery. Each step brings all of us closer to a more complete historical picture: newly-published personal recollections, such as Fred's, send us in search of related discs; while newly-discovered discs encourage exploration for explanations.

It is not my intent to try to sort out and list the current value of each disc. The pricing situation is far too volatile at this point in time; there are too many unknowns. How many 1948 Flyin-Saucers are there still in existence? How many American Trends Pluto Platters? How many collectors want them and what are they willing to pay? Prices published by Victor Malafronte in *The Complete Book of Frisbee* in 1998 were, by his own admission, a first attempt to establish a relative guide for the collecting market. Values were suggested to him by a panel of informed disc enthusiasts based on what discs were known in the mid-1990s. But much has been and is still being brought to light almost daily. Some prices have soared while others have plummeted. Once things settle down, more reliable, consistent price lists will begin to appear. What does this mean for present disc collectors? It means that there are some awesomely overpriced transactions occurring at the same time that there are some incredible opportunities. These are exhilarating days!

The following story is a case in point.

FINDING THE HOLY GRAIL

I vividly remember the *exact* moment when I became a disc collector. One gorgeous afternoon in the spring of 1976 I was tossing my faithful early-1957 Pluto Platter to a stranger from Florida I had just met in Elizabeth Park. He was the first person I ever saw throw a sidearm and I was immensely impressed! He informed me that I "really should put that one away because people in Florida and the West Coast are paying a lot of money for those...like *25 bucks!*" It was a moment of epiphany. A split second before it had been a favorite plastic toy, a cherished remnant of my happy childhood. Suddenly it was a valuable, coveted commodity in need of protection. That was the last day that disc flew in public and, although for many years it served in an honored role as my (since PDGA-illegal!) golf marker disc, it now rests peacefully encased in its baggie...a first-magnitude star of my collection.

Having been alerted that plastic had investment potential, two other good friends and I began poking around the back shelves of old toy stores, checking out what was flying around the parks and playgrounds, buying a few extra tournament discs, and sending for some special items offered in the back of *Frisbee World* magazine.

Stancil Johnson's recently published *FRISBEE: A Practitioner's Manual and Definitive Treatise* was the bible on everything to do with discs, and we devoured it! The lore surrounding the misty birth of the plastic disc in the late-1940s most fascinated us and the part about a PIPCO disc with a Li'l Abner label being a disc collector's dream (page 35) seemed truly unattainable.

But I was one of the lucky ones who was at a tournament in Amherst, Massachusetts around 1977 when Daryl Elliott showed up with an unopened carton of Li'l Abners that had recently been discovered by Roger Barrett at a California flea market. At nine dollars per disc, I picked up a set of all three colors for myself, and sets for each of my friends. Since few of the discs had ever made it to market due to a flap between Warren Franscioni of PIPCO and Al Capp, the creator of the "Li'l Abner" cartoon strip, 1,600 of the original 5,000 discs have survived in mint condition and regularly show up for sale.

A few years ago, while perusing eBay, I spotted a listing for a "Li'l Abner Flyin' Saucer circa 1950 near mint" and decided to have a look. I, and probably several other knowledgeable collectors, saw a picture of a red "Li'l Abner-Style" disc without the label on top and a second picture of the underside with its printed paper insert laying on top of the disc. Text gave a cursory story about the disc and the comment that the insert was loose and that it would be up to the buyer if s/he wanted to push it down into the disc. I thought, "another ho-hum offering," and almost clicked the back button.

Something stopped me from making that fateful click of the mouse. Why was the paper insert loose? Why was the label missing on an otherwise mint disc? And what was going on where the label was supposed to be?

The rather nondescript photo seemed to show a depression. Did that indicate a poorly molded disc, or, wait a minute...

(I didn't dare think it!)

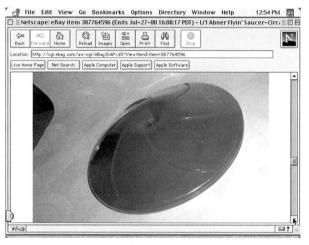

The vision of the Holy Grail—as appearing on eBay!

I tore open *The Complete Book Of Frisbee* and scrutinized the section on early PIPCO discs. The only PIPCO disc with a center depression shown was the original 1948 Style and it has large, raised, decorative lettering around the dip. Back to the photo on my screen and sure enough, there was the lettering! Or so I imagined seeing in the vague, pixelated image. I couldn't be certain, so I put in a rather modest bid of $51.00 in case I was mistaken.

As the bidding was pushed up towards my limit, I began to have second thoughts. Too much was at stake! I wasn't going to be around when the bidding closed so I decided to put in a substantial bid to insure I would win it. At the worst, I'd have an expensive, less-than-ideal example of a Li'l Abner. The next day I was thrilled to find that no one had outbid my original maximum.

A perfectly flat, uninserted insert? There had to be a wrinkle!

Thrill turned to ecstasy when I received the disc. Sure enough, it was a First Style Flyin-Saucer, the very first plastic disc ever produced...in as close to mint condition as then-current molding methods allowed! But what about the insert? The colorful inserts were printed on both sides of a heavy paper stock, then die-cut as a circle slightly larger than the discs. When they were hand-pushed into the underside of the genuine Li'l Abner models, they wrinkled and buckled, especially at the edges. *This insert was perfectly flat!* Here was a disc with a story, and I had to try to find it out.

My best guess was that someone at PIPCO or the molding company had used the disc as a prototype for the Li'l Abners... a sort of trial run of the printed inserts before the new Second Style mold was run. I emailed the dealer who had sold me the disc to find out if she had any further information.

Her answer was totally unexpected and floored me! She told me that she had acquired the disc from a relative of an artist who had worked for Al Capp. I had been on the right track but going in the wrong direction! I now had in my hands the very disc that had been sent to Al Capp by Warren Franscioni as a sample of what was in the works. This was *THE* disc and insert that enjoyed a front row seat throughout the ill-fated deal. What exactly went wrong? If only this disc could speak! With the promising deal dead and a threatened lawsuit to be reckoned with, the end of PIPCO was not far off. Warren abandoned the business, re-enlisted, and went off to war— never again to be as fully involved in flying disc promotion.

The rest, as they say, is history. But if the deal *had* gone through...if PIPCO *had* been a continuing success, Southern California Plastic never would have had the opportunity to market Saucers on their own. When the urge struck again in 1954, would Fred Morrison have bought Saucers from PIPCO to promote through his own American Trends Company? Or would he have rejoined his old partner Warren? Would the Pluto Platter ever have been produced? Without the Pluto Platter, would Wham-O have been interested in another, more poorly-performing flying disc? I think it's fair to say that no other single disc has had as profound an impact on the early progress of flying discs!

And, assuming that $51.00 is a *bit* below its true value... *how would you put a value on such a disc?*

Chapter 58 — The Thrills of Disc Collecting

HOLY MOLY!...AN EVEN HOLIER HOLY GRAIL?

What could *possibly* be more thrilling than unearthing Al Capp's prototype?!

"Fresbee Type Flyin Saucer" was the item's title on eBay. That sparked my interest. The misspelling of "Frisbee" was obviously unintentional...either a typo or a sign of ignorance. But "Flyin Saucer" might be more carelessness, or...?

The game was afoot!

A quick click...a moment's pause for the download, and... a surge of adrenaline! Even before my collaboration with Fred, I would have been able to correctly identify the disc as an original 1948 PIPCO Flyin-Saucer. That fact was significant enough, since only a scant handful of FS1s are known to still exist. That alone would have justified some hearty bidding.

The crude jpeg image showed a blue Saucer. I had read that Southern California Plastic had produced blue FS1 discs. While none of those has yet come to light, logically they were molded using the same bright, royal-blue plastic as the much more commonly found FS2 discs made in 1950 with Li'l Abner labels (see page 250, Fig. 1).

But this disc was *light* blue. Was that due to the poor lighting in the homespun photo? Or was the disc severely faded? In my experience, the bleaching effect of sunlight is never perfectly even. Usually, at the very least, the thicker rim shows less color shift than the thinner flight plate. However, the poor quality of the photo left my questions unanswered.

Quiz time! Why is *light* blue especially significant? If you paid attention while reading Fred's history, you should know!

Light blue plastic was used once…*and only once*. According to Fred, the very first molding of the Flyin-Saucers, the very first plastic flying disc in history, was run in "powder" blue.

Recognizing the immensity of the moment, I placed a bid guaranteed to succeed…and won. But I still would have to wait until the disc was in my hands to solve the mystery of the "blues."

Then in a new twist, I discovered that the seller lived only seven miles away. I could pick the disc up in person! (I must abashedly admit my frugal Yankee upbringing evoked warm, fuzzy thoughts of saved shipping costs.)

A phone call elicited a cordial invitation from the seller, who turned out to be a collector/dealer *extraordinaire* of old toys. His basement—a veritable museum—was packed to the ceiling with memorabilia. "Name a toy you played with as a child," he goaded. I recalled the Nichols Stallion 45 Mark II cap gun (with separate bullets, brass casings, and an extra set of pearl hand grips!) that was the envy of the neighborhood. "Here's one mint in the box," he proudly exclaimed.

After a fascinating hour of polite touring, I just *had* to ask… "Any other flying discs?" Just one, it turned out: a Regular Model issued by Wham-O sometime after 1966…still in its package that was now ratty with age. "I won't sell it," he stated resolutely. *That* one's gotta be worth a *lot!*" I was still champing at the bit. "That old Saucer you bought? Oh, yeah…here it is," he mumbled almost absentmindedly.

Trumpets blared a royal fanfare in my head. It was the same muted light blue all over…through and through! "Yep!" Fred later emailed back after seeing the photo attachment I sent, "That's powder blue!"

Chapter 58 — The Thrills of Disc Collecting

It is indeed a privilege being caregiver to the archetype of all flying plastic. But a lot of luck was involved. It was the fortunate combination of a misspelled name, a poor photograph, understandable ignorance on the part of the seller, as well as other disc collecting bidders (after all…only Fred and I knew about "powder" blue) that allowed me to so easily secure the World's Oldest Plastic Flying Disc…for only $82.00.

"Knowledge is power," the seller proudly asserted, referring to his encyclopedic memory of toys in general. But here was a case where broad-based knowledge bowed to highly-focused knowledge. Having done my homework, I recognized the significance of this priceless relic.

As I departed, we shook hands. The seller was obviously quite satisfied. I was absolutely thrilled to pieces, but kept it to myself. There was no need to spoil the moment with braggadocio. I didn't have the malice in my heart to break the news that he had, up until a moment ago, been in possession of the Holiest of Holy Grails in all of Discdom!

*The World's Oldest Plastic Flying Disc…
as revealed on eBay!
(See color photo, page 248, Fig. 1)*

59

GETTING INTO DISC COLLECTING

1. GET INTERESTED — Success rarely rewards those who are half-hearted about getting involved. The reason we have flying discs to collect today is because Fred ran his butt off for hours and days at a clip infecting fairgoers with his enthusiasm for tossing Saucers and Platters. Develop a passion for collecting. Have a reason for wanting to…or a goal to achieve. My first disc, a First Style Wham-O Pluto Platter which I bought in 1957, has kept me spellbound all of these years. I wanted to know more about this bit of yellow plastic which has given me so much enjoyment. Today I'm lucky to have assembled a collection of over 40 Pluto Platters representing nearly every Style and color Pluto Platter ever made.

2. GET EDUCATED — Maybe this book is your first introduction to disc collecting. If so welcome aboard! If you're an old hand you already realize how ignorant we still are about certain discs and their history. Whatever your level, part of the thrill is in the "findin' out." Read anything and everything you can. Even the yellowing pages of books written back in the 1970s can teach you some things—even wrong things help put history in perspective. Learning is a growth process that takes time. If you're lucky…a lifetime!

Chapter 59 — Getting Into Disc Collecting

3. GET SOURCES — Flying discs are everywhere! Sailing around playgrounds, wafting on a beach breeze, half-buried in the ooze on the bottom of your town park's pond. They're also to be found at flea markets, swap meets, thrift shops, secondhand stores, bargain basements, garage sales, tag sales, church fairs, antique boutiques, and aging, nearly defunct five-and-dimes. Ask your parents, grandparents, in-laws, out-laws, and other relatives, neighbors, and friends what's hiding in the remote corners of their homes and garages. Surf the Internet, use Google® and other search engines. Check out the sites listed in the Bibliography. Visit the chat rooms of disc clubs and special offerings of on-line disc stores. Check out not only the current items listed on eBay, but also the "Completed Items" to see who got what for how much. Contact buyers of discs you want… they might have other things to trade.

Dave Johnson swaps Frisbie Pie tin for Pluto Platter at a national fly mart. Photo ©Kraig Steffen.

And most importantly, observe your world. Keep a constant eye open for rare opportunities. Years ago I was returning to our Ultimate playing field with two good friends. We were engaged in a conversation about the disc golf round we had just completed. Suddenly, I spotted two neighborhood lads about 400 feet away tossing a green disc. Not just *ANY* green… pistachio green…*Pluto Platter green!*

As nonchalantly as I could compose myself, I excused myself from my friends (who had suddenly morphed into mortal disc collecting foes) and sauntered over to where the action was. "Hey, guys, toss me that disc, will ya?" I asked. They did. (A First Style!) "Where'd 'ya get it?" I inquired. "Oh, our neighbor was cleaning out his closet and gave it to us a few minutes ago," one of the 10-year-olds replied. "Here, try this one," I suggested as I tossed them a brand new 119G disc. Their throwing technique immediately improved and so did their obvious enjoyment. When I suggested a swap they couldn't believe I was *SO* stupid. "I like collecting those older discs, and besides I have more of those new discs, so keep it!" All of us were ecstatic with the trade...except for my friends, who were now "green" with envy.

4. GET A SPECIALTY — Disc collecting has rapidly grown from the original naïve mentality of "I've got to collect every disc ever made," to "Whoa...what happened to my bank account? I'd better specialize!" What you decide to focus on will depend on your personal reasons for collecting: fun, profit, bragging rights, nostalgia, etc. Since my first disc is a yellow WPP1 it's not surprising that I settled on Pluto Platters (and their ancestors) and yellow discs in general. Here's a list of some of the categories to specialize in:

Antiques — Any discs over 25 years old.
  (See special Legendary category, below)

Club Discs — All Styles of discs with decorations from disc clubs and organizations.

Fastbacks™ — Includes the original flat-topped Wham-O model and its many knockoffs. Most overlap with the Premium category.

Flying Rings — While not considered "true" discs, they are of interest to many devotees of flying plastic.

Foam and Rubber Discs — Nerf® Disc, Flying Pickle, and the Flapjack are good examples.

Foreign Discs — (Foreign to *whose* country?) Usually considered any discs manufactured outside of the U.S.

Frisbie Pie Company Items — Includes pie tins, pie display cases, postcards, pencils, razed factory bricks, etc. (These *may* relate to the history of the *name* "Frisbee," but *NOT* to the development of plastic flying discs.)

Games — Horseshoe sets and Sky Croquet, for example.

General Retail — Any discs designed to appeal to the mass toy market rather than the sport market. Examples: Regular, Master, All-American; many manufacturers.

Glow In The Dark — Any discs made of plastic containing phosphorescent material, such as the Moonlighter.

Golf Discs — Any discs designed specifically for use in the game of Disc Golf. These are usually identified by their lower profile, smaller diameter, extra density and weight, and sharper beveled edge…but not always. The earliest and most valuable are adaptations of general sport models.

Legendary — Any discs or series designed before 1964 (the last year of the Pluto Platter). Includes: PIPCO Flyin-Saucers (and Li'l Abner-Style), Sky Pies, Buck Rogers Flying Saucers, all polyethylene Flyin Saucer Styles, Space Saucers, Pluto Platters (all Styles), Sailing Satellites, Mars Platters (all Styles), Zo-lars, Wham-O Flying Saucers, Mystery-Ys, Jumping Jupiters, Sky Saucers, and a few others. To serious collectors these are the "crème de la crème" sometimes commanding four-figure sales stickers.

Miscellaneous Accessories — Books, magazines, ads, sales literature, tee-shirts, tote bags, posters, pins, belt buckles, and hats all fall into this category.

Mini Discs — Any discs under 5 inches in diameter.

Multi-Piece Construction — Any discs made from two or more separate components.

North American Series — An extensive line of G-Series discs from Wham-O which promoted the North American Series of tournaments during the mid-1970s through the early-1980s.

Novelty-Engineered Discs — Battery-powered effects, lights, whistling devices, etc.

Novelty, General — Interesting thematic twists of the basic disc concept such as discs made from fabrics or carpeting; discs with handles, or indentations to help catch with a finger or stick, etc.

Novelty, Mimetic — Discs molded to resemble other objects such as tires, cookies, records, bottle caps, space ships, sombreros and cow flops.

Packaged Discs — Any discs still in their original packages; including complete store displays.

Premiums — Any discs with a message promoting a commercial product, service, company, celebrity, or event not otherwise related to flying discs.

Prototypes — Any discs from initial test runs, not released for general sales.

Single Color — Collect any and all discs of one color or unpigmented (clear) only.

Single Disc Model — Pick one particular disc design and collect all its Style and color variations. Popular choices are: Pro Models, Super Pros, Pluto Platters, Midnight Flyers.

Single Manufacturer — All discs made by one company.

Special Events Series — Collect all of the discs commemorating the Olympic Games, political elections, etc.

Tournament Discs — All types of discs with graphics advertising or commemorating flying disc competitions.

World Class Signature Series — An extensive line of G-Series discs from Wham-O featuring each year's World Champions during the mid-1970s through early-1980s.

5. GET CONNECTED — It's your choice: go it alone or pull together. Some like to quietly putter with their collection, cloistered within their sanctum sanctorum. Others enjoy the social interaction at a lively "fly-mart." But sooner or later everyone needs help or advice about their collection. Connections you create along the way fall into two main camps: "Facilitators," who collect or deal in other types of antiques and discs than what you do, but help get you what you want, and "Friendly Rivals," who share your passion, interest, and knowledge of a specialty. Either way it's a good way to build up a stronger collection more quickly.

6. GET A BUDGET — There's a plan for every pocketbook! Discs range from free to over $6,300 (to date) so set a spending cap that works for you. Be realistic. If you're working up a colorful wall of pretty plastic purely for aesthetic reasons, don't steal from your IRA because you'll probably never sell or trade them and recoup your investment. But, if your collection *IS* your IRA...read on...*and invest carefully!*

7. GET INFORMED — When you're considering a trade, purchase, or how much to bid in an auction...knowledge is power! First and foremost you need to know about the disc. Hopefully you've done your homework and already know about it. Ahhh...it's the one you've been lusting for! Great, but it's way too easy to get swept away in the passion of the moment. (Will you still respect yourself in the morning for getting into that !%#! bidding war late last night?)

What is the disc's true condition? Look closely for little details which might spoil its value to you. If you suspect the disc is a one-of-a-kind, fifty-year-old relic you may need to forgive a few blemishes because no finer example exists. Most disc collectors are not pure investors (yet!) so each person must decide what makes any particular disc a "keeper" or a "reject." Personally, I use a price guide as just that...a guide. But, I also keep written and mental notes on what similar discs are going for in auctions. And, well...every now and then something comes along which you simply *CAN'T* do without...one of life's little rewards!

8. GET SKEPTICAL — If a deal sounds too good to be true, it may be. Many dealers don't know how to properly describe a disc and some unscrupulous bastards (you know who you are!) purposely don't want to tell you the gory details which would lessen the sales price. Inspect a disc carefully. If it's a photo, ask questions about things that may not show up well...

even if you have no reason to suspect hidden flaws. Descriptions of older discs often quote erroneous history which, since you are reading this book, you can now put into proper perspective. Remember that the burden of proof is always on the claimer, not the claimee; and that extraordinary claims require extraordinary proof!

9. GET MORE THAN ONE — Whenever you can, buy extras. There are many opportunities to pick up future trading/selling stock along with the one for your own collection. If you spot a nice tournament disc at an event, take a few spare ones home and sock 'em away. They will be hard to come by in just a few years. I was in one of those closeout bargain stores once and spotted a stack of about twenty Tee Birds from the early 1970s sitting on the floor. At 79 cents each I walked out with the lot. Now they fetch between ten and thirty dollars apiece.

Buy more than one copy of this book…and keep one in mint condition for your collection! ☺

10. GET THE STORY — Like people, some discs live interesting lives…others dull and humdrum. Any unusual, rare, or celebrated disc—young or ancient—deserves to have its story preserved for posterity. The best time to collect a disc's history is when you obtain it. Ask the previous owner where s/he got it, while the particulars are still fresh. Most will feel complimented and honored to be a part of history. Write down the account and keep it with the disc.

Occasionally, important new revelations clear away the mysterious fog obscuring legendary saucers. When I was fortunate enough to obtain an absolutely dead-mint American Trends Pluto Platter, naturally one of my first questions was how did this priceless treasure manage to escape decades of damage? The fact that it was still enshrouded in its original plastic bag certainly helped—the package had clearly taken the abuse, protecting its valuable contents. But these packages were never sealed. Why was the disc never removed and played with? Even once?! I had to know…so I asked.

Here's the story I received back:

> When my father was a young boy, he and his brothers played with a Pluto Platter in the yard. They loved this new toy that their dad had come across in Los Angeles. The neighborhood children also loved to come over and play with the Pluto Platter. They had a great time together. So my grandmother thought that it would make a great birthday present for all of their friends. Grandma would have the boys pick out a Pluto Platter, from red, green, white or yellow to give to the lucky birthday boy. She would also carefully enclose a $1.00 bill to go along with the gift to make it look like a more expensive gift. Little did we know that today those gifts would fetch such a price! So now, 50 years later, this Pluto Platter was still in the old barn. We saw that similar ones sold on eBay and we decided to put it up for the auction. We never expected it to be such a popular item!

Apparently, fifty years ago, this intended gift missed the party! And so it sat alone and forgotten on a shelf in a rural Utah barn with only curious mice as companions.

Besides sentimental value, what makes this story so important? It has been known for thirty years that American Trends Pluto Platters came in red and yellow. The first green one was finally discovered in 2002. It has always been logically assumed that they were produced in blue as well…that their discovery was imminent. According to this anecdotal account, we should also search for white!

But a good reporter verifies his facts by checking additional sources. That proved to be astonishingly easy: indisputable evidence came along with the deal! As part of his mail order fulfillment shipment Fred included a return card to encourage additional sales. Nestled under the disc, the card had also miraculously survived. And, lo and behold, listed on the card are the color choices then available—red, yellow, green, and white (Fred has since confirmed there were blue)—providing confirmation of our storyteller's childhood memories!

11. GET 'EM HOME SAFE AND SOUND — You can't do anything about a disc's past life but you can make the rest of its days pleasant, comfy and safe. Plastic is by nature very delicate stuff. If you're going to a tag sale or swap meet, bring along some plastic storage bags, just in case. One-gallon bags work well for most discs; two-gallon for those occasional behemoths, or packaged goods. If you've just won an on-line auction, contact the seller and ask him/her to please separately bag each disc to protect it from whatever else is in the box. (Did I tell you the one about the naked yellow disc and the fresh newspaper packing?) Ask that discs be shipped in boxes rather than in bubble-pack envelopes…double-boxed for really expensive gems. Always pay for insurance on sales over $20. Get a tracking number. Have a system in place so that once the disc arrives home it immediately receives your TLC.

12. GET 'EM CLEANED UP — I always scrutinize a new disc first, not only to make sure there is no unanticipated damage to report, but to prepare for the next step: cleaning. Some collectors never clean a disc, figuring, I suppose, that any accumulated grime is each disc's badge of its proud heritage; but I don't buy into that philosophy. A disc carefully restored to as near its original condition as feasible is not only prettier to look at, it's definitely worth more money and attains higher trade value. If there are any non-plastic components, such as paper or foil labels or metal gizmos…*STOP!* They need to be completely sealed off before giving the disc a washing. It may not even be worth the risk; you might decide to accept a little dirt.

When two of my American Trends Pluto Platters arrived home, I decided they deserved some freshening up. Since they still carry Fred's original paper AT stickers, I figured it *might* be important to keep that area dry. So I cut out squares of heavy acetate a bit larger than the labels and taped them down securely to the discs, completely sealing the edges…then minimized the water usage in those necks of the woods. I still sweated bullets until those babies were dry!

When it's bath time, first remove any rings, then clip and file your nails. Better yet, wear light rubber gloves. Use a stream of tepid (not hot) water and mild liquid hand soap first and see what comes off easily. Try hand washing first, or a very soft cloth if necessary. Be very careful about grit that comes loose: it will scratch a disc in an instant! Rinse off the soap, dry it, and inspect the disc. Dirt lodged in scrapes around the rim can often be extricated under running water with the very gentle action of a really soft nail brush. (I have one so soft it won't clean my nails!) If there is any foreign gummy residue left after you dry the disc, you can try some waterless hand cleaner or even something like citrus-based Goo Gone®, but be really careful that you keep those away from any applied decorations which may not be "permanent."

If you do end up using stronger cleaners, wash them away immediately with soap and water afterwards. You may find that the disc has a slight whitish, patchy film or existing scratches are more obvious (especially true on red discs). I'm guessing that some of the natural oils in the polyethylene have been removed from the surface temporarily, because I've found that the discs return to their original luster after they've sat in a bag for a few days.

13. GET CURIOUS — Now, while your new baby is squeaky clean, take the time to carefully inspect it top to bottom. There may be clues to wondrous new discoveries staring you in the face. Early plastic manufacturing processes were cruder and less controlled. The Production Department wasn't required to pass every little mold modification by the Marketing Department (*IF* there even was one) for final approval. So, small differences in the discs sometimes occurred between runs due to minor retoolings or damage to the mold. Some of these changes may define whole new Styles, while others merely constitute factory flaws. Occasionally, you may be the "Sherlock" who solves a mystery already on the books.

Perhaps one of you "Mars Platter Fanatics" out there has already come up with an unpublished working theory, but I had always wondered what was going on with Premier Products to cause them to make so many seemingly non-essential changes to their Platter. While the various Styles are adequately shown and identified in *The Complete Book of Frisbee,* it wasn't until I had enough actual specimens in my hands that a clearer picture began to emerge. What was it that Premier was up to?

It was 1958…the year after Wham-O had begun to market the Pluto Platter and the first year it was beginning to show significant commercial growth. Success begets competitors and Premier seized the moment. Why take the riskier approach of designing a brand new flying disc when you can swipe one already bringing in the bucks? (Ensuing legal action soon told them why not!) So they knocked off the Pluto Platter: planets, instructions, windowed observation dome and all... even putting their name on an esker for no apparent reason other than Wham-O had done it (without a clue as to *why* Wham-O had needed an esker!). A short time later they realized they had goofed with the design—the order of the planets was wrong! Their Second Style switched the names of the planets to exactly ape the Pluto Platter. Order had been restored to the universe! A few years later, after Wham-O eliminated their esker, Premier issued a Third Style Mars Platter without an esker plus the (by then Wham-O-registered) name "Frisbee" emblazoned on the underside in large letters.

That was the last straw for Wham-O, who sued and settled, acquired the mold, modified it, and began producing two Styles of their own Mars Platters in the 1960s.

Here's another. The defining element of the WPP7 is its backwards "1" (so-called "mold number") located in the center circular area on the underside. Ever notice that it's turned differently in relation to the address lines on different discs of that Style?! The numerals on all seven presently in my collection have different rotational orientations to the type lines. How could that be?

Knowing a little about the molding process, it was unreasonable to consider that the numbers had been added by an independent manufacturing step. If the digit had been inscribed into the same part of the die which created the text on the underside, then there would have to have been a retooling between each of my samples. No way. The only reasonable explanation left was that the center area (the "puddle") was created by a separate piece of the mold… one that could turn.

It's been reported that the loss of the "window panes" (ribs or spokes) on the "observation dome" (the "nipple," in molding industry parlance) which occurred between the WPP2 discs and the WPP3 discs was caused by a retooling or replacement of a separate nozzle component at the plastic injection point on top. But how to independently verify that there WAS a separate component? A *very* careful inspection showed that the window panes on the WPP2 discs are turned ever-so-slightly counter-clockwise when compared with the ATPP and WPP1 discs. (Once the panes were gone on the WPP3 and later discs, there are no rotational indicators left.)

So if the nipple on top was created by a separate component, how about its counterpart on the bottom?…the part on the WPP7 with the mold number. Curious, I wondered if there was evidence of a possible fourth part to the mold.

First, I noticed that the edge of the puddle is different from any of the rest of the molded designs on *ALL* Pluto Platters. It is sharper, more delicate, more easily damaged…like you might expect to be formed by a seam between two abutting machined-metal parts.

Second, with the appearance of the WPP3, the shape of that center area changed from being a smooth continuation of the bottom plane of the disc to that of a distinct "crater" having a raised rim and depressed center. That fits nicely with the timing in the "new nipple-maker" theory. It seems that *both* of the center parts of the mold were replaced at that time. How about rotational action as confirmation? Until the mold number on the WPP7 there were no molded-in indicators.

Or were there? One definite advantage to building up your collection of similar discs is the ability to make accurate comparisons. With twenty examples of WPP3 through WPP7 discs at my disposal, resources were *NOT* a concern! But flaws were. When looking for subtle clues, the scratches, scrapes and dings which discs easily accumulate over the years can be confusing. Fortunately, many of the discs in the collection are in pristine condition, making it easier to discern unique marks.

And there it was!! Off to the right side of the rotating "1" on *each* WPP7 disc was a subtle, 1/8-inch-long, slightly-curved nick. How long had *THAT* been there? Out came the WPP6, then the WPP5s, the WPP4s and finally the WPP3s before reaching the end of the trail: no nick on the WPP3s. [Other tooling marks later discovered *only* on the ATPP have since confirmed this story.]

But *WHY* was there a separate component that formed the center of the underside? What function did it serve? A nagging, unresolved question resurfaced. An object to be formed in a two-part mold is usually not designed with sides beyond perpendicular to the parting line, allowing it to slip out of the mold easily. But the Pluto Platter (along with many later disc designs) has a slightly "undercut" or back-sloping surface to the inner rim…where your fingers normally grip the disc. Wouldn't that cause the disc to get hung up in the mold?

Manually prying each disc from the mold seemed a labor-intensive, inconsistent operation that might inflict warpage on the newborn discs. Could there possibly have been a mechanical process to force or "pop" the discs out of the mold? Was there some sort of "plunger" to poke them out? Was that the fourth part of the mold?

Chapter 59 — Getting Into Disc Collecting

So I asked Dan Mangone, who has a great deal of molding experience, how discs are handled when the mold opens. "The mold operator simply pulls them out and sets them on a flat table," was his answer.

But after being confronted with the evidence for a fourth part to the mold, he was inspired to consult with some "old-timers" he knew in the molding business. Sure enough, they confirmed that "ejector pins" were sometimes built into the mold to force out stubborn parts.

Apparently, the ejector pin that was part of the original ATPP mold was replaced or retooled to make the WPP1 Style; and again when the WPP3 was produced. Later, at the time that the ® symbol was added after the Frisbee name on top (creating the WPP4), a "craftsman" dropped the loose pin or let his tool slip causing the nick…and then didn't bother to fix it. *Thank you Mr. Klutz!*

14. GET 'EM RESTORED? — For those trained in micro-surgery you might decide to "touch up" the worst dings and gouges. (WARNING — read the previous section about important, molded-in clues first!) If you're good, the disc will display better and no one will ever know. If you're not so handy… well, it might be best to leave things as you find them. Those little fuzzy hairs of plastic kicked up as road rash particularly annoy me. Unless it's very minor and already open, leave any peeling or blisters alone. Ditto broken lettering. I won't touch damage to labels, hot-stamped, or silk-screened designs, nor packaging either, although I did carefully use two strategically-placed small staples to minimize and protect a minor dog-eared section of an otherwise perfect corrugated cardboard box housing its First Style Pluto Platter Horseshoe set.

Cracked discs cannot be fixed, although some clear tape on the back may improve the disc's displayability. Slight overall warps (not creases) can sometimes be straightened using wide packing tape stretched across opposite rims to apply appropriate correctional tension while the disc rests on a flat surface for several months. A small, embedded dark stone or grain of sand can often be innocuously plucked from its lair using a needle. When I decide to perform a face-lift, I use an X-Acto® knife with a *NEW* blade, and an 8X photographer's precision loupe under strong light…and avoid alcohol!

15. GET 'EM IN STORAGE — Once you become a collecting fanatic (it does happen occasionally), things will rapidly get out of hand if you don't develop an effective and manageable storage system. I had over 700 discs before I finally got organized! The best I could muster was, "it's in that room… somewhere." Finally, I dragged them all out, sorted them in piles on the basement floor, numbered and cataloged them, put each into a fresh storage bag, and filled up 34 numbered cardboard file storage boxes obtained from Staples. Keep the discs loosely stacked vertically on their sides in a cool, dry location, and to minimize warping, rotate your crop occasionally. I've found a good way to number them is to apply a small strip of 3M Magic™ Tape to the inner rim and carefully write the number on the tape with a felt-tip pen. For the computer-enabled, a simple database program like Excel will complete the system. One of my columns lists in which numbered box each disc is stored for rapid retrieval. The next time someone wants to trade you their mint silver Sailing Satellite for your prototype Sky-Pro, you *NEED* to know right where it is! I keep a printout in a presentation binder and update it in pen as I acquire or trade discs.

16. GET 'EM ON DISPLAY — I enthusiastically collected discs in the 1970s and early-1980s and always had some proudly on display in our home. Then, when other priorities entered my life, I kept my collection hidden away in boxes and bags for many years. Out-of-sight, out-of-mind, as they say, it lay dormant. While the collection definitely accumulated some cash value, it gave no personal satisfaction in return. Now that I enjoy working out of a home office, part of the collection has come out of the closet to adorn my walls once again. I used two-foot-high (by appropriate length) Homasote panels with stretched burlap adhered to them, painted a medium blue, screwed to the walls. Discs hang from push-pins and are dusted with a very soft brush and rotated occasionally. It's easy to swap a disc or change the layout on a whim. At any moment I can divert my attention upwards and receive a small jolt of satisfaction gazing upon the historic, monochromatic plastic tastefully displayed. Besides that, a display is a great conversation starter…many a rewarding client meeting has started with "What are all those yellow things on your walls?"

17. GET A WEB SITE — This idea is really just a new way to display your collection, but to a much wider audience, instantly and without you having to be available. Of course not everyone has the means or technical skills to make it happen…yet. But it's the wave of the future and the future will prevail. Software mavens and hosting services want you to climb on board and so are making it easier and less expensive. Techno disc collectors on the cutting edge have begun building sites which provide up-to-the-minute availability of data impossible to obtain a few years ago. If you do launch a site, try to provide space for others to share knowledge about their discs as well as links to other interesting sites.

18. GET GOING — If you're going to start with the expectation of quickly achieving impossible goals, you're in for a huge disappointment. If you simply *must* have the most complete or best representation of some particularly esoteric discs right away, today, at any cost, dream on. Many rare discs have been hoarded away by your predecessors and you must wait until a collector is willing to part with one. You have to have patience and wait for one to suddenly appear…and be ready to pounce quickly. I had to wait twenty-five years for the opportunity to acquire an American Trends Pluto Platter. The only four collectors who had one, wanted theirs and couldn't have cared less that I wanted one too. I kept the flame alive, but it wasn't an obsession. In the meanwhile, many, many other fine discs came along and were collected. Finally, out of the blue, a yellow ATPP became available and another goal was realized. One of the truly best, but one of many.

19. GET A LIFE — If you catch yourself checking eBay® for new listings 47 times a day…find you can rattle off every Style/color combination of Pluto Platter ever produced while simultaneously filling in the long form of your federal income taxes…or mistakenly call your spouse Zo-lar, maybe it's time to slow down and assess the situation.

As yet there is no Disc Collectors Anonymous, so you may have to cure your obsession on your own. Remember, disc collecting is just an interesting adjunct to our real passion. It's a means to one end, not an end-all. Save some discs and some time just for pure throwing enjoyment…put on the sun tan lotion, get outdoors, and toss 'em!

60

GRADING A DISC'S CONDITION

WHEN YOU GAZE UPON A DISC, turning it slowly in your hands, observing it from all angles, your eyes collect objective information about its appearance while your brain processes that data into a subjective opinion about its condition. You compare what you actually see with how you know (or assume) it should look in its original, ideal state. You then make a personal decision whether you like it or hate it…if it's destined for the display wall or the dustbin.

If you're considering buying, selling, or trading a disc which isn't on hand for personal inspection, there needs to be a method of communicating that disc's condition relative to others of its ilk. This section will help you learn to look for, recognize, and evaluate important clues, and then express (or assess) a disc's overall condition using a categorical rating system understandable to other collectors.

In the interest of maintaining consistency, I will be building upon the momentum of two pioneers of disc collecting: Jim Palmeri, whose 1980 articles, which appeared in his superb *Flying Disc Magazine*, established the first published professional standards; and Victor Malafronte, who re(de)fined and extended the discipline in *The Complete Book of Frisbee*. Since the process of grading discs is so subjective, the reader is encouraged to absorb these earlier works (and others) to obtain the most complete understanding possible. (Jim, originally a science teacher, professes the academic approach to disc collecting; Victor, ever the original victor, waxes prophetic; while I shall *disc*ourse the role of the *pund*it.)

PERFECTION…A GOAL RARELY ACHIEVED!

The only ideal state for a disc design is in the mind of the designer! Maybe on paper. But when it's time to reproduce the concept in metal and then plastic, the real world takes over. If you assume a disc always pops from its mold in perfect condition…think again. Even if the original tooling is flawless, a mold over time acquires tiny scratches, dings, and glitches which are faithfully reproduced in plastic. (Read the story of the nick which first appeared on the WPP4 in the "Get Curious" section beginning on page 301.)

Inside the hellishly hot, dark cavity, mutations occasionally occur. Molten plastic may not flow evenly. Stray impurities can become embedded. Bubbles may form. Once the disc leaves the warm womb it faces a cruel world. Factory (mis)handlers cart discs en masse to the packager. Labeling, silk-screening, or hot-stamping operations exact a toll on the plastic as well as introducing imperfections of their own. Blister-packing, shrink-wrapping, or boxing are not gentle experiences for the young, impressionable discs. By the time a disc is delivered to the expectant buyer's waiting arms it may have suffered further trauma in shipping, shelving, and selling.

And once the disc arrives at the home of its new caregiver, it faces the inevitable disfiguring scars of unspeakable abuse committed under the guise of having fun.

WHAT'S THE DAMAGE?

So, if we can't have perfection, what do we get? Flaws. Fortunately not all imperfections are alike…at least as they impact the value of a disc. Just as some facial scars can be disfiguring handicaps, while a mole in just the right spot on just the right face might be considered a "beauty mark," there is a wide range of considerations for the damage discs can sustain. Most of these flaws are easily recognizable even to the neophyte collector, but my intent is to provide a common vocabulary for accurate, consistent descriptions.

Here, rounded up in alphabetical order, are the usual suspects:

BLEMISHES — These are the result of molding misadventures unique to each individual disc. Uneven flow of the injected plastic can sometimes leave gaps or bubbles. Double impressions have occurred. Marks from mishandling or embedded foreign matter are fairly common. All are undesirable and discs exhibiting these imperfections should be passed over… if there is a choice.

BLEMISH — An imperfectly molded nipple

BLISTERS — These unappealing sores result when the top skin of the plastic separates from the rest of the disc. Resist the urge to pop them or they will peel.

BURNS AND MELTING — There are a few overly-curious characters out there who get their dubious kicks from seeing what happens when a disc encounters a burning butt. Stay away from them!

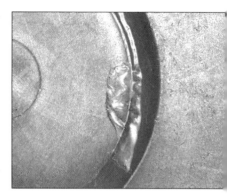
BLISTER — No remedy available...let it be.

CRACKS — There really is nothing worse that can happen to a disc than to have it split completely apart. For all intents and purposes, it's totally ruined...for tossing...for collecting. But if it is merely a

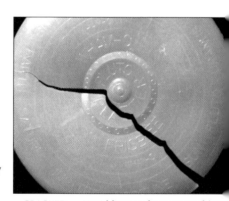
CRACKED — You'd have to be to want this!

HAIRLINE CRACK — Looks like a scratch.

CRACKED RIM — Busted by a bus?

hairline crack (defined as one which is only visible when the two sides are pushed apart) then the loss of value is minimal. Protect it from spreading or the disc will not be worth all that it's cracked up to be.

CREASES — These are a particular form of warping usually caused by some catastrophic event, such as getting folded while being run over by a bus. Since the plastic has been severely stretched, there is no way to reverse the process. A crease will greatly decrease the worth of the disc.

CREASE — Folded, spindled & mutilated.

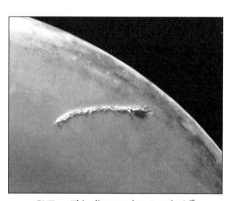
CUT — This disc needs a Band-Aid®.

CUTS — Not a topic for the squeamish. Basically a large scratch deep enough to raise a plastic edge, allowing dirt to accumulate within. Cuts can often disfigure lettering or other designs.

DAMAGED OR MISSING DECORATIONS — Any of the damage a disc can sustain may also affect its embellishments, such as stickers,

DAMAGED LABEL — Still priceless!

silk-screening, hot-stamp applications, etc. But there can also be value-diminishing problems unique to the decorations themselves. Missing or torn labels, incomplete graphics, overprints, ragged printing, wrinkling, yellowing, and glue stains all fall under this heading. There is a small subculture of collectors who deem misprinted discs to be highly desirable.

DELAY MARKS — Those shiny, concentric spiral marks (most often found on the bottom) were left by someone trying out their freestyling ability. Delaying (balancing the spinning disc on a fingernail) is a no-no to the collector. Silicone (or an equivalent) may have been applied to reduce friction. A few marks will lower the rating slightly. If the disc has been through a complete three-minute choreographed routine, maybe you should delay collecting that Style disc.

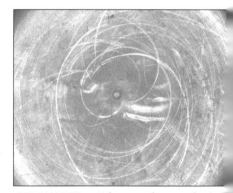

DELAY MARKS — Value on a downward spiral

DISTORTION, TIME — Not what you'd experience while getting sucked into a wormhole, but the shape-altering process that has occurred in several early disc Styles...presumably caused by design stresses acting on the less-pliable plastics used. For example, many of the FS1 discs have similar sunken center areas, while other FS1 and FS2 discs have raised centers.

TIME DISTORTION — Many FS1s are depresse

Chapter 60 — Grading a Disc's Condition

As with mold flaws, since most (all?) of the discs of each Style exhibit the same distortion to the same degree, the values of the discs cannot be affected by the change.

DOG BITES — It is hard to ignore a disc's toothy encounter with our canine companions. Certainly those pits from Fido's fangs are ruinous to the collector. But to what extent will be determined by the depth and quantity of chomps. A few slight dimples noticeable only under sidelighting will not greatly affect the price the disc will fetch. Multiple disc-piercing stabs might lead one to sadly consider euthanasia (for the disc). Occasionally you will find gnawings of other creatures which have worked plastic into their diets!

EMBEDDED OBJECTS — Sometimes a disc will land on a sharp object producing a small stab wound. Often you will discover the culprit, such as a stone or sliver, still embedded.

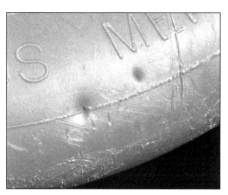
DOG BITES — Toss Spot a Gumabone instead.

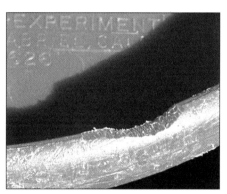
BITES — This mouse prefers Double Eskers!

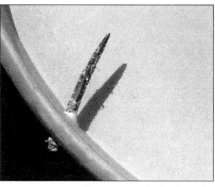
EMBEDDED — This Puppy got body pierced!

If so, you may be able to tease it out with a needle, to minimize the effect of the damage. If not…it's the pits!

FADING — One of the main attractions of plastic flying discs—right from the very beginning—is their (usually) vivid, primary colors. Intense, bleaching sunlight turns those saturated, eye-catching hues to wimpy tints…fine for bathroom walls but not the collection wall. Since this is continuous damage over time, the effect can vary from very mild to disastrous. But even at its worst, fading doesn't lower a disc's value as much as physical damage such as warping, holes or cracks.

One of the most common problems and concerns to the collector caused by fading is the confusion raised when trying to identify the true color of a disc which came in several close colors. For example, many dealers cannot distinguish between a faded red and an apricot Pluto Platter.

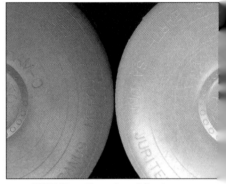

FADING — The color of (less) money.

While it is true that there are slight variations between batches of plastic pellets, the industry maintains rigid standards for color consistency. Fading normally has a *tinting* effect rather than a *color hue* shift. One good indicator of probable fading is when the thin flight plate of a disc is markedly lighter in color than the thicker rim and nipple…even when laying down so it's not subject to backlighting. Unfaded discs are more consistent in their overall appearance. If you can't see the disc itself and you're suspicious of a false identification, get a refund guarantee!

Chapter 60 — Grading a Disc's Condition

FISHEYES — If you hold a disc up to the light and see small, round, lighter-colored or clear areas embedded in the plastic, those are fisheyes staring back at you. These could be formed by improperly mixed plastic, bubbles, or foreign matter. While less than desirable, they usually do not scale back a disc's net worth.

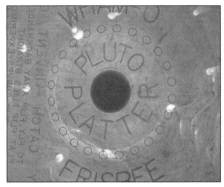

FISHEYES — This disc AKA "Catch of the Day" and "The Fisherman's Platter"

GRAFFITI — From identifying a former owner to Op Art embellishments, extraneous doodlings on a disc will mark down its worth. Multicolored patterns on the top in bold felt-tip pen are much less desirable than initials in pencil on the bottom. Unless, of course, we're talking autographs from the Legends of Discdom!

GRAFFITI? — Every rule has its exception!

HOLES — Complete penetration of the disc. The more catastrophic the chasm, the more it voids the value.

HOLES — Cleats meet Platter.

317

MARBLING — If you notice uneven color swirls or patterns, usually radiating from the injection point…that's marbling. It can be quite subtle, observable only when the disc is held up to the light, or quite overt (like a tie-dyed shirt). Caused by incomplete mixing of different-colored plastic pellets, marbling can be intentional or the result of sloppy quality control. Patterns are unique to each disc and can be beautiful or incredibly ugly eyesores. Those resulting from mold purging (switching colors during a nonstop molding run) are often treated as rare, collectable anomalies. (See Fisheyes and page 255)

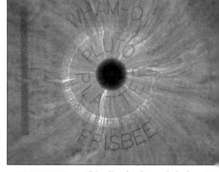
MARBLING — This disc looks mah-belous!.

MOLD FLAWS — Nicks, dings, pitting…whatever you want to call them, they are molded-in imperfections. Since they are the faithful reproduction of a part of the actual mold, as undesirable as they might appear, they cannot detract from the value of a disc because *ALL* of the discs have 'em. (Duh!) If otherwise identical discs are found which were made before a mold flaw occurred, they might be slightly more desirable.

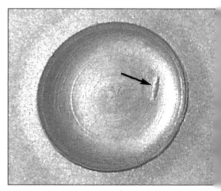
MOLD FLAW — Courtesy of Mr. Klutz.

Chapter 60 — Grading a Disc's Condition

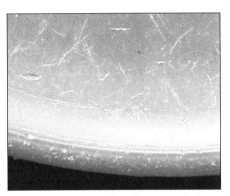
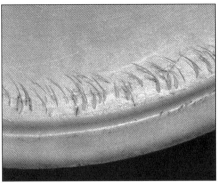

NAIL MARKS — Random digs, normal play.   *NAIL MARKS — Golfer's power-grip gouges.*

NAIL MARKS — Unless a disc has received the "white glove" treatment all of its life, it most likely will show telltale scars from tossers' fingernails. How many and how severe they appear varies greatly, but since they are usually found only on the underside, nail marks do not degrade a disc's display value as greatly as top-side damage.

PEELING OR "WELLISHES DISEASE" — Ever notice a little broken blister on a disc that begged to be picked at, or a tiny flap of raised plastic that asked to be pulled? Don't do it! Peeling occurs because the plastic often behaves like it's

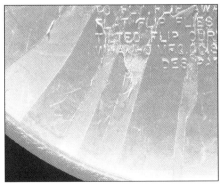

PEELING — Beyond sunscreen!   *PEELING — Can display well if on back only.*

comprised of thin layers instead of a solid mass. Pull on an edge and it behaves like the aftermath of a bad sunburn— the top skin sheds in shreds. Peeling strips a disc of its value.

SCRATCHES — Give polyethylene plastic a dirty look and you've marred the surface. It's a filthy world out there, full of abrasive elements, so protecting a disc takes extra TLC. Scratches range from microscopic to proto-cuts. The more, the un-merrier!

SCRATCHES — This Platter played hard!

SCUFFING — Ever fall off your bike and skin your knee on the pavement? Ouch! Same thing happens whenever a disc touches down on terra extra-firma. Unfortunately, discs don't heal with time, so road-rash behavior will last a lifetime.

SCUFFING — Plastic & concrete don't mix.

STAINS — Discolorations can be temporary surface phenomena or have permanently permeated deep into the plastic—removable or color-fast. There are cleaning agents ranging from plain tap water to caustic dissolvents which can be utilized only with increased daring and mounting trepidation.

Chapter 60 — Grading a Disc's Condition

WARP — Not a Trekkie's trans-light speed, but distortion of a disc's natural or intended shape. This can range from barely perceptible to incredibly distorted. Sometimes a disc is warped while still warm from the mold. Poor long-term storage, an afternoon spin in a hot car (temperature-wise), or getting run over by a bus are other warp-producing events. Most warps cannot be removed.

WARP — Not the smooth airfoil Fred designed.

If it wobbles on a flat surface…it's WARPED!

WEAR — While you might consider *all* forms of damage to be wear and tear, here we specifically mean the overall erosion of a disc's appearance. Most designs and lettering appear crisp when new but gradually give in to the onslaught of time. Worn, elderly discs have a smoother, less-distinct physiognomy than their youthful-looking siblings…and get less respect!

WEAR — My first disc…worn proudly!

61

A DISC'S CONDITION... CATEGORICALLY SPEAKING

WHILE THE FOLLOWING LIST is comprised of seven distinct categories, actual discs reside along a smooth continuum. What might seem at first glance to be a disc in Excellent condition may, upon closer inspection, be found to contain a fatal flaw such as a cracked rim. There is also the inevitable balancing act between two abutting categories. Some collectors handle this by adding a plus or minus to a rating, such as "Good Plus." Many folks are used to rating various things on a scale of 1 to 10 with 10 being perfect, so I've added a numerical equivalent (in parentheses) to each category based on that thinking. Whatever system communicates a disc's condition accurately to the satisfaction of all is the best …but still a poor substitute for being able to inspect the disc face-to-face.

MINT CONDITION (10) — In a word…*FLAWLESS!* No imperfections of *ANY* kind to the disc, adornments, or applications are permitted in order to achieve this lofty stature. It is rare, but possible, to find a disc in this elusive condition, and it will command the highest value for that particular Style. Mint discs can most often be found inside unopened packaging, but discs inside unbroken packaging are not always in mint condition (see Chapter 60). If the packaging is also to be included in the Mint rating, it too must be flawless.

NEAR-MINT CONDITION (9) — Any flaws appearing on a disc which deserves this rating must be those related to normal production and handling processes...and they must be minimal! No damage from play, warping from improper storage, or color fading is permitted. Packaging and decorations can have only the slightest wear associated with sales operations.

EXCELLENT CONDITION (8) — Your non-collecting, freestyling, (former) friend decides to see if your (formerly) near-mint Mystery-Y has any "delaying" potential. (It doesn't!) The disc makes (almost) one rotation before you (gently) rip it off his wayward digit and (not so gently) show him the door. He has just reduced the value of your prize a notch! A few boo-boos are permitted in this category if they are signs of very gentle, normal play on soft surfaces. There can be no signs of contact with hard surfaces such as heavy scuff marks, gouges, or broken lettering. Several digs from gripping fingernails are permitted on the underside as are a few innocuous scratch marks overall.

GOOD CONDITION (7) — If your "buddy" had continued his "delaying tactics" your disc would be Good Plus at best. Other demoting flaws include minor scuffing and scratches from more extended play, but still no signs of major abrasions from concrete, deep cuts, or obvious color fading. There can be only the slightest warp to the shape undetectable except when the disc is placed on a perfectly flat surface, but no creases. The surface should retain its original luster, and damage to decorations must be minimal.

AVERAGE CONDITION (5) — Most discs which have enjoyed a healthy, active life fall into this category. There will be clues all over the disc of normal, happy play. A few chance meetings with rocks or pavement will leave telltale abrasions...

mostly on the rim. There may be moderate scratches and minor cuts, a few damaged letters, and delay marks. Decorations can show similar flaws. Any names written on the disc must be discreet and on the back. There must be no major cracks, piercing dog tooth marks or significant color fading.

FAIR CONDITION (3) — Our descent rapidly continues with evidence of really hard play and some abuse. Consider carefully whether the disc is really worth your time. Expect obvious warping, damage from contact with pavement, embedded small stones and dirt, obvious color fading, a *few* gentle chomps from Fido, a bit of graffiti on the front, hairy road rash, mild blisters, and minor localized peeling. (Hopefully *ALL* of these won't appear on one disc!)

POOR CONDITION (1) — Besides the infractions above, any signs of severe creasing or warping, open blisters, and large areas of peeling plastic, severe color shifts, burns, holes, shredded or misprinted decorations (or lack of expected accoutrements) should convince you not to waste your time and resources on the disc.

DIS(C)TROYED CONDITION (0) — These discs deserve to be in your collection only if they are truly unique and of the highest historical importance. In the mid-1970s I spotted the shards of a yellow Giant Mystery-Y lying scattered on the ground, off to one side, at a dive shop in New Hampshire. I asked the owner if I could have it (them), endured his quizzical look, and proceeded to gather up all of the sections I could find. When I got the puzzle home and proceeded to assemble it, a piece of the picture was missing. A dozen deep dog bites added to the disc's obvious suffering. But, for a while, after I taped it together, I had bragging rights around the neighborhood.

CATEGORIES — COMPARATIVELY ILLUSTRATED

The following photos will help the reader understand how the overall look and condition of any disc fits into the general rating system. While most of the discs shown appear better in real life under soft, room illumination, they were photographed under the harshest, most uncomplimentary lighting conditions possible, then digitally enhanced to bring out the blemishes.

THE RATINGS GAME

There are a number of highly desirable, collectable discs which, if you take the criteria literally, don't neatly fit into one or another of the rating categories. How should an otherwise Near-Mint condition mold #1 Pro Model disc be rated if it is missing its label? Or a Near-Mint condition Sky Saucer with its former owner's name penciled on the front? Strictly speaking, they are no longer Near-Mint, but is it fair to call them in Fair condition?

A few years ago, I was contacted by a well-known, respected disc aficionado. He had noted my interest in a Flyin-Saucer auction and wanted to know if I was interested in another. (Another? There are only a tiny handful of these known to still exist!) I was intrigued, of course, but he was insisting on a trade for some rare items to add to his specialized collection of mini-discs—a specialty we didn't have in common. He wanted nothing else and I had nothing to bring to the table. Somehow the subject turned to Pluto Platters and the green WPP1 he had been pining for. I had one in Good-Plus condition to trade, attached a photo to an email and waited for his reply. "Perfect!" he shot back. "Would you consider trading it

MINT IN PACKAGE — Perfect disc, bag, sticker

MINT — Perfect ATPP, it doesn't get any better!

NEAR MINT — A few slight non-play marks

EXCELLENT PLUS — Minimal play marks

EXCELLENT — A few gentle play marks

EXCELLENT MINUS — More light play marks

GOOD — A few scuffs & very slight warp

GOOD-MINUS — More noticeable scuffing

AVERAGE PLUS — Slightly above average

AVERAGE — Normal scratches, scuffs & wear

AVERAGE-MINUS — Slight dog bites

FAIR-PLUS — Dog bites & name etched on top

FAIR — Cleat mark & minor crease

FAIR-MINUS — Warping & excessive abrasions

POOR-PLUS — Severe crease & dog bites

POOR — Major crack & warping

POOR — Excessive & intentional peeling

DIS(C)TROYED — Splitsville!

for a 'Double-Esker' (WPP5) also in Good-Plus condition?" "You bet!" was my response. But, in the process of taking some pictures of his disc to send me, he discovered a one-inch hairline crack (in Jupiter)…"not too obvious at all." That proved not to be a fatal flaw, because when I received the disc, it was in better, overall Excellent condition. What about the crack? Normally, an obviously cracked disc would fall to Poor condition…maybe a Fair-Minus. But here's a case where a crack so innocuous that you have to be told where it is to find it on a super-rare, highly-prized disc in Excellent condition has virtually no effect on its worth…to me, anyway.

There are three lessons here. First, rating the impact of flaws on the value of any single disc can be complicated and highly personal. Second, honesty when describing a disc's condition is paramount. My trading partner sincerely revealed the existence of the crack and left it to me to decide its effect on the value of the disc…to me. And third, any descriptive system needs flexibility. Beyond tagging the overall condition of a disc with one of the names of the seven categories above, and in addition to the pluses and minuses that may be tacked on, it is still best to accurately describe (or show) potentially value-impacting flaws individually.

After all, isn't the goal of the perfect deal for everybody to walk away perfectly satisfied?

62

A FEW OF THE MOST IMPORTANT DISCS TO COLLECT

HERE, IN MY QUESTIONABLY HUMBLE OPINION, are the very best discs and other paraphernalia to look for in rough order of importance and desirability...not necessarily dollar value. Your order may be different or I may have overlooked one of your special discs. Don't get mad, just get even...by writing your own list!

- ❏ 1948 PIPCO Flyin-Saucer (FS1) in powder blue or black (very first run of the very first plastic flying disc)
- ❏ 1948 PIPCO Flyin-Saucer (FS1) in any other colors
- ❏ American Trends Pluto Platter (ATPP)
- ❏ Flyin Saucer/American Trends— *MUST* have AT label, label residue, or order card to be considered an FS5/AT or FS7/AT.
- ❏ Flyin-Saucer with Li'l Abner label & inset (FS2 & FS3)
- ❏ Wham-O Pluto Platter, First Style (WPP1, especially white)
- ❏ Pluto Platter Horseshoe set
- ❏ Double-Esker Pluto Platter (WPP5)
- ❏ Sixth Style Wham-O Pluto Platter (WPP6)
- ❏ Flyin Saucer (FS7)

- ❏ Brown Pluto Platter (WPP2)
- ❏ All other Styles of Pluto Platters
- ❏ Flyin Saucer with Disney label & package (FS7/D or FS8/D)

- ❏ All other later Styles of Flyin Saucers (FS9–FS13)
- ❏ Professional Frisbee (#1 Mold, white, single band)
- ❏ Sky Pie (original Style)
- ❏ Space Saucer (the earlier the Style the better)
- ❏ Sailing Satellite (especially silver, first run)
- ❏ Zo-lar
- ❏ Mars Platter (any Premier Style)

Chapter 62 — A Few of the Most Important Discs to Collect

- ❏ Wham-O Flying Saucer (Especially the First Style—WFS1)
- ❏ Speedy model
- ❏ Mystery-Y (regular and giant sizes)
- ❏ Sky Saucer (Copar)
- ❏ Night Flyer (DGA 40 mold, first release)
- ❏ Innova-Champion Eagle or Aero (especially a prototype)
- ❏ 1976 NAS 40 and 50 mold with black hot-stamp (the "Black Jimmy")
- ❏ 1978 Discraft Sky Pro
- ❏ Wham-O Mars Platter (especially the pre-grooved Style)
- ❏ Wham-O (from Mystery-Y mold)
- ❏ Classic Frisbee (pre-Super Pro)
- ❏ Wham-O Mini 2 or 4-Pack (1967)
- ❏ Wham-O Moonlighter, raised letters
- ❏ Master Model Frisbee with raised letters & low number
- ❏ PFI Flying Saucer
- ❏ Twirl-A-Boom
- ❏ CPI Saucer Tosser
- ❏ 1982 Hall of Fame Dedication disc
- ❏ *The Official Frisbee Handbook* by Goldy Norton
- ❏ *Frisbee* by Stancil Johnson
- ❏ *Flying Disc Magazine* (1980 — especially the first issue)
- ❏ *Frisbee World Magazine* (any issue, but especially the first, 1976)
- ❏ Buck Rogers Flying Saucer
- ❏ Frisbie Pie Tin (any Style) — de rigueur?

63

TOOLS OF THE TRADE

TO BUILD AN EXCITING DISC COLLECTION you'll need the proper assortment of gadgets and gizmos in your toolbox. The very same instruments, skillfully applied, will help a seller or trader craft the perfect deal.

While some of the information provided in this chapter is generally valuable in the construction of *any* disc collection, you will also find highly-specific data precisely honed for the task of building an impressive assemblage of Flyin-Saucers and Pluto Platters.

How many permutations of Fred's original 1946 Whirlo-Way concept have been identified to date? In what colors? Flip to the Flyin-Saucer Fact Finder and find out. Its companion Pluto Platter Fact Finder will give you everything you need to know to become an expert on the availability of these highly-collectible direct ancestors of the Frisbee.

To help you learn the proper terminology for identifying Pluto Platters, the anatomical structures of all Styles have been combined in one set of idealized, annotated artwork.

And since the task of identifying one Flyin-Saucer or Pluto Platter Style from another has traditionally been addling and onerous, you will stroll through simple, step-by-step, fail-proof methods published for the first time ever.

Chapter 63 — Tools of the Trade

TIPS ON PHOTOGRAPHING DISCS

If you like what you see in the Colorful History section, I'd like to share some photography tips to help you improve your own pictures.

- Become familiar with your camera, particularly its metering and close-up capabilities.

- Film-based cameras still provide the ultimate image quality, but require professional scanning to maintain that advantage as the images are translated into an electronic format.

- Digital cameras let you see results and make changes immediately and eliminate scanning. Higher pixel capture specs don't always ensure better images. Spurious image noise, particularly in darker areas, can easily degrade detail.

- Make sure your film type or white balance setting on your digital camera matches the (color) lighting you are using. While color casts can be removed later, the process will degrade the image in subtle ways.

- To avoid polluting the color of the disc, use a neutral color environment and background. I always digitally silhouette out the disc and drop in a desired background later.

- Discs taken from an angle look more dramatic and attractive, define the shape better, and reveal more detail.

- Close-up views with wide-angle lens settings *may* create unappealing distortion; telephoto views flatten the appearance. Some zoom lenses can't take very sharp close-ups.

- Brighter lights will allow you to use a higher *f*-stop (smaller lens opening), giving you more apparent depth of focus.

- Smaller, undiffused, direct-light sources (like the sun and bare bulbs) will cast harder, detail-defining shadows…and show flaws! Avoid shadows cast in more than one direction. If needed, soften contrast with diffusers and fill dark areas with white reflector cards propped off-camera. To eliminate hot spots and wash-out, avoid on-camera flash.

- For crisp images always use a tripod.
- Develop a standard, easily-repeatable setup of location, camera, lights, disc position, and background.
- Discs with foil labels or designs are tricky to shoot. Think of them as mirrors. If you want a shiny gold design to sparkle, try propping a yellow or gold card out of the picture so it will reflect in the foil when seen through the camera's viewfinder.
- Shift the lights and reflectors slightly to maximize the appearance of each disc.
- Turn off unnecessary room lights; close the window shades.
- If it's built into your camera, learn how the auto-focus feature functions. Particularly with smooth objects such as discs, you may need to preset the focus on another nearby object with sufficient contrast before reframing and snapping the shutter.
- Use a standard exposure setting target: tear out a magazine page with both black text on a white background and varied color images; hold it in front of the disc and preset the exposure, white balance, and focus; then remove it just before taking the shot.
- While everything is set up, take several views of each disc.
- For ultimate control and creativity, enhance your shots digitally in an image-manipulation program such as Photoshop.
- Have fun, experiment, and don't get *disc*ouraged!

TIPS ON SELLING AND TRADING DISCS

No matter what your original motivation was for amassing a pile of discs, eventually you'll decide something has to go.

- There are two basic roads to travel: selling and trading. Both have their rewards—and their proponents. Most antique dealers and estate sellers understandably regard discs as profit-deriving commodities…income. A few disc-collecting purists perish the thought of mixing money and memorabilia and insist on swapping. Most practical collectors do some of both.

- Either way, to get the most out of the deal, know exactly what you've got, and be able to accurately describe, communicate, or advertise both the disc's Style and condition.

- When describing a disc, put yourself in the acquirer's shoes. What would make you interested in the disc? What detractions would you want to know about?

- Be honest in your description. Don't exaggerate or hype its condition. Save the term "rare" for those that truly are. If you aren't sure about any aspect, don't guess or fabricate. Your reputation is at stake! Ask for help, read up, or simply say you don't know.

- If you're dealing on-line, a nice picture will reap rewards. Make sure it's sharp…fuzzy pics hint at a fuzzy deal! If an important detail (or flaw) doesn't show up in an overall view, show an informative closeup.

- Find out what else your buyer/trading partner is interested in. It could be a short-cut to your next deal!

THE SIMPLE WAY TO IDENTIFY ANY PLUTO PLATTER

To the casual saucer owner, general antiques dealer, and budding collector…even to some old hands, identifying a Pluto Platter has always been a confusing and daunting task—more of a job than a joy! Previous books and articles have adequately described the particular details of each type, but the experts have always left it to the readers to sort out the specifics on their own. More often than not, the unfortunate result is an inadequately described or misdiagnosed Platter…or another frustrated soul giving up in despair.

WHY is accurate identification so important? Because not all Styles are of equal value to the collector, the trader, or the seller. Several common Styles are flooding the market. Certain other Styles are extremely rare, making them highly-prized for their collectability, tradability or salability. Do you know which Styles are missing from your collection? Do you know which ones will fetch the big bucks? Do you honestly know for sure what you're advertising for sale? Do you confidently know what you're buying or trading?

Here, for the first time, is a simple, step-by-step method (based on the Kennedy System used throughout this book) to quickly and positively identify *any* and *all* of the eight different Styles of Pluto Platters which have been recognized and cataloged to date. (After more than fifty years, it is *still* possible, although highly implausible, that other Styles still await our discovery!) Experienced disc collectors who are familiar and comfortable with earlier taxonomic systems for categorizing Platters will find a cross-reference on the Pluto Platter Fact Finder page.

Chapter 63 — Tools of the Trade

You will find it most helpful to refer to the color photos of Pluto Platters the first few times you apply this method, paying particular attention to the detail photos. Soon you will learn to immediately recognize particular, key features which will speed the process, but until identification becomes second nature, always start at the beginning and resist skipping ahead.

AMERICAN TRENDS OR WHAM-O PLUTO PLATTER?
Hold the disc with the top side facing you. Turn it so the name Pluto Platter in the center reads naturally. Now look about two inches above the name Pluto. Does the name WHAM-O appear lightly in 3/16-inch-high lettering?

- If it doesn't, *congratulations,* you are the proud beholder of an American Trends Pluto Platter...an ATPP in the Kennedy System! (Turn the disc over and verify that the address in fact lists AMERICAN TRENDS CO.) Fainting is permitted, but set the disc down safely first!

- If WHAM-O appears...*Oh, well!*...go to Step 1.

STEP ONE
Look between the name Pluto and the small WHAM-O described above. Does the name WHAM-O appear again in large 3/8-inch type?

- If not, the disc is a WPP1 (Wham-O Pluto Platter, 1st Style in the Kennedy System).

- If the large WHAM-O is present, go to Step 2.

STEP TWO

Look at the one-inch diameter, raised bump at the very center (the Observation Dome). Does it have six radiating lines that look like spokes on a wheel? (These parts of the design in combination with the inner concentric circle form the twelve window panes of the Observation Dome.)

- If the lines are present, the disc is a WPP2 (Wham-O Pluto Platter, 2nd Style).

- If the lines are missing, go to Step 3.

STEP THREE

Under the word PLATTER is the name FRISBEE in 3/8-inch letters. Look to see if there is a ® after the last "E."

- If the symbol does *NOT* appear, the disc is a WPP3 (Wham-O Pluto Platter, 3rd Style).

- If there is a ® symbol, proceed to Step 4.

STEP FOUR

Turn the disc over. Does the address line for WHAM-O MFG. CO. appear on a long bar raised slightly above the background plane of the disc? (This is referred to as an "esker.")

- If it does, and "PAT. PEND." appears below the esker, the disc is a WPP4 (Wham-O Pluto Platter, 4th Style).

- If it does, and there is a *second* esker, with "DES. PAT. 183626" on it, go to Step 5.

- If there are no eskers (the WHAM-O address and "DES. PAT. 183626" appear on the same plane as the rest of the type), go to Step 6.

STEP FIVE
- *Congratulations!* The disc is a very rare WPP5 (Wham-O Pluto Platter, 5th Style).

STEP SIX
Look in the circular area at the very center of the back.

- If it is void of any designs (ignore flaws), the disc is a very rare WPP6 (Wham-O Pluto Platter, 6th Style).

- If there is a 1/4-inch, backwards-appearing numeral "1," go to Step 7.

STEP SEVEN
- The disc is a WPP7 (Wham-O Pluto Platter, 7th Style).

- If it is blue, *gently* flex it by the edges to see if it might be one of this Style that was made of an experimental softer, more "rubbery" plastic…the less common WPP7R (This can best be ascertained by having versions made from both types of plastic on hand for comparison.)

That's all there is to it!

Identifying *any* Pluto Platter is now as easy as 1, 2, 3…7!

THE SIMPLEST WAY TO IDENTIFY FLYIN-SAUCERS AND THEIR DESCENDANTS.

While the steps to identify a Pluto Platter may at first seem complicated, the procedure to identify a Saucer can feel positively daunting: there are thirteen different Styles which have been identified to date! As with Pluto Platters, it is possible that others await discovery and identification…perhaps even more so with Saucers since the mold passed through many more hands over a longer period of time than the Pluto Platter mold. In fact, just as this book was nearing completion, a new Style (FS3) came to light, necessitating shifting all of the subsequent Style numbers by one. Future discoveries may require similar adjustments to the system.

We will proceed with a step-by-step method (based on the Kennedy System used throughout this book) to positively identify *any* and *all* of the thirteen different Styles of Saucers. Since there are no earlier taxonomic systems for categorizing Saucers (as with the Platters), it is even more important to cross-reference the Flyin-Saucer Fact Finder page in this chapter as well as the pertinent color pages. And, once again, it is important to resist the temptation to skip ahead until the differences between Styles become second nature.

STEP ONE—What Kind of Plastic? Hard Considerations.
This question is easy (and essential) to answer. If it is pliable, it was made after 1953 and you may skip ahead (just this once) to Step 4. But, if the disc is hard and inflexible then begin at the beginning by looking at the center of the top.

- If it has *"FLYIN-SAUCER"* in large raised italic letters, *congratulations!* It is an FS1…the first plastic flying disc made. Only about ten have been located by collectors to date and thus, they are one of the discs most sought-after by collectors. If it is either light blue (Fred describes the color as "powder blue") or black, it is from the very first mold run of the very first ever plastic disc. If the name *"FLYIN-SAUCER"* is missing, go to Step Two.

STEP TWO
Look in the center of the top (if there is a label, see note below).

- If the words: "Pat. Applied For" plus a tiny PIPCO logo appear, then the disc is an FS2. If the words and logo are missing, go to Step Three.

STEP THREE
- The disc is an FS3. (See note below.)

NOTE: The ill-fated Li'l Abner promotion appears to have used both FS2 and FS3 Style discs. As part of the promotion, a label was glued to the top center of each disc, covering up the area critical for distinguishing between the two Styles. Thus, it may be impossible to differentiate an FS2/LA from an FS3/LA without resorting to mutilation of the labels. However, based on my very limited experience (four discs), I was able to ascertain through careful tactile examination of the labels, backed up with tissue paper rubbings, that all four are almost certainly FS2s. (The one "sacrificed" for Figure 2 on page 250 turned out to be an FS2 for sure!) The FS3 shown as Figure 3 on the same page is the only example I've verified so far.

STEP FOUR—The Age of Polyethylene.
Beyond this point, all Saucers were made using softer, more flexible polyethylene plastic. Take a look at the top center once again.

- If the disc is missing any lettering or designs (in other words from the same mold that produced the FS3), check the level of the outer circular center area.

- If it is *SUNKEN* about 1/16", it is an FS4.

- If it is *FLUSH* with the rest of the top of the disc or *RAISED*, proceed to Step Five.

STEP FIVE
- If it is *FLUSH,* and there is no lettering or designs, it is an FS5.

- If there is lettering, go to Step Six.

STEP SIX
In late-1953 or early-1954, SCP restored a name for the disc in small letters on the top. Whether by accident or design, the hyphen in *"FLYIN-SAUCER"* was dropped, and thus the disc is referred to as the FLYIN SAUCER.

- If the name "FLYIN SAUCER" appears, and the center circular area is *RAISED* about 1/16", the disc is an FS6.

- If the center circular area is *FLUSH* with the rest of the top of the disc, go to Step Seven.

STEP SEVEN

While polyethylene Saucers are not as glossy as the original hard plastic *FLYIN-SAUCERS* (FS1–FS3), they are at least semi-shiny. (Normal wear will also reduce the shine!)

- If the disc is as described in Step Six, with a flush center, and has a "semi-shiny" surface, it is an FS7.

- If the surface is best described as *evenly* "dull" or "MATTE," with a slight texture, go to Step Eight.

STEP EIGHT

At some point SCP decided to lightly sandblast the surfaces of the mold. Both top and bottom have a dull, lusterless, roughened surface, with the exception of the area on the bottom still retaining the original PIPCO information and logo. (This area was masked off during the sandblasting and is thus shinier.) So far the only example I've seen is the mint example shown in the color pages with its Disneyland label.

- If the surface is "MATTE," it is an FS8.

- If the "Arcuate Vanes" on top don't extend from near the outer rim to the center circular area, go to Step Nine.

STEP NINE

From 1953 until into the 1960s, SCP continued to produce the Saucers with the slight variations described above, primarily selling them after 1956 through their Disneyland contracts …all the while retaining the original PIPCO information on the bottom. Although PIPCO, Inc. had been dissolved by around 1951, SCP continued to pay commissions to Warren

Franscioni. Then, in the mid-Sixties, SCP recognized an opportunity to further capitalize on the Saucers. The "Flyin Saucer" name (by then considered unnecessary) was removed and the decorative "Arcuate Vanes" were trimmed back from the center to provide a large flat area suitable for imprinting with commercial promotions. (Thus the Saucer precedes the Wham-O Fastback model as a Premium disc.) Turn the Saucer over and look at the center.

- If the SCP logo is present, *PLUS* the name "Republic Tool and Die Corp."—the company that rebuilt the die (including adding their name)—it is an FS9.

- If the name of Republic Tool is missing, go to Step Ten.

STEP TEN

A good guess is that a short time after the mold was altered, SCP decided that having the two names on the disc was confusing (or contributed to lost business), so they required Republic Tool to remove its name.

- If the SCP logo *ALONE* is present, the Saucer is an FS10.

- If the SCP logo is not present, go to Step 11.

STEP ELEVEN

Sometime before SCP went bankrupt about 1970, the Saucer mold was altered by replacing the SCP logo with the name Royal Krafts International and its RKI logo. (The Saucer mold was not among the defunct SCP's frozen assets acquired by Molding Corp in 1971.)

- If the RKI information is present, it is an FS11.

- If there is what appears to be crudely obliterated information, go to Step Twelve.

STEP TWELVE
Events and timing become undetermined at this point. The Saucer mold again changed hands, winding up in the possession of an unknown company which crudely and partially obliterated the RKI information without adding their own identity.

- If two crude "eskers" and a *PARTIAL* RKI logo is present, the disc is an FS12.

- If the back side is blank (except for vague remnants of the structures described above…observable only under a magnifying glass) turn the disc over.

- If there are three major concentric *RAISED RINGS* inside of the truncated Arcuate Vanes, go to Step Thirteen.

STEP THIRTEEN
- The disc is an FS13. The last Style cataloged to date.

FLYIN-SAUCER FACT FINDER

IDENTIFYING A FLYIN-SAUCER (FS)

(See color images, pages 248–259)

FS STYLE NUMBERS, Kennedy System

	Distinguishing Features	1	2	3	4	5	6	7	8	9	10	11	12	13
Full Size "Arcuate" Vanes — Hard Plastic	Large "FLYIN-SAUCER"	✔												
	"Pat. App. For" ONLY (Li'l Abner label)		✔											
	NO graphics on top (Li'l Abner label?)			✔										
Full Size "Arcuate" Vanes — Polyethylene Plastic	NO graphics on top, SUNKEN center				✔									
	NO graphics on top, FLUSH center					✔								
	"FLYIN SAUCER" (no hyphen), RAISED center						✔							
	"FLYIN SAUCER" (no hyphen), FLUSH center							✔						
	MATTE (sandblasted) finish; most (all?) have a Disneyland label								✔					
Shortened Vanes — Soft Polyethylene	SCP logo AND Republic Tool Co. name on back									✔				
	SCP logo ONLY (faint traces of Republic Tool) on back										✔			
	RKI name & logo on back											✔		
	RKI name & logo PARTIALLY TOOLED OUT on back												✔	
	3 RINGS on top inside of shortened vanes, no name on back													✔
	RARITY* (Low numbers rarest)	4	8	?	1	2	3	5	7	6	?	?	?	

PRODUCTION COLORS FOR EACH STYLE

	1	2	3	4	5	6	7	8	9	10	11	12	13
Red	✔	✔	○	–	–	–	✔	✔	○	○	✔	✔	○
Yellow	✔	✔	✔	✔	✔	✔	✔	○	○	✔	✔	○	
Blue (*Powder* blue = 1st run FS1)	✔	✔	○	–	–	–	✔	○	✔	✔	○		○
Green	✔	–	–	–	–	–	✔	○	○	○	○		
Orange	✔	–	–	–	–	–	✔	✔	○	✔	✔	○	
Black (1st run FS1)	✔	–	–	–	–	–	–	–	–	–	–	–	
White	✔	–	–	–	–	–	–	–	–	–	–	–	
Variegated	✔	–	–	–	–	–	✔	–	–	–	–	–	
Pink	–	–	–	–	–	–	–	–	–	–	–	–	

✔ = Verified color   ○ = Likely; unverified by author

PRODUCTION YEARS*   '48–'50   '50   '50   '53   '53   '54?   '54-?   '56-?   '60s   '60s   '68?   '70s   ?

© Copyright Phil Kennedy 2006

*Best guess based on current opinions.

PLUTO PLATTER FACT FINDER

IDENTIFYING A PLUTO PLATTER (PP)

(See color images, pages 262-271)   **STYLES, Kennedy System** (AT=American Trends, W=Wham-O)

Distinguishing Features	ATPP	WPP1	WPP2	WPP3	WPP4	WPP5	WPP6	WPP7
American Trends name on back	✔							
Only one small Wham-O on front		✔						
3 Wham-Os on front, paned observation dome			✔					
Non-paned observation dome, no ® after Frisbee on front				✔				
® After Frisbee on front, single esker on back					✔			
Double eskers on back						✔		
Design Patent on back, no eskers, no backwards "1" in center circle on back							✔	
Design Patent on back, no eskers, backwards "1" in center circle on back								✔
Palmeri/Jensen System Periods	AT	1	2 Early	2 Late	1 Trans.	2 Trans.	3 Early	3 Late
Malafronte System Periods	AT	1	2	3	4	5	6	7
RARITY* (Low numbers rarest)	1–3?	7	8	5	4	1–3?	1–3?	6

PRODUCTION COLORS FOR EACH STYLE

	ATPP	WPP1	WPP2	WPP3	WPP4	WPP5	WPP6	WPP7
Red	✔	✔	✔	✔	✔	✔	✔	✔
Yellow	✔	✔	✔	–	–	–	–	–
Blue	✔	✔	✔	✔	–	–	–	✔
Green	✔	✔	✔	–	–	–	–	–
White (very rare)	✔	✔	–	–	–	–	–	–
Apricot (WPP5 ultra rare)	–	–	✔	✔	✔	✔	–	–
Blue Rubbery Plastic (rare)	–	–	–	–	–	–	–	✔
Brown/Root Beer (extremely rare)	–	–	✔	–	–	–	–	–

✔ =Verified color

PRODUCTION YEARS	'55–'56	'57	'58–'59	'59–'60	'60?	'61?	'61?	'61?–'64

© Copyright Phil Kennedy 2006   *Best guess based on current opinions.

ANATOMY OF THE PLUTO PLATTER—TOP

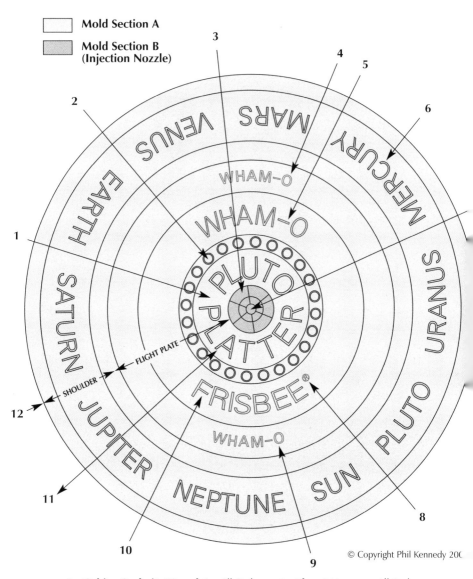

1. **Cabin, Cockpit, (Cupola)**—All Styles
2. **Portholes**—All Styles
3. **Observation Dome (Nipple)**—
   All Styles: ATPP, WPP1 & WPP2 have 12 window panes (spokes); later Styles have mid-ring only (no spokes).
4. **1st Small Wham-O**—WPP1 & later
5. **Large Wham-O**—WPP2 & later
6. **Planet Names**—All Styles
7. **Injection Point**—All Styles
8. **Registered Symbol**—WPP4 & later
9. **2nd Small Wham-O**—WPP2 & later
10. **Frisbee Name**—WPP2 & later
11. **Pluto Platter Name**—All Styles
12. **Rim & Mold Parting Line**—All Styles

© Copyright Phil Kennedy 200

ANATOMY OF THE PLUTO PLATTER—BOTTOM

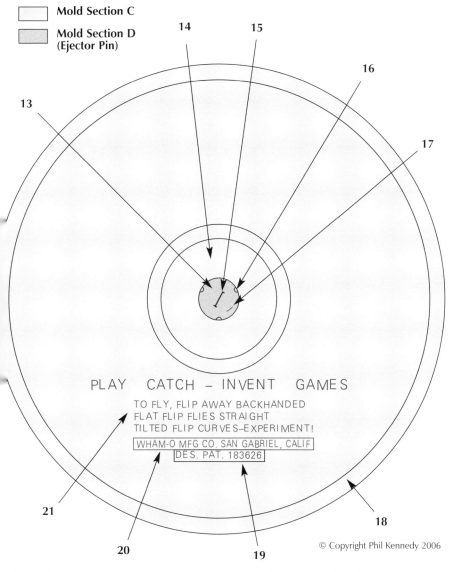

© Copyright Phil Kennedy 2006

13. **Observation Dome "Floor"**—All Styles (also called the Puddle)
14. **Cabin, Cockpit "Ceiling"**—All Styles
15. **Backwards 1 "Mold Number"**—WPP7 only. Ejector Pin could turn, creating many rotational orientations.
16. **3 Semi-hemispheres**, along with tooling marks across center. ATPP only.
17. **Small Nick (Flaw) on Ejector Pin**—WPP4 & all later Styles.
18. **Rim**—All Styles
19. **Patent Esker**—WPP5 Style only.
20. **Address Esker**—WPP1 to WPP5. All bottom characters flush on later Styles.
21. **Lu's Throwing Instructions**—All Styles

351

FLAT FLIP FLIES STRAIGHT!

Index to Appendices

A	Whirlo-Way Design Drawing, 9/10/46	354
B	SCP Cost Quote for Flyin-Saucers, 3/15/48	355
C	SCP / PIPCO Contract Addition, 3/17/48	356
D	SCP Invoice for Flyin-Saucers, 6/30/48	357
E	Franscioni / Burandt Letter, 3/20/50	358
F	Capp Enterprises / PIPCO Letters, 4/6/50 & 4/27/50	360–361
G	Flyin-Saucer Flight Instructions and Game of Heckle	362–364
H	Flyin-Saucer Advertising	365–367
I	SCP / Franscioni Letter, 8/26/53	368
J	Franscioni / SCP Letter, 9/18/53	369
K	American Trends Mail-Order Forms	370
L	Jacobson / Franscioni Letter, 4/18/56	371
M	Wamo / Morrison Contract, 1/23/57	372
N	SCP / Franscioni Letters, 3/21/57 and 8/7/57	373–375
O	Wham-O Product Line Literature, 1957	376–378
P	Pluto Platter Article, *People & Places*, 6/58	379
Q	Pluto Platter Patent 9/30/58	380
R	Patent Infringement Letter, 10/9/58	381
S	Wham-O Corporate Image, *Life*, 12/3/65	382
T	Wham-O Trade Ad, 3/66	383
U	Franscioni / Johnson Letter, 8/14/73	384–385
V	Franscioni / Johnson Letter (Undated)	386–387
W	"Where the Frisbee First Flew," by Jeff McMahon	388–396
X	Timeline of Events	397–404
Y	Spinnin' Yarns	405–409
Z	Glossary of Terms	410–421

APPENDIX A — The First Design for a Flying Disc — 9/10/46

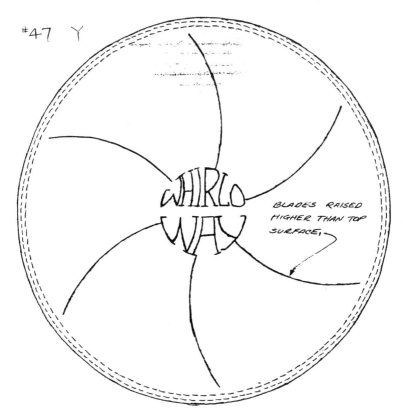

#47 Y

BLADES RAISED HIGHER THAN TOP SURFACE,

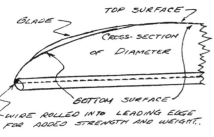

BLADE
TOP SURFACE
CROSS-SECTION OF DIAMETER
BOTTOM SURFACE
WIRE ROLLED INTO LEADING EDGE FOR ADDED STRENGTH AND WEIGHT.

A DEVISE DESIGNED BY WALTER FREDERICK MORRISON SEPT. 10th, 1946. WHEN SPUN OR WHIRLED CREATES A DIFFERENCE BETWEEN AERO-DYNAMIC PRESSURES ON TOP AND OR BOTTOM OF A SURFACE,

IN THIS CASE, THE BLADES CA. TOP OF THE DEVICE CAUSES THE AIR TO BE THROWN OFF WHILE THE AIR UP UNDER THE DEVISE IS CONFINED.

ALSO, THE LEADING EDGE OF THE DEVISE SIMULATES THE LEADING EDGE OF AN AERO-PLANE WING.

WHEN THE DEVISE IS WHIRLED AND MOVED THRU THE AIR AT THE S& TIME, IT WILL TEND TO RISE, FLOAT OR DESEND ACCORDING TO THE MOMENTUM FIRST GIVEN TO IT, IF IT IS MOVING IN A HORIZENTAL PLA

APPENDIX B — SCP Cost Quote for Flyin-Saucers — 3/15/48

Southern California Plastic Company
2773 W. Broadway, Eagle Rock 41, Calif.

Telephone: CLeveland 64119

N° 131

Name: W. R. Franscioni & W. F. Morrison
Date: March 15, 1948
Address: 884 North Broad Street
City: San Louis Obispo, California
Tel.: San Luis Obispo 3195 ~~Home 3099W~~

We are pleased to submit the following proposal for your consideration:
We offer to manufacture for you the following priced items for the consideration and upon the terms and conditions hereinafter stated:

Name of Part: Flying saucer
Material: Fortical Color:
- In lots of 5000 — $ .3025 per unit
- In lots of 25,000 — $ .28 per unit
- In lots of 50,000 — $ .275 per unit
- In lots of 100,000 — $ .26 per unit

Name of Part: Flying saucer
Material: Ethylcelluose Color:
- In lots of 5000 — $ .265 per unit
- In lots of 25,000 — $ .2425 per unit
- In lots of 50,000 — $ .2375 per unit
- In lots of 100,000 — $ .225 per unit

These prices are for castings cut from the gates and bulk packed with the regular finish as is obtained from the molding process, and F.O.B. our plant, unless otherwise specified below.

Remarks: If it is possible to buy material at lower than base cost we will pass this savings on to you.

Terms:
Molds for producing the above castings $ 1690.00 (Plus any taxes) Estimated Daily Production of castings 1900 units a day based on a 24 hour
Terms on molds: 50% before starting die, and balance before start of production.
Sample castings will be submitted within 8 weeks after approval of drawing, and/or models.
Remarks: The die cost is based on your design, any changes will be at a time and material basis.

THE GENERAL CONDITIONS PRINTED ON THE REVERSE SIDE HEREOF CONSTITUTE A PART OF THIS OFFER, AND YOUR SIGNATURE AND RETURN OF ORIGINAL COPY DENOTES YOUR ACCEPTANCE HEREOF. UNLESS ACCEPTED FORTHWITH THIS OFFER SHALL BE DEEMED TO HAVE BEEN WITHDRAWN.

We wish to thank you for the opportunity of quoting and assure you of our best efforts in your behalf, should we be favored with your order.

SOUTHERN CALIFORNIA PLASTIC COMPANY
By _____

Customer's Acceptance: Date _____ By _____
Signature of person authorized to sign.
Firm Name _____ Capacity _____
Owner, Partner, President, etc.

Payment when due for the above products and any repeat orders and of all expenses of collection thereof is hereby guaranteed; and I waive demand and notice of default, and consent to alteration, and to extension of time to the obligor, without further notice to me.

_____ Individually
_____ Individually
_____ Individually

APPENDIX C — SCP / PIPCO Contract Addition, 3/17/48

SOUTHERN CALIFORNIA PLASTIC COMPANY

March 17, 1948

NEW ADDRESS
1805 FLOWER ST.
GLENDALE 1, CALIF.

W. R. Franscioni & W. F. Morrison
884 North Broad Street
San Luis Obispo, California

Gentlemen:

This letter is to be made a part of our Contract Form #131, dated March 15, 1948.

It is the intention that this letter will take care of certain sections of Contract No. 131 and clarify and set forth certain conditions.

1. If for any reason our organization (Southern Calif. Plastic Co.) is unable to produce the parts as required by you, (within the terms of our agreement) then Southern Calif. Plastic Co. will release this die until such a time as Southern Calif. Plastic Co. can and will produce your parts, at which time the die is to be returned in the same conditions as released.

2. The title to the die at all times shall remain in your name. However, the die will not be removed from Southern California Plastic Co. until a minimum of 150,000 parts have been produced from the dies. Also to provide for the removal of the die from Southern California Plastic Co. upon a payment of 50% in addition to the original tooling cost.

Warren R. Franscioni

Walter F. Morrison

SOUTHERN CALIFORNIA PLASTIC COMPANY

Stanley J. Gray, President

APPENDIX D — SCP Invoice to PIPCO, 6/30/48

INVOICE

SOUTHERN CALIFORNIA PLASTIC COMPANY
1305 FLOWER ST. • GLENDALE • CALIFORNIA

A 04700

LOS ANGELES PHONE
CHapman 5-1027
CItrus 3-4274

MANUFACTURERS

LD TO: W. R. Franscioni & W. F. Morrison
884 North Broad Street
San Luis Obispo, California

DATE: June 30, 1948

YOUR ORDER NO.	DIVISION NO.	SHIPPED VIA	TERMS	OUR JOB NO.	DATE WANTED	DATE SHIPPED
			Net Cash	Stock		

QUANTITY	DESCRIPTION	UNIT PRICE	AMOUNT
301	Flyin Saucers	.25	75 25

pd. by Fran.

ORIGINAL

APPENDIX E — *Franscioni / Burandt Letter* — *Chapter 47*

XXXXX. 1432-J

P O BOX 679

March 20, 1950

Robert J. Burandt
359 San Benito Way
San Francisco 27, Calif.

Dear Mr. Burandt:

We have received your letter, dated March 13, 1950, in which you request information concerning our "FLYIN-SAUCER" operation in it's entirety. I trust that the following will be of assistance.

Enclosed you will find copies of our advertising matter, which should do for some of the information requested. Also included are a few copies of the glossy prints. These are not the best, but seemed to be the only ones available at the moment. Most of our photo work has been in connection with the development of a 16MM color film with sound. We came up with 250' of pretty good stuff; however the film is in the East right now. Further assistance on the photo or demonstrational angle could be supplied by contacting FRANZ & ROTHROCK, our representatives in your city. Thier add. is 354 -55 Irwin Street, San Rafael. Or you can call Mr. C. J. "Chuck" Franz at Townsends, 129 Geary St., Exbrook 2-7000; who I am certain will be happy to assist in any way possible.

Now for the general information, if I can do so without becoming too wordy and involved. Mr. Walter F. Morrison and myself, are sole owners and developers of the item. The idea originated from the practice of sailing ordinary domestic cake tins. Cutting high school one spring day, we found ourselves at the beach thoroughly enjoying our illegal holiday; someone suggested that we do something other than just lay in the sun. Fred, as Morrison is called, picked up a cake tin we happened to have brought along, and started to sail it. It seemed he had been swiping his mother's cake tins and practising for some time. Before long we were all being instructed by him in the rare art of sailing cake tins. This went on for several seasons, including the experience of earning extra funds by commerciallising, in a minor way, on our unique abilities. We would buy a couple dozen of the tins, find a spot where things seemed to be quiet, start playing, work up interest, then start peddling the tins. We did'nt do too badly either.

Nothing was done to really push the idea at that time; and as time passed we merely grew up and more or less went our seperate ways. Then came the war. I had been flying, and working as a Primary Army Air Corps Flight Instructor, so-- went the full time as a memberofothe Air Transport Command; spent two years in the C.B.I., working the HUMP deal, and wound up with nothing more serious than one Bail-out to my credit.

FLAT FLIP FLIES STRAIGHT!

--- 2 ---

Fred too wound up as "Fly-boy". After his training here in the States he wound up in a Fighter Group in Italy. Just 45 or 50 days before V-E Day, and on his 58th mission, as he puts it, he was shot down in flames. He to used the Nylon Pack, and hitting the ground was the most serious part of his inglorious end. However he was taken prisoner, and spent the time up to V-E Day as a guest of the Gerry visiting such places as Nuhrenburg and the like.

Came the Post-war adjustments and in the course of events Fred went to work for me in the little business that I had started, peddling Bottled Gas. In talking over old times as we went from one job to the next, our cake tin experiences came back into focus. After that things moved pretty fast. More than one, while watching us flip the thing back and forth would exclaim, "here'd you get the Flying Saucer?".

With the flight experience and what little book learning we could remember our cake tin took on a streamlined appearance. The metal, which was noisy, would eventually break and cause cuts, became a tough flexible brightly colored plastic. All this, after hours of redesigning and test, working on lift, gyroscopic balance and the like.

Plastic dies, and all that goes with it soon went right through our meager savings. So as a last effort, the little business went by the board, and all our coconuts gathered in one basket. It has been almost two years now and things have just begun to really roll.

We have learned the hard way. Personal demonstration, knocking around at Fairs and what have you. Gradual progression has brought us up through a group of direct representatives, such as Franz & Rothrock; now Manufacturer's Representatives, and finally Jobbers, Dealers and a flow of orders which is so essential to the success of any venture.

Present manufacturing equipment is capable of a monthly output of 75,000 units. At the present rate, this output will be reached by early summer.

The reprint from PACIFIC PLASTICS runs pretty true to form. The shot of the young fellow gives about as good an idea as any on how to launch the thing. By running through the instructions, etc., you will see that we repeatedly point out that an easy smooth snap of the wrist is all that is necessary. From your own observations you should have learned that a lot of "beef" is a hindrance rather than a help.

Once the SAUCER is properly launched, with a good fast spin, it is guided by use of regular aeroplane Flight characteristics, if. bank it, and it will turn, sail it level and it will go straight.

I trust my disertation has been of assistance. And I most certainly want you to know that your interest in our little gadget is gratefully accepted.

Thank you, I am

                Very truly yours,

                PIPCO

                Warren R. Franscioni
                Co-partner and Sales Manager

APPENDIX F — Capp Enterprises / PIPCO Letter — 4/6/50

This letter of introduction was received by PIPCO about two months after Fred Morrison parted company with Warren Franscioni.

April 3, 1950

SALES PROMOTION MANAGER
PIPCO PRODUCTS
San Luis Obispo, Calif.

Dear Sir:

While shopping in Abercrombie & Fitch, I noticed your amazing new game, THE FLYIN-SAUCER, and, being impressed by your sense of timeliness and promotion, immediately purchased several.

The LI'L ABNER comic strip will, in the very near future, carry a picture of our hero, LI'L ABNER afloat in a flying saucer and this of course ties in perfectly with your item.

Will you be kind enough to read the enclosed story regarding the appeal of our comic strip. Please note, also, the photostat attached which shows the actual flying saucer with LI'L ABNER in it.

I feel certain that an affiliation with our comic strip would prove most advantageous to you at this time.

I look forward to hearing from you and hope that we will be able to work together on this promotion.

Cordially yours,
CAPP ENTERPRISES, INC.

GLADYS MURRAY

GM:s

APPENDIX F — Franscioni / Capp Enterprises Letter — 4/27/50

This letter shows that Franscioni proceeded rapidly with contract negotiations and payments to Capp Enterprises, and that PIPCO was to be incorporated.

April 27, 1950
1805 Flower Street
Glendale, California

Jerome B. Capp
CAPP ENTERPRISES, INC.
17 East 45th Street
New York 17, New York

Dear Mr. Capp:

Enclosed you will please find our certified check for $2,000, as per terms of the contract, and the four copies of the signed contract. Also enclosed are the copies of the original contract, which were not used when the changes were entered prior to our signing.

You will find the changes made, covering listing of the licensee, renewal option, and the starting date. These were all made in accordance with our telephone conversation of April 24th, with Ruth Astor of your office.

Listing of the licensee was changed, since we are not yet a corporation. In this same connection I should like to state, it is assumed we will be allowed to assign, to the corporation, since our corporate counsel informs this is permissable under California Law, and it is assumed the Laws of the State of New York are not to the contrary. Confirmation on this point would be appreciated.

The renewal clause was added, since this was the understanding in your letter of April 6, 1950; signed by Gladys Murray.

I trust you will find the above alterations in order.

We are going ahead full speed. Formation of a corporation is being rapidly brought to a close; in order that we might have the ability to fully justify the expectations of the job to be done from this end. Full production of all sales material should have commenced before the end of this coming week. Increased production rate of the item is but a matter of giving the full speed ahead signal at the desired time. All other problems are being cleared as rapidly as possible.

Personal contact is tentatively planned immediately following the May 8th date mentioned by Gladys Murray. It is possible that we shall be able to clear a contact with a New York representative at an earlier date.

I trust this is the beginning of a mutually satisfying association.

Sincerely yours,

Warren R. Franscioni

WRF:bm

APPENDIX G — *Original Flyin-Saucer Instructions*

FLIGHT INSTRUCTIONS

FLYIN' SAUCERS have flight characteristics very similar to airplanes. The SAUCER IS launched in identically the same manner as sailing your hat onto a hook—by spinning and forward motion.

In order to fly in a straight line, the SAUCER must leave the hand in a level position. To curve the SAUCER, it must leave the hand banked or tilted in direction of desired curve—for example: for left curve—the left side of the SAUCER must be tilted down.

FOR BEST RESULTS — The spinning of the SAUCER is most important and most difficult to master. Because the spin creates a gyroscopic action which controls the attitude of the SAUCER in flight, a smooth, fast spinning delivery should be developed Do not hold the SAUCER too tight.

Analyze your mistakes and make corrections by tilting or banking SAUCER. The correction must be applied to the SAUCER as it leaves the hand.

SAIL 'EM BACK AND FORTH - PLAY CATCH !

Begin by flying your saucer about 10 feet. The distance you are able to fly it will quickly increase with practice.

MAKE 'EM TURN !

By releasing the SAUCER in a tilted manner, you can make it turn to the left or right. Bank it the way you want it to turn. It is advisable to learn to fly straight before starting to make turns.

MAKE 'EM COME BACK !

After learning to fly straight and make turns, you'll be able to make your SAUCER return to you by sailing it into the breeze at a sharp angle. The harder a wind blows, the flatter an angle you can fly it to make it return. Spin SAUCER as much as possible.

MAKE 'EM SKIP !

Right-handers launch SAUCER so that left side strikes hard surface. Right side for left-handers.

HARD SURFACE

APPENDIX G (cont.) — Instructions for the Game of Heckle

THE GAME OF HECKLE

THE GAME OF HECKLE provides a means of utilizing the unique manner in which the FLYIN' SAUCER can be guided. Rules and regulations are provided, forming the basis for skill and competition.

PLAYERS — Four — with two on each team.

OBJECT — To fly SAUCER around HECKLERS into your partner's circle.

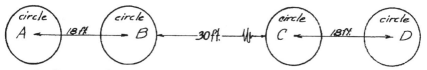

ALL CIRCLES ARE 6 FEET IN DIAMETER -- CENTER SPACE MAY VARY WITH ABILITY.

All players must remain in their circle until SAUCER is airborne.

The game begins with the Flier (A) attempting to sail the SAUCER around the HECKLERS in the circles (B) and (C) so that his partner in the Receiver's circle (D) can catch it.

Flier (A) must remain in his circle when serving the SAUCER.

HECKLER (B) must remain in his circle at all times while his team is defensive. He may attempt to stop the flight of the SAUCER, or distract the Flier in any manner. Should he step or fall out of his circle, his team forfeits 1 point and the offensive team retains serve.

HECKLER (C) remains in his circle until SAUCER is airborne. He may then leave his circle to heckle the Receiver (D) in any manner so long as he doesn't interfere with flight of SAUCER or touch the Receiver, or step into the Receiver's circle. Hecklers forfeit 2 points for each infraction.

Receiver (D) attempts to catch the SAUCER in his circle. Should he do so, then his team receives 2 points. Should it be necessary for the Receiver to leave his circle to catch the SAUCER, then his team scores but 1 point. Should he drop or miss the SAUCER, no points are scored, and the teams change positions. (A) changes with (B) and (C) changes with (D).

(C) is now the Flier, and (B) the Receiver. HECKLER (D) must remain in his circle, and the HECKLER (A) becomes the roving HECKLER.

Teams change positions when the Receiver fails to catch the SAUCER.

In the event that no Referee is available, disputes will be settled by mutual agreement, or the flip of a coin.

First team to score 25 points wins the game.   KEEP 'EM FLYIN'

This is a PIPCO PRODUCT   San Luis Obispo, Calif.

APPENDIX G (cont.) — Later Instructions & Reorder Form

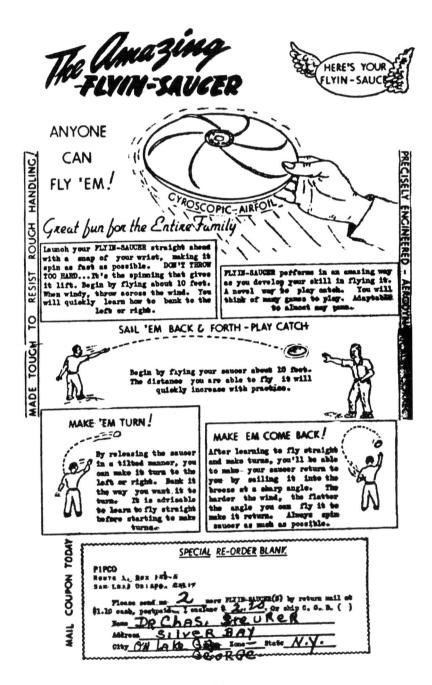

APPENDIX H — Flyin-Saucer Advertising & PR

COUNTER SPY
By Hazel Stall

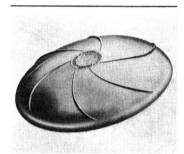

FLYIN' SAUCER ... an authentic, scientifically designed gyroscopic airfoil—flying disc to you (and me) that's fun for the whole family. Curved fins give it the required lift, and simple instructions enable you to zoom it up 100 feet or more, even control long distance flights to play catch with a friend. You can make it bank, turn and return like a boomerang. Rugged plastic 8½" in diameter; in red, yellow or blue, $1 postpaid. Par Sales Company, Dept. F, 6912 Hollywood Blvd., Hollywood 28, Calif.

PIPCO — PR article (circa 1950)

PIPCO — Generic ad (circa 1950)

APPENDIX H (cont.) — Flyin-Saucer Advertising, Full Page Ad

Exciting Fun for Everyone!

The FLYIN-SAUCER
(A Gyroscopic Airfoil)

- **GREAT SPORT FOR KIDS – FASCINATING FOR ADULTS**
- **PRECISELY ENGINEERED – AERODYNAMICALLY CORRECT**
- **TOUGH, FLEXIBLE PLASTIC – ALMOST UNBREAKABLE**

HERE IT IS! The most exciting, contagious new fun game since ping pong. The sport that is giving recreation to men and women, boys and girls. An engrossing outdoor pastime that's making new converts every day.

It's the FLYIN' SAUCER. A bowl shaped disc that sails and floats like a bird. Thrown by hand it can be made to curve, boomerang, fly straight or skip off a hard surface.

Made of pliable, high grade plastic to take a good beating, it was brought to this country by a couple of Army fliers who flew the Hump. They applied aerodynamic design to it, named it the FLYIN' SAUCER and introduced it on the California and Florida beaches. It swept the beaches like a mammoth bulldozer and moved inland to the parks, front yards, high school and college campuses — anyplace there was room to play catch.

Available in rich red, friendly blue or flashing yellow. Complete instructions and rules for the game of HECKLE with every cellophane wrapped FLYIN' SAUCER. They're 9½" in diameter and weigh six ounces.

YOU CAN'T BUY MORE FUN FOR $1.00

Distributed by

CRANDIS ASSOCIATES
P. O. BOX 306   RED BANK, NEW JERSEY

APPENDIX H (cont.) — Monsanto Ad Featuring Flyin-Saucer

*m the back cover of a comic book, circa 1950. Note upsidedown Saucer & baseball-style toss!)

APPENDIX I — SCP / Franscioni Letter — 8/26/53 — Ch. 49

On 7/13/53, after several years without any contact, SCP wrote Franscioni asking to reobtain the Flyin-Saucer mold. This letter is SCP's response to Franscioni's reply.

SOUTHERN CALIFORNIA PLASTIC COMPANY

1805 FLOWER • GLENDALE, CALIFORNIA • PHONE CHapman 5-1027

August 26, 1953

Major Warren R. Franscioni
P.O. Box 342
Ellsworth Air Force Base
Rapid City, South Dakota

Dear Maj.:

Thanks a lot for your interesting letter of August 16, giving us the painful details in regard to the Flyin' Saucer and bringing us up to date on your own activities. It certainly looks like the Capp organization let you down on the promotion, as their original correspondence showed a terrific potential. You and Fred certainly worked hard enough to put it over.

We are still receiving calls here for the Flyin' Saucer. We believe we could handle some over-the-counter sales here, provided the Saucers were made out of Polyethylene. Do you still have the single cavity die, or was it incorporated into your dual cavity mold? If you still have it in your possession, and it isn't in "hock", we would like to run a few Saucers on it here and pay you some kind of a royalty on the ones sold. We would not want to purchase the die, but merely figure on a royalty basis. This would give you some extra "petty cash", befitting a man of your Rank and Distincti Let me hear from you on this.

I believe I forgot to mention in my letter to you that Stan Gray died suddenly of a heart attack a year ago this last March. He had been ill for some time, but the suddenness of his death was unexpected by all of us. Clyde Gray left the Company shortly before Stan's death and is no longer connected with us.

Glen and I are doing our best to keep the place solvent and Jack Stout is still in the molding room. We would certainly like to see you if you get down our way and we will promise you a few "beers" on the house at MacDonalds.

Best regards,

SOUTHERN CALIFORNIA PLASTIC COMPANY

Ed Kennedy

Edward L. Kennedy, President

ELK/kbm

CREATORS OF THE FAMOUS Stoway LINE

APPENDIX J — Franscioni / SCP Letter — 9/18/53 — Ch. 49

In this letter Franscioni agrees to allow SCP to produce and market the new polyethylene Saucers. Note the left-over modified PIPCO letterhead.

PIPCO

Telephone 3099-W

Warren R Franscioni
~~Box 348 Ellsworth AFB~~
Rapid City, S D

1767 Conejo Drive
San Luis Obispo, Calif.

18 September 1953

Edward L Kennedy, pres.
Southern California Plastic Company
1805 Flower Street
Glendale, California

Dear Ed:

You will find numerous enclosures to this thing. First you will be able to tell from the first that I have heard from my many business associates in the saucer venture. And as always, with a bunch of big brains like us, time must be taken for us to get our heads together. So since we seem to be in accord on the main point, that of trying to get together with you and make some sort of a deal, I have proposed that you deal direct with all of the power up San Francisco way. For the sake of business on our part I will let Rothrock get the dope to you on the agreement, but I think you will be able to get a few of the points that I made to the boys when I first wrote them about your proposal and I trust that you might feel that I dont think any agreement we may make should be strictly a one way deal, regardless of the direction that any one individual might be interested in going. I also trust that the figures I originally proposed to them will be used, because I think they are fair, and give you the room you will need to ply around.

For my money Ed, I am willing to drop the die in your plant and say here it is, you always thought this thing had lots of merit, it's your baby and as long as you want to go at it you are the only one who has the whip by the handle and if you can do something with it we will all make a little dough.

For this reason and not to get all of those brainsdoing double time again in the wrong direction, I am sending enclosure two and three. Bower is a lad who used to move a few for us down there on the southern beaches. As you can see, this is the first time I have heard from him in quite a spell. The last time was at our last Pomona Fair day, and apparetnly, since it is about that time again this year he seems to have thought of us. Dont know if anything will come of this, but you got it. If I were to send this one to S F, those lads would probably want to dump some of that stuff we have warehoused up there even though we might be trying to make a deal with you at the time. I would like to see him get some of those new poly jobs when you get them run. As a matter of fact I would like to see them myself.

Enclosure four, I think you will get a bit of enjoyment out of this one. I am sure you will recognize the type craft and hope you will agree that the A F method of check out, preflight and run-up meets all requirements, encompasses all details and is suficient.

«« Designers of the amazing FLYIN' SAUCER! »»

APPENDIX K — American Trends Mail-Order Forms

> AN XLNT GIFT AND XMAS IS COMING
> FOR EACH SAUCER SEND $1.00 PLUS 10¢
> FOR SHIPPING. SEND TO
> NAME _____
> ADDRESS _____
> CITY AND STATE _____
> QUANTITY ( ); COLORS (RED); (YELO); (ORANG
>
> HOW TO FLY — SPIN SAUCER AWAY
> FROM BODY WITH BACK-HANDED SNAP
> OF WRIST, (AS YOU WOULD SAIL A HAT.)
> TO CONTROL — SPIN SAUCER AWAY
> LEVEL. SAUCER TURNS THE WAY ITS
> BANKED OR TILTED. (LIKE A PLANE)
> START CLOSE TOGETHER - AVOID WIND.
> HAVE FUN - GET ANOTHER !!!

AMERICAN TRENDS — Flyin Saucer Mail Order Form back side (late 1954) — (See page 253)

ENLISTMENT FORM

Being of sound mind and complete control of my finances, I would like to become a PLUTO PLATTER PILOT.

Name..
          Please Print
Address...
City and State..
                                    Intestinal
Age............... Height................... Fortitude................... Devout.........................
                                    Amount   Yes or No (if neither explain)

I would like a ☐ Red; ☐ Yellow; ☐ Green or ☐ White PLUTO PLATTER (S) as sanctioned by ADMIRAL ASTEROID, Conqueror of the Cosmic All.

All answers are true to the best of my knowledge and I enclose $1.10 for each PLUTO PLATTER and SPACE LICENSE.

Send to Space Headquarters
AMERICAN TRENDS CO.
15838 HARVEST MOON, LA PUENTE, CALIFORNIA

SEND THIS CARD   We Will Mail Prepaid or C.O.D.

AMERICAN TRENDS — Pluto Platter Mail Order Form (1955-1956) — (See page 263)

APPENDIX L — Jacobson / Franscioni Letter — Chapter 51

In this letter Franscioni's lawyers advise him to have his application prepared and submitted for a design patent rather than a mechanical (or utility) patent. Also shown is reference to Warren's original (abandoned) patent application.

CLARENCE A. O'BRIEN (1883-1942)
HARVEY B. JACOBSON
JOHN H. LEWIS

FRANCIS N. GLADDING
PHILIP E. BARNES
JESSIE W. KARSTED
GEORGE E. POPPER
NORMAN E. MILLER
JOHN H. LEWIS, JR.
KENNETH S. GOLDFARB
CHARLES E. BROWN
WILLIAM E. BECK
DONALD M. SELL
HOMER A. SMITH
SAMUEL MEERKREEBS

CLARENCE A. O'BRIEN
AND
HARVEY B. JACOBSON
REGISTERED PATENT ATTORNEYS
UNITED STATES AND FOREIGN PATENTS
PATENTS, TRADE-MARKS AND COPYRIGHTS
DISTRICT NATIONAL BUILDING
1406 G STREET, NORTHWEST
WASHINGTON 5, D. C.

REGISTERED
IN UNITED STATES
PATENT OFFICE

CABLE ADDRESS
"O PATENT" WASHINGTON
PATENT CODE

April 18, 1956

Major Warren R. Franscioni
205 Frank Avenue
Ellsworth AFB, South Dakota

    In re: Walter F. Morrison and Warren R. Franscioni
           TOY
           U. S. Ser. No. 24,346 - Abandoned

Dear Major Franscioni:

        This will acknowledge receipt of your communication of April 12 forwarding a remittance of $100.00 to apply on account and instructing us to proceed with a design application covering the above invention.

        If an application for design protection is filed in the Patent Office and a patent granted thereon, it will then be too late to obtain mechanical patent protection for your invention. The design patent will be available as a reference against any mechanical claims which we may make.

        In addition, where alleged design and mechanical inventions reside in substantially identical structures, as in this case, it has been decided by the Court that the issuance of a second patent would not be justified. In other words where an invention is susceptible to design and mechanical protection and in each case the structure is substantially the same and there is merely one inventive concept present, as in the situation in this case, an election must be made as to whether an application for design or mechanical patent is to be filed.

        As we previously advised it is our opinion that it would be preferable for you to proceed with a design application rather than a mechanical application. However, we are holding this matter in abeyance pending your further instruction.

        Cordially yours,

        CLARENCE A. O'BRIEN & HARVEY B. JACOBSON

JAG:ch   By *[signature]*

APPENDIX M — Wamo / Morrison Contract, 1/23/57 — Ch. 29

Shown is the first page of the three-page document. Note that the company is still called Wamo (not Wham-O) on this date.

AGREEMENT

This Agreement made at San Gabriel, California, this 23rd day of January, 1957, by and between Walter Frederick Morrison and Lucile E. Morrison doing business as American Trends Co., hereinafter called "First Party", and Wamo Manufacturing Co., a California corporation, hereinafter called "Second Party".

WITNESSETH:

WHEREAS, First Party has conceived and developed a new and unusual idea of a plastic flying saucer type toy and

WHEREAS, said new and unusual idea or process consists of plastic molding, suitable for a game.

WHEREAS, First Party desires that said idea or process be exploted on a nation wide basis; and

WHEREAS, Second Party desires to exploit same;

NOW, THEREFORE, for and in consideration of the mutual promises and covenants hereinafter contained, it is agreed by and between the parties hereto as follows:

I

First party, does hereby lease one injection type molding die and any and all patents, patent applications, and copyrights which have been or may hereafter be filed or acquired in connection therewith, and agree to execute any necessary papers and rightful oaths to secure said right, title, and interest to said second party, it being the intent and understanding of the parties that, subject only to the express limitations hereinafter set forth, second party shall have full exclusive right to use said dies and/or process, manufacture, sell, lease, use, and otherwise exploit said idea and disc on world wide basis.

II

It is the present intention of the parties that said idea or process be exploited by advertising and selling a number of toy saucers. Second party hereby agrees to pay to First party a royalty of six and six-tenths percent of all wholesale sales (after refunds for returned merchandise) on any and a such sales made by Second party. For the purpose of this paragraph, a sale

APPENDIX N — SCP / Franscioni Letter, 3/21/57 — Chapter 52

SOUTHERN CALIFORNIA PLASTIC COMPANY

1805 FLOWER • GLENDALE CALIFORNIA • PHONE CHapman 5-1027

March 21, 1957

<u>AIRMAIL</u>

Lt. Col. Warren R. Franscioni
205 Frank Avenue
Ellsworth Air Force Base
South Dakota

Dear Warren:

If you think you are confused on the "Flying Saucers", I can only say that we are much more so.

I called Chuck Franz approximately a month ago and told him that we had just found out that Fred Morrison had had another die built on the Flying Saucer and was merchandising the product under the name of "Pluto's Platter". During the time that he was having the Saucer made, he was also accepting sales commissions from the company here.

I knew nothing about the fact that he was having the Saucer built until the time he started demonstrating it in the various fairs and he was also calling on our accounts.

I promptly told him that he had to bring his account up to date with us as, at one time, it ran over three thousand dollars. He has now sent in a check to clear up the account and we are mailing you a commission check which brings us up to date on the Saucers sold.

In my opinion, Fred acted completely unfairly on this entire thing and we certainly will never do business with him again. Fred's dad, Duke Morrison, has tried to sell both Saucers at the same time. I feel sorry for Fred's dad, but I too am completely confused as to where he stands in the picture. We have told him that we will be unable to do business with either one of them again and are setting up our own sales.

We have cinched Disneyland for the next year and they are going to have their own cellophane bag with some of the Disney characters on it. I regret to state that they can no longer demonstrate the Saucer out there as one of the Saucers got loose over the fence and hit some women on the head. This suit has been settled by Disneyland but it appears to be impossible to get them to demonstrate at the present time. They are, however, going to display the Saucers all over Disneyland and also, are going in for a mail order business on this item.

CREATORS OF THE FAMOUS  LINE

Lt. Col. Warren R. Franscioni
March 21, 1957
Page two

Only this morning, I found out that Fred had also been out there in order to try to get the account away from us. However, we lowered the wholesale price from forty-five cents to thirty-five cents per Saucer and I believe that Fred will find, before he gets through, that he is working on a very slim margin.

I certainly hope you will be able to get down here again soon and this time, I will definitely plan on spending more time with you than when you were down here before.

               Best regards,

               Ed.

               Edward L. Kennedy - President
               SOUTHERN CALIFORNIA PLASTIC COMPANY

ELK:sa

APPENDIX N — SCP / Franscioni Letter, 8/7/57 — Chapter 52

1805 FLOWER • GLENDALE CALIFORNIA • PHONE CHapman 5-1027

August 7, 1957

Lt. Col. Warren Francioni
1100 Felder Avenue
Montgomery, Alabama

Dear Warren:

As I recall it, you said that you would be stationed in Montgomery for the next year so I am taking a chance on writing to this address.

I have a copy of the letter to you from Dr. Walter F. Morrison which is entirely misleading.

It is true that an eastern company is putting out a very cheap flying saucer using reprocessed material which has made the sales increasingly difficult, however, Disneyland is selling more of our saucers than ever and we have several boys in the area working the fairs and ready to work the colleges when the fall term begins. We also have the original Frisbee distributors handling our product in the east.

Mr. Morrison called me to change the construction of the die along the lines he suggested in his letter to you. I told him that we had nothing to do with ownership of the die and that it was up to you and Franz to change the die at any time. I would certainly advise against it and put some kind of a stop to Dr. Morrison's corresponding with you. Naturally, the royalty which you get, is none of his business at all. I wanted to get this letter off in a hurry so that you won't be taken completely by surprise when he honors you with a phone call.

I received a summary from Lyon & Lyon on the points discussed with you regarding patent rights on the saucer. I forwarded a copy of this correspondence to Franz in San Francisco.

It certainly was nice to see you while you were in Los Angeles, and I hope that it won't be too long before you come our way again.

Best regards,

Ed Kennedy

CREATORS OF THE FAMOUS Stoway LINE

APPENDIX O — Wham-O Product Line Literature — 1957

In early 1957 the Pluto Platter ("Flying Saucer," bottom row, center) was merely a hopeful newcomer…out of place in an extensive Wham-O product line dating back to 1948.

This small folder was included in some of the earliest WPP1 packages.

Note that it still bears the older "wamo" logo and does not yet mention the name "Frisbee," the Sailing Satellite model, or Hula Hoops—all products introduced later that year.

Many of the products easily justify the origin of the Wham-O name!

FLAT FLIP FLIES STRAIGHT!

WHAM-O THROWING KNIVES
Balanced to stick!
Mayan
TARGET SPORT **3 for $3.98**

Now everyone can enjoy this knife-throwing game. With very little practice you can stick these balanced knives every time. Outdoors—Indoors. Lots of fun for entire family. Three 10" knives. Tempered steel, leather handles. With target.

Golfers WHAM-O for practice
NEW! GROOVE YOUR SWING AT HOME! DEVELOP FORM - CORRECT HOOK AND SLICE!

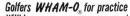

$1.75
USED BY PROS

No ball to chase! Simply push into ground and hit. Returns to position after club swing. Practice just 5 minutes a day with our instructions and play 100% better on Sunday! Folds to 8" for golf bag. Use to warm up at starting tee. Tough pliable plastic, ash hardwood stock, 5" steel spikes. Withstands violent abuse. Only $1.75 complete.

wamo FENCING FOILS

These handsome swords are made of fine carbon spring steel and are ideal for learning the art of fencing.
special price 41" long SET **$4.98**

Can be hung as wall display in den, polished metal guards with blood red and silver cordons, beautifully set off the solid alder grips. Once used in deadly combat, now an exciting sport. A real bargain, $4.98 with fencing instructions, safety tips and 2 masks.

NEW LAWN SHUFFLE
Now you can play shuffle board on your lawn. No expensive cement court necessary. Pucks are rolled on lawn onto numbered scoring courts. The special pucks are balanced to give real accuracy. This is a more exciting version of the game made famous by Luxury Liners. Complete with two shuffle cues made of top quality ash hardwood, four brightly colored shuffle pucks, two scoring courts. Satisfaction guaranteed. Only $9.95. 30 ft. court.

NEW POOL GAME
Everyone plays! It's fun!

Only **$3.98**
LARGE **3 x 4 ft.** reg. complete with balls and cues

Now you can have your own pool table! Just set this 3 x 4 ft. pool table frame on your rug and you're ready to play! Swell party game! Folds compactly—sets up in seconds. Comes complete with sturdy wood frame, six pool pockets with ball traps, ten numbered balls, two cues, and instructions on the different pool games.

WHAM-O BLOWGUN SET
for target and hunting
SPECIAL **$2.98**
This amazing gun has the accuracy of a rifle. Compression of breath in barrel gives terrific air power. You won't believe your eyes! 5" long. Average person can hit a 2" bullseye at 30 ft. Excellent for shooting small game. For target fun with friends, set up in patio or den. Set includes metal blowgun, rubber mouthpiece, four 5" steel darts and range target. Extra darts 6 for $1.

RIFLE BLOWGUN

Collapsible to 2½ feet with connector
5 ft. takedown
Guaranteed to go thru ¼" plywood **$6.95**

only **$2.98**
Catch and throw game
WHAM-O Jai-Alai
It's new---It's different---It ZOOMS!

Curves...light as a feather---in spectacular curves. Can be thrown straight or made to curve upward against gravity, depending upon the manner thrown. Basket-like jai-alai racket makes exciting catches easy. Only takes 5 to 10 minutes to become an expert and keep two balls in the air. Requires no court. If you miss a catch, opponent gets a point. 10 points in a game. Comes complete with rackets, 2 balls, and instructions.

new floor tennis
Special Only **$2.98**

OR SETS ON ANY TABLE

Exciting game! Takes the place of $50 table tennis set
It's really fun! Special light ball travels more slowly than ping-pong ball—long rallies are easy! It's portable—sets up in a minute. Plays like table tennis but there is no bulky table to get in the way. Play indoors or outdoors. Kids love the game. Set comes complete with paddles, net, brackets, court mark.

WHAM-O tether baseball

Only **$1.98**

It's fun to bat the ball again and again - no ball to chase. Teach your boy to bat. One player twirls ball thru strike zone. Keep score - 20 hits out of 30 strikes wins game. Practice slugging, bunting to sharpen your eye, improve your batting average. The whole family can play right in the backyard. Swell for parties. OK for tennis practice too. Complete with rubber baseball, swivel, cord, handle.

Powermaster
.22 MATCH PISTOLS
BRAND NEW $16.95

Automatic ejection
The new Powermaster is a fine single action .22 pistol. Shoots long rifles, longs, shorts. Features recoil action with automatic ejection for rapid load and fire. Form fitted grips, 5" barrel, 11" overall, 10-land rifling, extreme accuracy. Balanced for fine shooting. 2-way adjustable sight. Entirely U.S. made. Satisfaction guaranteed.

WHAM-O SPORTSMAN
$1.50 35-LB. PULL!
HITS LIKE A RIFLE—
KILLS RABBITS, SQUIRRELS.
Powerful, silent, accurate.
For hunting, target, routing pests.

HUNTING SLINGSHOT
Heavy duty 7" ash stock.
40 steel balls, extra rubber, target.
* Professional model of National Slingshot Assn.

WHAM-O amazing
FLYING SAUCER
really flies! **79c**
aerodynamic design

FLICK OF THE WRIST—and your saucer sails away, up to 100 ft. Will fly straight, curve right or left, or return to you depending upon the angle you throw it. You can even play catch around a tree! Scientific airfoil causes lift—spinning stability in flight. Made of unbreakable polyethylene.

APPENDIX O (cont.) — Wham-O Product Sales Literature — 195?

By Fall 1957 Wham-O added the name "Frisbee," the Pluto Platter Horseshoe Game and their first original flying disc design, the Sailing Satellite, to their product sales literature.

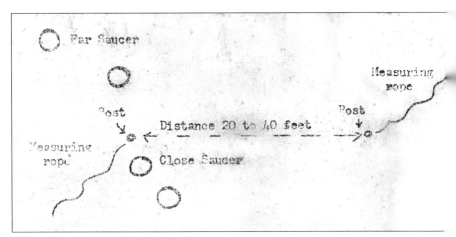

The earliest Pluto Platter Horseshoe Games had Mimeographed, hand-drawn instructions.

APPENDIX P — Pluto Platter Article (People & Places 6/58)

The Hoornbeeks, Paul & Marge (Lu's sister) shown "hooping it up" with WPP1s.

flying saucers

Small fry find a more utilitarian use for saucers. Game is often played by groups in park, but can be enjoyed at home as well.

FLYING saucers, as more and more people are discovering, are not optical illusions. They are real in at least one version, a popular new game manufactured by Wham-O, specialists in unusual toys. The object of the game is to get the saucers (made out of a flexible plastic material) into or around or through nine targets, earning a maximum of points. The targets, named for the planets, vary from loops to swinging pans to pools of water behind an obstacle.

Topix

Everyone in the family, from children to grandparents, will want to try their skill. Game can be played singly, or by teams.

APPENDIX Q — *Pluto Platter Patent* — Chapter 32

United States Patent Office

Des. 183,626
Patented Sept. 30, 1958

183,626
FLYING TOY
Walter Frederick Morrison, La Puente, Calif.
Application July 22, 1957, Serial No. 47,035
Term of patent 7 years
(Cl. D34—15)

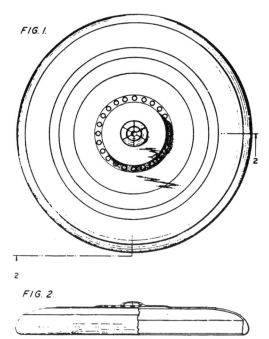

Fig. 1 is a top plan view of a flying toy, showing my new design;
Fig. 2 is a side elevational view thereof, partly in cross section taken on line 2—2 in Fig. 1.
I claim:
The ornamental design for a flying toy, as shown.

References Cited in the file of this patent
UNITED STATES PATENTS

D. 137,521	Davidson	Mar. 28, 1944
1,404,132	Manes	Jan. 17, 1922
2,690,339	Hall	Sept. 28, 1954

FOREIGN PATENTS

890,001	France	Oct. 25, 1943

APPENDIX R — Wham-O Attorney Patent Infringement Letter

In 1958 Premier Products produced the Mars Platter and Empire marketed the Zo-lar...both knockoffs of the patented Pluto Platter design. In the early 1960s Wham-O sued both companies, settled out of court and obtained the molds for the Mars Platter as well as Empire's two "Mystery-Y" models (see pages 274–275).

JAMES B. CHRISTIE
ROBERT L. PARKER
C. RUSSELL HALE
R. WILLIAM JOHNSTON
M. ROY SPIELMAN
ASHLEY STEWART ORR
ANDREW J. BELANSKY
HAROLD L. JACKSON

CHRISTIE, PARKER & HALE
LAWYERS
595 EAST COLORADO STREET
PASADENA 1, CALIFORNIA
SYCAMORE 5-5843 RYAN 1-5637

SACRAMENTO OFFICE
826 J STREET
SACRAMENTO, CALIFORNIA
GILBERT 3-9148

October 9, 1958

Re: Case No. 1771
FLYING TOY
Walter F. Morrison

Mr. Walter F. Morrison
15838 Harvest Moon Street
Puente, California

Dear Mr. Morrison:

We have received the original patent deed to the design patent on this application. The design patent issued as of September 30, 1958 under number 183,626.

The original will be kept in our files because of the possibility of litigation in the near future with respect to this patent. Therefore, I enclose Thermo-Fax copies of the original patent deed.

I suggest that you discuss with Wham-O Mfg. Co. whether or not you wish to bring suit against the Premier Products Company and the Empire Plastic Company for infringing the design.

Very truly yours,

Jack Gribble

W. J. Gribble

WJG:ct

Enclosure
cc: Wham-O Mfg. Co.

APPENDIX S — Wham-O Corporate Image — 1965

Wham-O was featured in the December 3, 1965 issue of LIFE Magazine in an article captioned: "The Ups and Downs of the Novelty Game." At that time the company was cleaning up with sales of recently introduced Super Balls. Also mentioned was the rise and fall of Hula Hoops, Air Blasters and kits of fish eggs. Conspicuously missing are Pluto Platters, which had just been converted into the new Professional Model Frisbee (or is that one lying upside down on the table?).

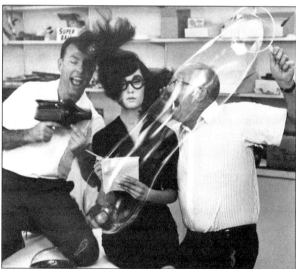

Top: Rich Knerr demonstrates the Air Blaster. Below: Spud Melin and Rich ham it up with a "secretary" for LIFE's camera.

APPENDIX T — Wham-O Trade Ad — 1966

This ad appeared in the March 1966 issue of *Toys & Novelties*, but would have been conceived and produced in late 1965 when Ed Headrick was at the height of reinventing Wham-O's marketing strategy. The Pluto Platter had just been retooled to make the Pro Model. This ad features a Flying Saucer, which was about to be replaced by the Regular Frisbee. Because Headrick's patent application had not yet been completed, the ad still lists Fred's recently expired Design Patent!

APPENDIX U — Franscioni / Johnson Letter, 8/14/73 — Chapter 53

Lt. Col. Warren R. Franscioni
Box 216, A.F.N.E.
APO New York 09085

14 August 1973

Stancil E. D. Johnson, M. D.
716 Lighthouse Avenue - Suite C
Pacific Grove, California 93950

Dear Dr. Johnson:

In response to your letter of 24 July 1973.

From the time that Cozzette first wrote about your interest in the history of the Flyin' Saucer and the receipt of your letter I have had time to evaluate my initial concern about whether your book might interfere in any future legal proceedings about the subject. I have come to the conclusion that your book, if based upon the facts, would not.

From the beginning and during the years since my recall to active military duty I have attempted to keep a fairly complete file of the Flyin' Saucer venture. Most of this I have here in Oslo; but, because of the bulk, the balance of the file is in temporary storage in the states pending my return. I believe I have what is necessary here to answer questions for your history.

I first met Fred Morrison in late 1947. He was a struggling WW II veteran trying to build a home for his family at Baywood Park, a developing residential area just outside of San Luis Obispo, California. At that time I was attempting to establish a bottle gas business, with a partner, George Davis, in San Luis Obispo. We needed someone to assist in the installation of home heating appliances, and Fred went to work for us. We had all been pilots during WW II.

As Fred and I became better acquainted our discussions went back to pre WW II during the "great depression days" which included tossing or sailing things like pie or cake tins, either for our own enjoyment or to pick up a bit of extra change. From this bit of thought, plus stimulus from the then current flying saucer craze, we began to ponder the possibility of developing our thoughts into a saleable toy.

With a brief education and knowledge of aeronautical engineering I tackled the job of working up a design that would transform the pie tin shape into what we believed would be the best configuration of an injection molded plastic Flyin' Saucer.

We then contacted Mr. Stanley Gray (President) and Mr. Ed Kennedy of Southern California Plastic Company, 1865 Flower Street, Glendale, California for advice on the feasibility of using plastic as the basic material. This resulted in an agreement with So. Cal. Pl. Co. for fabrication of a single cavity die and their assistance in developing the sales of the item.

The very first test model was machined from a solid block of Tennessee Eastman's "Tennite", a rather tough and stiff cellulose base material. Before disintegrating, it served to confirm our theories regarding the use of plastic materials from the standpoint of aerofoil configuration and specific gravity. The next step was to turn Stan and Ed's boys loose on fabrication of a die for use in the injection molding process. I dont think anyone thought of putting any of those early birds aside for posterity!

As Mr. Kennedy may have told you, the experiences and business of trying to find and develop an early market for product could be a story in itself. Your research into the activities of PIPCO may have brought much of the past to light.

Your research should have also revealed much about our attempt to exploit the association with Al Capp and his Li'l Abner; also, the demise of PIPCO INC following this abortive and mismanaged venture.

Shortly after all of this, in the Fall of 1950, I was recalled to active military duty for the Korean War effort. From here on Fred and I began to drift further and further apart. So much so that the odd sized Frisbees you mentioned, with the "one-on-one guts" instructions molded on the inner surface, are unknown to me.

Since I do not know at this point the extent and depth of past history that will serve your purpose I will await further word from you. I do want to see what Fred has stated for your interview. Also I have lost contact with Ed Kennedy, his address I will appreciate.

For your information, my tour here takes me up to September 1974. I hope the Air Force and I can decide on Sacramento, California as the area for my next place of duty.

I look forward to your next letter.

        Sincerely yours,

        Warren R. Franscioni

APPENDIX V — Franscioni / Johnson Letter — Chapter 53

~~I find~~ the opening chapter, of your ~~to your~~ indicates that you have spent considerable time at research into determining how the "Flyin' Saucer" came to be known as Frisbee. I have no doubt that all you report regarding Mr. William Russell Frisbie in 1871 to date is factual. May I only state, from the time Morrison and I began thinking about the "Flyin' Saucer" and until my recall to active military duty in 1951, there had been no mention of Frisbie/Frisbee in our "little" part of the world.

You asked about the first flights. I mentioned our theory "test" model, machined from solid plastic. This was early 1948. Production from the first mold was in the late summer 48'. Sales attempts were through Woolworth stores. The first being the Glendale outlet, set up by So Cl Plastic. We soon found the item was a dead issue laying on the counter. Which prompted our offer to demonstrate, in the store. Woolworth put Fred and me in a "cage", to protect the customers. It worked, but, it not for long. We soon realized the only place to demonstrate was outdoors. Next came the Pomona County Fair.

I "like" the way you have Morrison scrapping up enough money for the mold; because, after all these years that is the way I feel, scrapped, or if you please, "scrapped" in the whole deal. In the first place, I can not accept that you give Morrison full credit for putting things in plastic. Whether Fred got some of his ideas as a youngster in Utah, or the beaches of Calif as we later compared notes, I do not know. But I do know that/when we compared some of our past experiences at sailing things, it came out plastics, with no intermediate steel ringed tin models. There was only one signature on the check that paid for that mold, mine, against my personal bank account. Anyway, I am the "compatriot" he talks about at Pomona. And I must say that he did come up with the "wire" concept. This, after we had numerous comments from the "tip" (crowd) " I'll bet those guys fly that thing by wires". By this time we had become so proficient that at 20 yds one of us would hold out his hand and the other could deliver the "Saucer" such that reception was made with imperceptible displacement OF THIS HAND, to catch it. For a couple of "pitch men" we held them spellbound. We said and did a lot of screwy things with the wire gag. It was a crowd (tip) builder, and we did so well at Pomona that the next couple of years this aw was how we spent most of our time promoting sales.

I am no so sure you are accurate in your description and evaluation of our application of the Bernoulli principle; but, all of that is neither here noe there. My point, you can do anything you want in the attainment of flight characteristics and performance. At the time that we were getting off the ground, we soon found that public acceptance (sales) involved safety. Conseguently the "Flyin Saucer" was kept light and flexible in body to forestall any claim that it could be classified as a "lethal" object in a crows. We knew then, as you later claim, with proportionate increases to the size and density of the leading edge mass we got a proportionate amount of "zing" in the forward velocity of the "Saucer". Many of our early demonstrations to prove safety to a potential merchant was tolaunch the thing, "hard", against the plate glass show window of his store. Try that one with your "Vic Malfontes' Super Frisbee!

It all gets back to keeping the past in perspective, and which did really come first in this subject that is of great interest to both of us. What ever the historical background of arriving at "FRISBEE", until "Flyin' Saucer" came on the scene, pie tins (or cookie box covers)were only for processing (or marketing) baked goods. And when you come to classifying what is desireable in performance of the plastic models, take time to give credit for the reason of each design. Mr Malfonte's model would have been a real "killer" at the Pomona Fair and at the time we were trying to get off the ground. The demonstration to our first potential merchant would have been disastrous.

APPENDIX W — Jeff McMahon's Article — July 24, 1997

WHERE THE FRISBEE FIRST FLEW

The Untold Story of the Flying Disc's Origin
50 Years Ago in SLO

By Jeff McMahon

Two men held a circle of plastic over a heater in a San Luis Obispo garage in 1948, trying to mold a lip onto the disc's down-turned edge. One of those men would be hailed as the inventor of the Frisbee. The other would die unknown, just as he began to fight for a share of the credit and millions in royalties the Frisbee generated.

THE FIRST TO FLY

Walter Frederick Morrison came to Warren Franscioni in 1947, looking for work. Both men had been Army Air Corps pilots in World War II. Maj. Franscioni served with the Air Transport Service in India and China; Lt. Morrison flew a fighter in 58 missions over Italy before being shot down and held in Stalag 13, Germany's infamous prison camp.

Franscioni's parents lived in Paso Robles, where his father had been mayor, so he settled after the war in San Luis Obispo. He founded a butane company as his father had done in Paso. He built a home on Conejo Avenue, in a neighborhood developing near San Luis High School, and he opened the Franscioni and Davis Butane Co. office at 884 Broad St., across Broad from Mission College Prep.

"I first met Fred Morrison in late 1947," Franscioni wrote in a 1973 letter. "He was a struggling World War II veteran trying to build a home for his family at Baywood Park, a developing residential area just outside San Luis Obispo, California."

"At that time, I was attempting to establish a bottle gas business with a partner, George Davis, in San Luis Obispo. We needed someone to assist in the installation of home heating appliances, and Fred went to work for us."

The bottled gas business moved too slowly in postwar SLO to sustain three men and their families. So Franscioni and Morrison dreamed up an enterprise on the side.

For decades kids had played catch with metal pie tins. The sport grew in popularity during the Depression, and soldiers spread it across the country during the war.

The game had a few drawbacks. The tins made a shrill noise, and if you didn't catch them just right, they stung. After a few crash landings they could crack or develop sharp edges that cut fingers.

Morrison and Franscioni thought of casting them in plastic, a material proliferated by wartime industry. Morrison took credit for the idea in later interviews, but Franscioni said they thought of it together.

"I do know that when we compared some of our past experiences at sailing things, it came out plastics," Franscioni wrote.

It seems like a simple idea today, but Morrison and Franscioni broke new ground. And after 49 years of improvements, the Frisbee has diverged little from their first plastic interpretation of a pie tin.

"People were throwing paint can lids and paper plates and pie pans throughout history, since they were invented," said Victor Malafronte, a Frisbee historian in Alameda. "The first plastic disc was that Flyin' Saucer in 1948."

Morrison and Franscioni used a lathe to carve their first model out of Tenite, a hard cellulose material now used in toothbrush handles and eyeglass frames. That disc confirmed the aerodynamics of the toy, but it shattered on landing.

"I tackled the job of working up a design that would transform the pie-tin shape into what we believed would be the best configuration of an injection-molded Flyin' Saucer," Franscioni wrote.

Franscioni's daughter, Coszette Eneix, remembers her father and Morrison working in the basement of their Conejo Avenue home.

"I remember one time—I was like 5—I remember standing in the basement downstairs, and I remember over the water heater they were trying to mold this plastic thing to try to get a lip on it," Eneix said.

Newspapers had coined the term "flying saucer" less than a year earlier when a pilot reported seeing disc-shaped objects skipping through the air above the Cascade Mountains in the Pacific Northwest. The Roswell incident in June 1947 fueled the flying saucer craze. Witnesses in Roswell, N.M., reported seeing the bodies of aliens at a UFO crash site.

Franscioni and Morrison named the new toy to capitalize on the publicity.

"Hundreds of flying saucers are scheduled to invade San Luis Obispo in the near future," the Telegram-Tribune reported in 1948. "Two local men, pooling resources after the words "flying saucers" shocked the world a year ago, have invented a new, patented plastic toy shaped like the originally reported saucer."

THE SAUCER CRASH

People have purchased more than 200 million Frisbees in the last 50 years, Malafronte estimates, more than baseballs, footballs, and basketballs combined. Those booming sales, however, began with a whimper. In 1948, people didn't know what to make of the Flyin' Saucer.

Morrison and Franscioni formed a company called Partners in Plastic, or Pipco, based in SLO. They contracted with Southern California Plastic Co. in Glendale to manufacture Flyin' Saucers for about 25 cents each. They sold them for $1 through outlets like Woolworth and Disneyland.

"We soon found the item was a dead issue on the counter," Franscioni wrote, "which prompted our offer to demonstrate in the store. Woolworth put Fred and me in a cage to protect the customers. It worked, but not for long. We soon realized the only place to demonstrate was outdoors."

Morrison and his wife traveled to county fairs to hawk the flying disc. Franscioni sometimes joined them, Eneix said, but he usually remained in SLO, handling national sales and keeping Pipco's books.

The demonstrations won people's attention. They hadn't seen anything fly like the disc, which remained aloft long after gravity would have pulled a ball back to earth.

Some observers thought the disc followed an invisible wire, and Morrison capitalized on that notion. He offered the disc for free if customers paid $1 for the invisible wire.

Teaching people how to throw the disc became another challenge. Americans seem born to the art of Frisbee throwing today, but it required a new skill in 1948.

"By running through the instructions you will see that we repeatedly point out that an easy smooth snap of the wrist is all that is necessary," Franscioni wrote.

Flyin' Saucers came with directions urging people not to throw the discs too hard or hold them too tight, and to launch them "in exactly the same manner as sailing your hat onto a hook."

Franscioni and Morrison's early marketing efforts occasionally backfired. A Disneyland employee demonstrating the Flyin' Saucer accidentally overshot a fence and hit a woman in the head. She sued, and Disney halted its demonstrations.

Then Morrison and Franscioni struck a deal with Al Capp, who agreed to include the Flyin' Saucer in his "Li'l Abner" cartoon strip. That strip appeared in national newspapers sometime around 1950. Franscioni and Morrison printed "Li'l Abner" inserts and packaged them with their Flyin' Saucers to capitalize on the publicity.

The inserts infuriated Capp, who felt they exceeded the terms of their agreement. Capp threatened to sue and demanded $5,000 in compensation.

"I was really hurt. How could Li'l Abner do this to my daddy?" Eneix said. "That was a hunk of change that put them down. That was quite a bit of money back then."

Franscioni and Morrison were already struggling to meet the cost of casting the original dies for the Flyin' Saucer. The Capp payoff devastated Pipco. Franscioni borrowed $2,500 from his mother and $2,500 from his mother-in-law, Eneix said, and the demise of the Flyin' Saucer began. Eneix and her sister went door to door in SLO selling the discs for 25 cents. Today, collectors will pay $500 for an original Pipco Flyin' Saucer.

THE PLOT THICKENS

The Franscioni and Davis Butane Co. crashed at about the same time as Pipco. In 1950, Walter Franscioni had to sell the Conejo Avenue home where the Frisbee was born. He moved to Greenville, worked as a trucker, and applied for reactivation in the Air Force.

"I remember us losing our home and how hard that was," Eneix said. "Korea was happening then, and my father then applied for being recalled back into the service, but he continued trying to get the Flyin' Saucer thing to go."

The Air Force moved the Franscionis to South Dakota in 1952. Morrison moved to Los Angeles, where he worked as a building inspector, and the inventors of the Flyin' Saucer drifted apart. Southern California Plastic Co. continued to produce the discs, and Morrison continued to sell them.

Eneix keeps folders full of yellowing letters and old business records to document what happened next. Some of those records show that Morrison began manufacturing his own flying disc on the side.

Morrison set up a new company, American Trends, redesigned the disc to make it look more like a flying saucer, and called it the Pluto Platter. Morrison began selling the Pluto Platter while still accepting sales commissions on the Flyin' Saucer, according to Ed Kennedy, the president of Southern California Plastic Co.

"We had just found out that Fred Morrison had another die built on the Flyin' Saucer and was merchandising the product under the name of Pluto's Platter," Kennedy wrote in a 1957 letter to Franscioni. "During the time that he was having the saucer made, he was also accepting sales commissions from the company here."

Kennedy accused Morrison of trying to steal Flyin' Saucer accounts by offering Pluto Platters at a lower cost.

"In my opinion, Fred acted completely unfairly on this entire thing," Kennedy wrote, "and we certainly will never do business with him again."

Southern California Plastic Co. severed its relationship with Morrison and contacted a patent attorney. The question of patent violations never went to court, however, and has never been resolved.

THE WHAM-O FRISBEE

Morrison was demonstrating his Pluto Platter in a Los Angeles parking lot in 1955 when Rich Knerr and Spud Melin spotted the unusual flying object.

Knerr and Melin had founded their own toy company back in 1948, the year Franscioni and Morrison were developing the Flyin' Saucer. Knerr and Melin had one product, a wooden slingshot. They named their company for the sound the slingshot's pellets made on impact—Wham-O.

Morrison signed a contract with Wham-O, and Knerr and Melin sold the Pluto Platter with a marketing expertise Morrison and Franscioni never showed. Knerr came up with the new name for the disc.

Knerr was visiting East Coast college campuses in the mid-1950s, giving away Pluto Platters to seed market demand. At Yale he encountered students tossing metal pie tins and yelling "Frisbie!" the way golfers yell "Fore!"

Historians have traced that tradition to a Bridgeport, Conn., baker named William Russell Frisbie. In 1871 Frisbie moved to Bridgeport to manage the local branch of the Olds Baking Co. He eventually bought the bakery and renamed it Frisbie Pie Co.

Frisbee historian Malafronte believes truck drivers for the company were the first to toss Frisbie Pie tins on the loading docks during idle times. The tins bore the words "Frisbie's Pies" and had six small holes in the center, in a star pattern, that hummed when the tin flew.

The sport moved to Eastern colleges, where students shouted "Frisbie!" to warn people of incoming pie tins. A sport developed and took on the name "Frisbie-ing." Knerr took the word home to Wham-O, misspelled it "Frisbee," and registered it as a trademark. In 1958, Morrison's Pluto Platter became the Wham-O Frisbee.

Southern California Plastic Co. continued to make Flyin' Saucers for Disneyland and a few other outlets. It handled sales and mailed royalty checks to Franscioni until the mid-1960s, when he headed to Vietnam.

THE BITTER TOY

Many American homes have housed a Frisbee, but Coszette Eneix's home is not among them.

"Every time I see a Frisbee I just want to cringe," she said. "I get angry inside. It shouldn't be called Frisbee. It isn't Frisbee. How come they're calling it Frisbee? That's not right. It's Flyin' Saucer."

Eneix hasn't decided whether to use her files of yellowing papers in a lawsuit or in a book, but she wants justice for her father.

"I want it in the history books, as it comes down, that my father was there, not Fred Morrison alone," she said.

"When you read about the history of the Frisbee, you always hear Fred Morrison. Fred Morrison did this. Fred Morrison did that. Bullshit. Excuse my language. Bullshit. It was Warren Franscioni and Fred Morrison. It was a partnership. I think they should have equal billing."

The International Frisbee Hall of Fame in Lake Linden, Mich., reserves its primary listing for Morrison.

"Fred Morrison, Inventor of the Frisbee," it says. "Walter F. (Fred) Morrison has provided pleasure to millions of people throughout the world. He was the first person to envision the creation of a plastic disc to be used as a substitute for a ball in a game of catch."

Wham-O went on to market the Hula-Hoop, the Super Ball, the Water Wiggle, and other toys, but Frisbee remained its most profitable product. In 1977, 20 years after Wham-O began selling Frisbees, it generated up to 50 percent of the company's annual sales. At the time, Wham-O estimated it had sold 100 million flying discs.

Morrison told the Los Angeles Times in 1977 he had made about $1 million in royalties.

Nearly all written histories of the Frisbee attribute its invention to Morrison. Stancil E.D. Johnson, a Pacific Grove psychiatrist, may have been the first to mention Warren Franscioni in a footnote in his 1975 book, "Frisbee."

Johnson heard about Franscioni from Ed Kennedy, the president of the Southern California Plastic Co. In 1973, Johnson contacted Franscioni, who was then an Air Force colonel stationed in Oslo, Norway. He asked Franscioni to write down his memories of the flying disc's origin.

Franscioni sent Johnson one letter in August 1973.

"I have had time to evaluate my initial concern about whether your book might interfere in any future legal proceedings about the subject," Franscioni wrote. "I have come to the conclusion that your book, if based upon the facts, would not."

Franscioni argues that he designed the first Flyin' Saucer, not Morrison, that he paid for the initial mold with his own money, and that the two men jointly developed the idea of casting it in plastic.

Franscioni began a second letter to Johnson in 1974, but he never completed it. He died of a heart attack at age 57.

"Fred Morrison never wanted to admit this," Johnson said. "Franscioni died and never was able to come back and get his share of the profits."

Franscioni might have acted earlier. Ed Kennedy urged him to take legal action against Morrison as early as 1957.

"Other people were asking my father to do something—stop him, sue him, stop him," Eneix said, "but we were in South Dakota. My father was getting his career going again as an officer in the Air Force, and that was taking a lot of his time. And I think my mom was leery of putting more money into this thing."

In 1957, the Frisbee had not yet made its millions. The rights to the toy hardly seemed worth the cost of a lawsuit.

"There was a lot of disappointment in the '50s, and they were hurt, really hurt," Eneix said.

"So we all started quieting down and not talking about it. That's what we do in my family. We don't talk about it. Then we didn't fly the Flyin' Saucer much anymore on picnics. It was too painful to keep remembering it because we were losing it."

THE SILENT INVENTOR

Morrison, 77, now calls himself "Walt" and lives near Monroe, Utah, a town of 1,700 people in the Sevier River valley. He owned a motel there and operated it with his third wife until he retired three years ago. Morrison has an old pickup truck, but he rarely drives it into town.

"He lives in a house in the country and seems to enjoy life," said Mark Fullenbaugh, publisher of the Richfield Reaper. "I haven't seen him in person in about six months. You don't see him out much, so I can't tell you much more than that about him."

Morrison declined to be interviewed for this story.

"Well, I'd like to be a nice guy and say yes, but I'm so tired of this shit," Morrison said.

"It's been done so many times, so many ways, that I just don't do it anymore. I'm an old man now and I just haven't got time for this. I want to just sit back in my chair and sleep."

Morrison has always been "cagey" about the facts of the Frisbee's birth, according to Malafronte, who met Morrison at Frisbee tournaments.

"I had asked Fred about his partner, and he owns up to it," Malafronte said. "The problem is, I think Fred has a lot of stuff he can lose and nothing to gain by talking."

Meanwhile, Mattel Corp. is celebrating the 40th anniversary of the Frisbee this year, even though the plastic flying disc turns 50 next year.

Mattel, the world's largest toy company, bought Wham-O in 1994. It dates the Frisbee's official birth as 1957, when Wham-O first marketed Morrison's Pluto Platter.

Mattel has no knowledge of plastic flying discs that may have existed before 1957, said Mattel spokeswoman Sara Rosales, nor of their inventors.

Jeff McMahon hurls amazing whirling adjectives for New Times.

"Where the Frisbee First Flew" by Jeff McMahon, originally printed in *New Times*, San Luis Obispo, July 24, 1997, vol. 11, no. 49. www.planetobispo.com.

©Jeff McMahon—Reprinted in its entirety with permission of the author.

APPENDIX X

TIMELINE OF EVENTS
Frisbee History in a Nutshell

1917(?)	Warren Franscioni born.
1920	Walter Fredrick Morrison born, Richfield, Utah. (Jan. 23)
1920	Lucile Eleanor Nay born. (June 7)
1935(?)	Warren Franscioni graduates from high school in the Paso Robles, California area.
1937	Fred and Lucile Nay meet in high school in L.A., CA.
1937	Fred flips his first (popcorn can) "lid" at a Nay family Thanksgiving gathering. (November 25)
1938	Fred graduates from John Marshall High School in L.A. (January)
1938	Fred & Lu begin selling cake pans on Santa Monica, California beaches.
1938	Lu graduates from John Marshall High School. (June)
1938	Fred works that summer in "The Pit."
1939	Fred and Lu get married. (April 3)
1940s	Both Fred & Warren serve in WWII as Army Air Corps pilots.
1946	Fred & Lu move into a tent while building a home in Baywood Park, California.
1946	Fred sketches a design for the world's first flying disc and names it the Whirlo-Way after the legendary racehorse Whirlaway. A draftsman translates it into a professional drawing which Fred mails to himself and copies to two others to establish priority.

1947   Fred & Warren meet; Fred works for the Franscioni & Davis butane business; Fred introduces Warren to flippin' cake pans.

1947   Pilot Ken Arnold reports nine UFOs flying by Mount Rainier. During an interview with him by Bill Bequette of United Press, Arnold states: "Well, they flew erratic, like a saucer if you skip it across the water." Bequette, in his write-up, coins the term "Flying Saucer." An alien craft is reported to have crashed near Roswell, NM.

1947   Fred & Warren discuss developing a plastic flying disc.

1947   PIPCO is born.

1948   A machinist is hired to turn Fred's eight design sketches into six prototypes on his lathe. Four survive flight tests. Fred converts the best flyer into a cardboard template.

1948   On March 15, Southern California Plastic Company (SCP) in Glendale, California submits a cost proposal to PIPCO. SCP is hired to create a mold. The name "Flyin-Saucer" is added to the top. The first FS1 Saucers are produced in powder blue and black.

1948-50 Flyin-Saucers sold extensively at fairs, in a few stores, and at beaches using "invisible wire" and other sales ploys.

1948-50 Franscioni uses Fred's Whirlo-Way drawing to support patent searches and applications.

1948-9? An attorney advises Franscioni that the Flyin-Saucer is not patentable.

1949   Hall Manufacturing develops The Sky Pie. While not a true saucer, it is an example of an early flying device.

1949   Fred and Warren meet with three Sacramento, CA businessmen who show interest in the Flyin-Saucers.

1950   Fred and Warren part company. (February)

1950   Franscioni begins negotiations on a deal with (Al) Capp Enterprises for a "Li'l Abner" promotional tie-in. SCP alters the mold to provide a flat area on top for labels. Five thousand (FS2) discs are produced. The Capp organization develops printed paper inserts. The deal is called off (presumably when PIPCO adds unauthorized stickers to the discs) and Capp threatens to sue.

1950   Franscioni engages Franz & Rothrock of San Francisco for additional financial and promotional support.

1950   PIPCO is incorporated and dissolved sometime between mid-1950 and early-1953.

1950   Franscioni applies for a utility patent (serial #24,356) sometime before November.

1950   Teller Hall files for a patent on the Sky Pie on December 15, 1950, and receives patent number 2,690,339 on September 28, 1954.

1951   Franscioni drives trucks for a while, then re-enlists in the Air Force, abandoning all Saucer promotions.

1951   Franscioni's patent application #24,356 is rejected by the Patent Office March 12.

1952   Patent application #24,356 appeals time expires; application is abandoned by the Patent Office.

1952   Fred and Lu move to San Dimas, California, about 30 miles east of Los Angeles.

1953   Ernest "Bill" Robes develops and sells the first version of the Space Saucer at Dartmouth College in New Hampshire without any prior knowledge of the Flyin-Saucer. He does not patent his design.

1953   SCP contacts Franscioni to reacquire the Flyin-Saucer mold (September).

1953-4   SCP slightly alters the mold, uses polyethylene for the first time, and begins to market Flyin Saucers (no hyphen) on their own, paying Franscioni commissions.

1954   Fred contacts SCP about the availability of Flyin Saucers for the upcoming fall fair season. He purchases 2,000 at wholesale cost (28 cents each) and applies labels for his new business, American Trends Company, to attract additional sales. Fred, Lu, and the Hoornbeeks demonstrate at fairs. A second order is placed during the fair season. A few leftovers are sold mail-order in bags.

1955   Having exhausted his supply of Flyin Saucers, Fred explores the possibility of developing and molding his own disc at a lower cost. Rainbow Plastics in El Monte, California quotes 11 cents each and gets the job.

1955   The birth of the modern flying disc. Fred designs the Pluto Platter (ATPP)—universally recognized as far superior to the Flyin Saucer in both flight performance and appearance!

1955   Lu Morrison coins the "Flat Flip Flies Straight" instructions.

1955   Fred markets his Pluto Platters at fairs and area beaches beginning in September at the L.A. County Fair. A few mail-ordered Platters are sent in printed bags with "Pluto Platter Pilot Enlistment Forms" for reordering.

1956   Wamo co-owners, Rich Knerr and Arthur "Spud" Mellin, observe demonstrations of the Pluto Platter at regional fairs. They agree that a flying saucer toy is of future interest to Wamo, but do nothing at the time.

1956   SCP begins selling Flyin Saucers (FS7/D) to Disneyland in special Disneyland-designed packaging.

1956   Warren switches his new attempt at obtaining a utility patent on the Flyin Saucer to a design patent application for an "Aerial Sounding Toy or Equivalent."

1956   During a demonstration in an L.A. parking lot in mid-December, Fred is encouraged by "a man in the crowd" to go talk to Wamo. Fred and Lu begin negotiations with Wamo.

Timeline of Events

1957   On January 23, Fred and Lu sign all rights to the Pluto Platter over to Wamo. The American Trends name is replaced with the new spelling "Wham-O" (on an underside esker), and one small "Wham-O" is added to the top side creating the first (WPP1) of seven Styles of Wham-O Pluto Platters. They are sold from bulk bins in test stores at first, then in unsealed bags, and finally in bags closed with a stapled header. A Pluto Platter Horseshoe Game is marketed later in the year.

1957   Franscioni's 1956 design patent application would have received approval with the correction of certain irregularities in the forms and Fred's signature on a new oath. By now aware of the Pluto Platter, Franscioni chooses to abandon application, which expires by late 1957.

1957   Wham-O first uses the name "Frisbee" (June 17; in commerce July 8).

1957-60   Fred, Lu and the Hoornbeeks continue to work the fairs selling Pluto Platters obtained from Wham-O. A few WPP1s have been found with an American Trends label.

1957   Wham-O submits an application for a design patent in Fred's name on July 22 (serial No. 47,035).

1957   Fred and Lu demonstrate wooden prototype Hula Hoops to fairgoers for Wham-O.

1958   The Pluto Platter mold is retooled, creating the Second Style (WPP2)...the first disc to bear the name "Frisbee."

1958   Wham-O applies for a trademark on the name "Frisbee" on July 28.

1958   Fred receives U.S. Design Patent No. 183,626 on September 30 for a "Flying Toy." Patent is for 7 years.

1958   Lawsuits for design infringement are first considered against Premier Products Company (for their Mars Platter) and Empire Plastic Company (for the Zo-lar).

1959	Wham-O receives Registered Trademark #679186 for the name "Frisbee" on May 2.
1959	Third Style Wham-O Pluto Platter (WPP3) created.
1960s?	SCP retools the Flyin Saucer mold, replacing the PIPCO information with their SCP logo (FS9).
1960-64	Fourth through Seventh Pluto Platter Styles (WPP4–7) are marketed.
1961	Fred becomes a building inspector for the City of Los Angeles, California.
1961	The Pluto Platter agreement is renegotiated in writing.
1964	Pluto Platters are demonstrated in the Better Living Pavilion at the New York World's Fair by players behind a glass wall. Discs are sold in shrink-wrapped packages with specially printed paper inserts.
1964	Ed Headrick, newly hired Vice President in Charge of Marketing and General Manager, has Wham-O alter the mold for the Pluto Platter to make the Professional Model Frisbee, released in October. Mold #1 is eventually sent to their Irwin Toy affiliate in Canada.
1965	Fred assigns his design patent to Wham-O on March 17. There is an oral agreement to continue royalties (later formalized in an August 10, 1970 written agreement).
1965	The Pluto Platter patent expires on September 30.
1965	Ed Headrick files a patent application for a Flying Saucer (Ser. No. 505,864) on November 1 based on the improved flight performance caused by "a series of concentric discontinuities" (rings) first used on the Pro.
1967	Ed Headrick is awarded the first utility patent on a flying disc, #3359678, on December 26. Headrick assigns the patent to Wham-O for ten dollars.
1967	International Frisbee Association (IFA) developed by Ed Headrick.

Timeline of Events

1968	Fred resigns from his building inspector post.
1968	Fred attends the first IFA Master's Tournament at the Rose Bowl in Pasadena, California on April 27.
1969	Fred and Lu divorce.
1969	The first International Junior Frisbee Tournament is held in Madison Square Garden, New York, NY.
1970	Fred opens and operates "Walt'z Hardware," on Foothill Boulevard and White Avenue in La Verne, CA.
1970	Fred and Lu remarry, and divorce again.
1970?	SCP goes bankrupt. Royale Kraft International replaces the SCP logo with its RKI logo (FS11).
1971	Molding Corp buys the assets of the defunct SCP, but the Flyin Saucer mold is not on the list of items.
1972	Fred marries his second wife, a real-estate broker.
1972	The first book on Frisbee, *The Official Frisbee Handbook* written by Goldy Norton is published.
1973	Fred is interviewed by Stancil Johnson for his book.
1974	Warren Franscioni dies.
1974	Fred attends the World Frisbee Championships held at the Rose Bowl in Pasadena, CA. (August 23–25)
1975	*FRISBEE: A Practitioner's Manual & Definitive Treatise* written by Stancil Johnson is published.
1977	Fred changes name of his store to "Go-Fer Hardware."
1977	Roger Barrett discovers 1,600 Li'l Abner discs (FS2) still packed in sawdust in their original shipping cartons at a San Jose, California flea market.
1978	Fred is inducted into the Frisbee Hall of Fame as a charter member.
1979	Fred closes Go-Fer Hardware.

1980	First definitive study of Pluto Platter history and collectability by Jim Palmeri, Lightnin' Lyle Jensen, and Dan Mangone, is published in the February issue of *Flying Disc Magazine*.
1982	Wham-O and the trademarked "Frisbee" name are bought by Kransco.
1983	Fred and his second wife divorce.
1983	Fred sells the hardware store property, moves back to Utah, buys the lease for the Richfield Municipal Airport and operates under the name Sunlight Aviation, Inc.
1984	Fred marries and divorces his third wife, a waitress.
1984	Fred owns and operates a motel in Richfield, Utah.
1985	Fred remarries his third wife.
1986	Fred begins breeding and racing quarter horses.
1986	Kransco cuts off royalty payments on May 15. Fred and Lu sue for breach of contract on November 11.
1987	Lu (Morrison) Bennett dies.
1987	Fred relinquishes his motel and the Richfield airport.
1987	Fred and his third wife redivorce.
1992	Fred wins a settlement against Kransco. Royalties are restored.
1993	Fred operates the Crooked Arrow Ranch (racehorses).
1994	Kransco sells Wham-O and the trademarked "Frisbee" name to Mattel.
1997	Jeff McMahon publishes "Where The Frisbee First Flew."
1997	Mattel sells Wham-O and the trademarked "Frisbee" name to Charterhouse Group International.
1998	Victor Malafronte publishes *The Complete Book Of Frisbee*.
2000	Fred sells his racehorse business.
2001	Fred discovers Frisbee "mis-history" on the Internet.
2002	Spud Melin and Ed Headrick die.
2004	A first-run, powder blue Flyin-Saucer is found in CT.

APPENDIX Y

SPINNIN' YARNS

30 Events from Published Frisbee History... That Never Happened!

1. **Fred's father invented the sealed-beam headlight.**
   (Stancil Johnson: FRISBEE, *page 19, and others)*
   Fred's father was an optometrist and never claimed to have invented the sealed-beam headlight.

2. **Fred Morrison and Warren Franscioni went to high school together.**
   (Warren Franscioni: 3/20/50 press release sent out by him)
   Fred and Warren did not go to high school together. Fred went to John Marshall High School in Los Angeles, CA, while Warren grew up 200 miles away in Paso Robles, CA.

3. **The Flyin-Saucer was designed by Warren Franscioni.**
   (Warren Franscioni in a 1973 letter as reported by Jeff McMahon: "Where the Frisbee First Flew")
   The Flyin-Saucer was designed by Fred using his 1946 Whirlo-Way drawing as a basis.

4. **Fred passed by the Frisbie Pie Company while visiting Bridgeport, Connecticut in 1948.**
   (Margaret Poynter: Frisbee Fun, *page 9)*
   Fred had never heard of the Frisbie Pie Company until long after Wham-O had used the name Frisbee; nor has he ever visited Bridgeport, CT. (See #27)

5. **PIPCO stood for "Partners In Plastic."** *(Widely reported)*
   PIPCO originated from "If it's a PIPCO product, it's a Pip." (Fred now wishes he *had* thought of Partners In Plastic!)

6. **Early design experiments for the first Flyin-Saucer included placing sheets of plastic over a water heater in Franscioni's basement.**
   (Victor Malafronte: The Complete Book of Frisbee, page 70, and Jeff McMahon: "Where the Frisbee First Flew")
   Fred says, "If it happened, I wasn't there."

7. **Prototypes for the first Flyin-Saucer were hand-carved.**
   (Stancil Johnson: FRISBEE, page 35, and others)
   Prototypes for the first Flyin-Saucer were lathe-turned by a machinist using Fred's handmade cardboard templates.

8. **Fred actually welded a steel ring inside the rim of a prototype of the Flyin-Saucer.** *(Variously reported)*
   Fred had thought of adding a steel ring inside the rim of a cake pan to increase stability. He showed one in the 1946 Whirlo-Way drawing, and briefly considered the idea for the Flyin-Saucers, but the idea was immediately rejected by SCP as too impractical for plastic molding.

9. **The first flying disc was called the Flyin' Saucer or Flyin'-Saucer.** *(Widely reported)*
   The spelling of the name as molded into the 1948 disc is Flyin-Saucer. The 1954 retooled Saucers made from polyethylene have Flyin Saucer (no hyphen) molded on top.

10. **Fred paid for the molding of the Flyin-Saucer in 1948.**
    (Stancil Johnson: FRISBEE, page 19)
    Warren Franscioni secured all funds for the molding and promotion of the Flyin-Saucer between 1948 and 1950. (See #11)

11. **Fred has claimed sole responsibility for the development and financing of the Flyin-Saucer.** *(Variously reported)*
    Fred has always given Warren Franscioni due credit for his role in the co-development of the Flyin-Saucer, and sole responsibility for arranging the funding.

12. **The 1948 Flyin-Saucer was made of polyethylene.**
    (Flaghouse web site)
    The 1948 Flyin-Saucer was probably made of ethylcellulose. Some have called it Butyrate. Flyin Saucers were not made of polyethylene until late-1953 or early-1954.

13. **Fred and Warren sold Flyin-Saucers through Disney.**
    (Jeff McMahon: "Where the Frisbee First Flew")
    Fred left Warren in 1950. PIPCO was dissolved before 1953. Disneyland opened in 1955. Flyin Saucers marketed by SCP directly (still with the PIPCO logo) *were* sold at Disneyland sometime after 1955.

14. **Fred was still with PIPCO during the Al Capp "debacle."**
    (Widely assumed & reported)
    Fred and Warren split up two months before (Al) Capp Enterprises first contacted Warren in April 1950.

15. **Al Capp was angry about the Li'l Abner inserts and sued.**
    (Widely reported)
    Capp Enterprises created the inserts themselves through Brian Specialties. Franscioni *may* have produced the labels on top of the discs in violation of the contract stipulations which *might* have initiated the threatened lawsuit.

16. **Fred and Warren continued to have personal contact after their February 1950 split.**
    (Inferred by Victor Malafronte: The Complete Book of Frisbee, *page 74-75 & others)*
    (See #14 & #18)

17. **Fred was a Los Angeles building inspector before or immediately after the breakup of PIPCO.** *(Widely reported)*
    After Fred left Warren in 1950, he continued working as a carpenter for eleven years. He served as a Los Angeles building inspector between 1961 and 1968...long after the 1957 Wham-O Contract.

18. **Fred and Warren were still selling discs together in 1953.**
    (Victor Malafronte: The Complete Book of Frisbee, *page 73)*
    After their split in February 1950, Fred and Warren never again had ANY form of contact. (See #14 & #16)

19. **Fred was receiving sales commissions on the polyethylene Flyin Saucers from Southern California Plastic.**
    (Ed Kennedy, in a 1957 letter as reported by Jeff McMahon: "Where the Frisbee First Flew"; see also the Fifties Web Index)
    Fred never received sales commissions on the Flyin Saucers from Southern California Plastic. Rather, in 1954 he had to *buy* them COD from SCP at wholesale cost.

20. **Fred designed the Pluto Platter in 1951.**
    (Stancil Johnson: FRISBEE, *page 19; also see Flaghouse, UK Ultimate & Yesterdayland web sites)*
    Fred designed the Pluto Platter in 1955; it was produced just in time for the September 1955 L.A. County Fair.

21. **Fred changed the name of the first disc from "Rotary Fingernail Clipper" to "Pluto Platter."** *(Discovery web site)*
    "Rotary Fingernail Clipper" was Fred and Warren's pet name for the 1948 Flyin-Saucer but it was not advertised as such. The 1955 Pluto Platter was a completely new disc. (See #20 & #22)

22. **The Pluto Platter is a "redesign" of the Flyin Saucer.**
    (Variously reported including Jeff McMahon: "Where the Frisbee First Flew"; see also The Fifties Web Index)
    The Pluto Platter was a completely new design and is universally recognized as far superior to the Flyin Saucer.

23. **Fred tried to steal Flyin Saucer accounts from SCP.**
    (Ed Kennedy, SCP in a 1957 letter as reported by Jeff McMahon: "Where the Frisbee First Flew")
    Fred was totally unaware of how (or even *that*) SCP was marketing their Saucers. Pluto Platters were sold at fairs and through a few mail orders, not through sales accounts.

24. **Fred was spotted by Rich Knerr and "Spud" Melin of Wham-O demonstrating Pluto Platters in a parking lot.**
    (Widely reported)
    Rich Knerr and "Spud" Melin, copartners of Wham-O, said later they witnessed demonstrations of the Pluto Platters at a few local fairs but didn't make any contact with Fred.

25. **Fred was approached by Wham-O to discuss acquiring his Pluto Platter.** *(Variously reported)*
    Fred and Lu first contacted Wamo in late December 1956 to see if they might have an interest in their Pluto Platter.

26. **Wham-O purchased the rights to the Pluto Platter in 1955.**
    (Flaghouse web site)
    Wamo contracted for the rights to the Pluto Platter on January 23, 1957.

27. **Fred told Wham-O about the Frisbie Pie Company.**
    (Margaret Poynter: Frisbee Fun, *page 15)*
    Fred never heard of the Frisbie Pie Company until at least the 1970s. (See #4)

28. **Fred has changed his name to "Walt."**
    (Jeff McMahon: "Where the Frisbee First Flew")
    Fred was born Walter Fredrick Morrison and has always answered to both Walt and Fred.

29. **The Frisbee was invented by Spud Melin.**
    (Widely reported in the media upon Spud's death in 2002)
    The first plastic flying disc (FS1) was invented/designed by Fred Morrison. The first disc to carry the name "Frisbee" was a Pluto Platter (originally designed by Fred in 1955), modified by Wham-O in 1958 (WPP2).

30. **The Frisbee was invented by Ed Headrick.**
    (Widely reported in the media upon Ed's death in 2002)
    (See #29) Ed had the Pluto Platter Frisbee mold reworked in 1964 to create the Professional Model Frisbee.

APPENDIX Z

GLOSSARY OF TERMS
The Essential Flying Disc Vocabulary

Accuracy—A competitive tournament event in which four discs are thrown at a standard target from seven different stations. Discs passing through the target are scored as "hits."

Airfoil—A part or surface, such as a wing, whose shape controls stability, direction, lift, and thrust; the cross-section shape of a well-designed flying disc.

American Trends Company—The business name used by Fred and Lu Morrison to sell Flyin Saucers at fairs in 1954, and then Pluto Platters at fairs, beaches, and (a very few) through mail orders from mid-1955 to 1960.

Arcuate Vanes—Raised spiral, rib-like structures first appearing in Fred's 1946 Whirlo-Way drawing (labeled as "blades") and added to the first Flyin-Saucers in an attempt to increase lift. They don't. (See Rotary Fingernail Clipper)

AT—The designation used in the Kennedy System for American Trends (as in FS7/AT or ATPP).

Bakelite—An early type of hard plastic used to make items such as telephones and appliance components.

Bernoulli's Principle—An effect of internal pressure reduction with increased stream velocity in a fluid. Named for Swiss physicist and mathematician Jakob Bernoulli (1654–1705).

Bernoulli's Principal—Currently valued at 10,000,000 Euros.

Blue Laws—State statutes which limit or prohibit the sale of alcoholic beverages.

Boomerang—A flying device originating in Australia which often is designed to return to the thrower. Also, the action of tossing a flying disc into the air at a steeper than usual angle so that it will return to the thrower.

Glossary of Terms

Butyrate—(Cellulose Acetate) Butyrate is the thermoplastic often reported to have been used to make Flyin-Saucers (FS1–FS3). Called "Tuffy" plastic on Li'l Abner inserts. SCP's original quote lists "ethylcellulose."

Cabin—Raised, flat, circular structure with Portholes and an Observation Dome first used on the Pluto Platter to simulate a UFO's control center or cockpit and copied thereafter on many knockoffs. (Also Cockpit and Cupola)

Caco Engineering—The builders of the Pluto Platter mold.

Cake Pan—Oven pan for baking cakes. One of the early devices which people couldn't resist throwing to each other!

California—Birthplace of plastic flying discs.

Cockpit—(See Cabin and Cupola)

Crock(ery)—Euphemism used by Fred Morrison for a flying disc-shaped object.

Cupola—The raised circular flat area on the top center of a Pluto Platter or any of its knockoffs. (See Cabin)

DDC—Short for Double Disc Court. A competitive two-disc game played by two teams of two players who each attempt to defend their home court.

Design Patent—(See Patent, Design)

Diaphragm—(Ask your mother)

Die—A device used for forming materials; herein used to describe a multi-part mold used to form plastic discs.

Discathon—A tournament event in which individual competitors run a course throwing discs around, through, or over obstacles while being timed.

Disc Golf—A popular flying disc game based on "ball golf." Courses are designed with tee-off areas, fairways, hazards, out-of-bounds, and targets of various types. Standardized targets include disc-catching devices utilizing chains suspended above a basket attached to a metal pole.

Distance—A competitive event in which players attempt to throw a disc the farthest.

Dome—The top center mound of plastic, as on a Pluto Platter. (See Injection Point and Observation Dome)

Esker—A raised bar or strip of plastic on a flying disc created by cutting into the metal die, usually to remove or alter an inscription such as an obsolete name or address.

Ethylcellulose—An early type of hard plastic listed as an option on the first SCP molding quote, and probably what was used to manufacture the FS1–FS3. Printed on Li'l Abner inserts is: "Tuffy" plastic by Celanese. (See Butyrate)

Flight Rings—A series of concentric grooves added to the outer one-third of the top surface of the Pluto Platter during the creation of the Pro Model (patented by Ed Headrick of Wham-O in 1967) with the intent of increasing lift and providing a better gripping surface.

Flittin' Dish(es)—Euphemism used by Fred Morrison for a flying disc-shaped object.

Flyin Saucer—The name on "PIPCO" discs (FS6–FS8) molded by SCP in polyethylene from 1954 to the early 1960s.

Flyin-Saucer—1948–1950 hard plastic PIPCO disc (FS1–FS3).

Flying Disc Magazine—A short-lived (3 issues), high-quality, bimonthly periodical edited and published by Jim Palmeri in 1980; the February premier issue contains the first in-depth study of the Pluto Platter and introduces the Palmeri / Jensen System for categorizing them.

Flying Saucer—Term for a UFO coined in 1947 by UPI reporter Bill Bequette; the name of a Wham-O disc which first appeared in 1958; and those from other manufacturers.

Fly Mart—An organized event (often at disc competitions) for the purpose of selling and trading collectible flying discs.

Fortical—An early hard plastic listed as an option on the first SCP molding quote; its higher cost probably excluded its use.

Franscioni and Davis—The LPG (butane gas) service and equipment business owned by Warren Franscioni & George Davis located in San Luis Obispo, CA in the late-1940s.

Freestyle—Activity based on creative throwing, catching, and handling of one or more spinning discs. Competitive Freestyle events use judges to subjectively rank the performing teams.

Frisbee®—The name Wham-O Mfg. Co. first used on June 17, 1957 and registered as a trademark on May 26, 1959 for its Toy Flying Saucers For Toss Games, class 22. The first disc to carry the name was the WPP2 in 1958.
Fred was ambivalent about the new name: "If the experienced folks [at Wham-O] who were going to promote the [Pluto Platter] disc believed a name change would be beneficial, so be it! 'Frisbee'...what a hell of a name to hang on anything! I think the name served its purpose because it's relative to nothing; a stroke of unintended genius. Surely there was much discussion concerning various names before 'Frisbee' was adopted. Consider the frivolous mindsets of the promoters. Everybody was having fun. The outrageous wasn't ridiculous."

Frisbee Hall of Fame—Located in Houghton, Michigan and giving honor and recognition to the legends of the sport, Fred Morrison was inducted as a charter member in 1978.

Frisbie—A reference to the Frisbie Pie Company, headquartered in Bridgeport, Connecticut from 1871 until bought out by Table Talk Pies (Wagner Baking Corp.) in 1956.

FS—The designation used in the Kennedy System for the Flyin-Saucer, Flyin Saucer, and Flying Saucer (as in FS4).

Guts (Frisbee)—A competitive game in which two teams of up to five players face each other 14 meters apart and attempt to throw the disc in a manner which will be within reach of but uncatchable by the other team.

Header—A separate strip of material (usually printed heavy paper) which is folded over the open end of a plastic bag and stapled closed. A punch hole is usually added to hang the package on a store display rack.

Horseshoe Game—A game marketed by Wham-O consisting of four discs and two ground targets based on the traditional game using metal horseshoes. The original 1957 version consisted of four WPP1 discs in various color combinations, two furniture-grade wooden stakes, two stout measuring cords and mimeographed instructions. The stakes had "wamo" stickers. Later versions used Mars Platter, Horseshoe Game model, and Regular Frisbee discs, and added metal hoops to the stakes.

Hot Stamping—The method of applying a metal-foil decoration to a disc using a heat-transfer process.

Hula Hoop—Wham-O's trademarked name for a plastic extrusion bent and fastened to form an approximately three-foot circle to be swung around the body using gyrations of the hips or other body parts. It was based on an old Australian game and became *THE* toy fad of 1957, upstaging the Pluto Platter.

Injection Molding—During this manufacturing process plastic pellets or granules are fed from a hopper into a heating chamber; a plunger pushes the plastic through the chamber where the material is softened into a fluid state. At the end of this chamber, the resin is forced under pressure into a cooled, closed, hollow-cavity mold. Once the plastic cools to a solid state, the mold is opened and the part is ejected.

Injection Point—The location at which melted plastic is forced into the mold, usually at the center of the top or bottom of a disc. There is often a bump or dome of plastic remaining with varying degrees of finished appearance. (See Nipple and Sprue)

Insert—A piece of cardboard or heavy paper, printed with throwing instructions and/or sales information, which is sized and shaped to fit into the concave underside of a disc or package.

Invisible Wire—The basis for the sales ploy developed by Fred Morrison to explain the accuracy with which he and his partners could direct Flyin-Saucers being demonstrated to the public. It was sold for a dollar in "lengths" of 100 feet, and came with a "free" Saucer.

Kennedy System—A simple descriptive method for categorizing both Flyin-Saucers and Pluto Platter variations by their unique Styles; developed for and used throughout this book. Refer to the color pages and Chapter 63 for specifics. (See Style, Palmeri System, and Malafronte System)

Glossary of Terms

Knockoff—A disk made to intentionally duplicate or mimic an already existing disc design. An "illegal knockoff" is a disc created in defiance of a patent. The Wham-O Flying Saucer is a knockoff of their own Pluto Platter, while the Premier Products Mars Platter was an illegal knockoff of the patented Pluto Platter design.

Kransco—The company which bought the Wham-O business from its original owners in 1982, and then sold it to Mattel in 1994. In 1986 Kransco shut off royalty payments to Fred and Lu Morrison who brought suit and won.

Label—A small printed paper or foil design adhered to a disc to display decorative, sales, or instructional information.

Lid—A container cover such as were used in the early 1900s to seal tins of cookies, candy and popcorn. Many are quite aerodynamic. Also, (originally) a Master Frisbee or (now) any other large flying disc.

Lift—The component of the total aerodynamic force acting on an airfoil perpendicular to the relative wind and normally exerted in an upward direction, opposing the pull of gravity. The elated feeling experienced when throwing a flying disc.

Li'l Abner—The main Dogpatch character in a cartoon series developed by Al Capp which had phenomenal success in the 1940s and 1950s. Warren Franscioni began a 1950 promotional tie-in using the Flyin-Saucers (FS2) which ended with PIPCO being threatened with a lawsuit.

Lying 101—An entry-level anti-truthful course which Fred claims Edward Kennedy of SCP would have flunked.

Malafronte System—The method of categorizing Wham-O Pluto Platters into seven Periods as published in *The Complete Book of Frisbee,* by Victor Malafronte. (See Period, Kennedy System, and Palmeri System)

Mattel—A toy manufacturer which bought the Wham-O business (and trademarked "Frisbee" name) from Kransco in 1994, then sold it to Charterhouse Group International in 1997.

Mold—A hollow form for shaping a plastic material. What may form on a disc which has been inactive for way too long.

Molding—(See Injection Molding)

Mold Number—A small code number or letter usually engraved into a mold to identify it from other copies of the same mold. None of the Flyin-Saucer/Flyin Saucer Styles have mold numbers, and only the WPP7 Pluto Platter has one.

Moonlighter—A version of the Wham-O Professional Model introduced in 1969 which is made of plastic containing a phosphorescent material. When exposed to light for a period of time, it will glow in the dark.

Morrison's Modulus—Fred's personally-developed mathematical formula for designing flying discs:

$$AP = \frac{\pi Tn(S+BVD)F^2}{TLC}$$

Where:
AP = Aerodynamic Performance
Tn = Atomic weight of Tin
S = The latest Spin
B = Bernoulli's principal (in francs)
V = Number of major Vanes
D = Diameter of circular reasoning
F = Fred's Fudge factor (from Penuche's Recipe)
T = Thrust of argument
L = Lifting experience
C = Coszette's Constant (drag)

Nipple—(See Injection Point) A molding industry term.

Nut—Total of expenses required for exhibiting at a fair.

Observation Dome—The center mound of plastic on the top of Pluto Platters (and several knockoffs), particularly on the ATPP, WPP1 and WPP2 Styles which have rib or spoke structures to simulate 12 window panes.

Palmeri System—A hierarchical method for categorizing Wham-O Pluto Platters into three major production Periods, two minor subdivisions, and two Transitional Periods; developed during a late-1970s collaboration of Jim Palmeri, Lightnin' Lyle Jensen, and Dan Mangone; first published in the February 1980 issue of *Flying Disc Magazine*. (See Kennedy System, Malafronte System, and Period)

Patent, Design—The legal protection granted by a government to an individual or business against illegal copying of the *unique cosmetic appearance* of a device.

Patent, Utility—The legal protection granted to an individual or business by a government against illegal copying of the *functionality* of a device based on *unique structures critical to its stated performance.*

PDGA—The Professional Disc Golf Association. The organization which governs, promotes, regulates and sanctions equipment and tournaments for the sport/game of disc golf.

Period—The time during which a disc is produced for normal retail sales…often applied as a descriptive name for the disc itself, i.e. Period One Pluto Platter. This term generally excludes unique discs and prototypes. (See Style, Palmeri System, and Malafronte System.)

Pie Pan (Tin)—A (usually) metal baking dish used to bake pies. One of the early devices which people couldn't resist throwing to each other! Tins from the Frisbie Pie Co. are now best remembered (and most valuable), but tins from most other bakeries around the world were sailed.

PIPCO—The DBA name for the business partnership between Fred Morrison and Warren Franscioni. It did *NOT* stand for "Partners In Plastic." PIPCO was incorporated shortly after Fred and Warren parted in February 1950 and dissolved before 1953. (See page 64)

Pipco Crab—A term coined by an early disc collector for the Flyin-Saucer due to its resemblance to a horseshoe crab.

Pitch—An aggressive (often exaggerated) selling effort by a hawker of small wares. (See Invisible Wire)

Pluto Platter—The first modern plastic flying disc. The size, weight, and overall shape defined the standards for the vast majority of flying discs which have followed over the past fifty years. Designed and produced by Fred Morrison in 1955 and sold under the American Trends Company name, its manufacturing and promotional rights were sold to Wamo in 1957. It was the first disc to be called a

"Frisbee." The mold was altered seven times over ten years, finally serving as the basis of the mold #1 Professional Model Frisbee in 1964.

Popcorn Can Lid—Yet another of those objects of yore which demanded to be thrown! One at a 1937 Nay family gathering introduced Fred Morrison to his destiny.

Portholes—The round designs inscribed on the side of the Cabin (see also Cupola, and Cockpit) found on the Pluto Platter and its mimics; meant to evoke the windows UFOs "have."

PP—Designation for Pluto Platter (i.e. WPP5) in the Kennedy System.

Precision Plastics—Machine shop in Pomona, California which created the molds for Fred's Krazy-Eight Bowling Balls and The Popsicle Machine.

Professional Model Frisbee—The direct descendant of the Pluto Platter. In 1964, Ed Headrick removed the Pluto Platter graphics and Observation Dome structure, added "flight rings," and increased the weight of the rim very slightly. The resulting Pro mold #1 was cloned to make additional molds before being sent to Irwin Toys, Wham-O's Canadian affiliate, in the late 1960s.

Prototype—An initial design Style which serves as a test pattern or model for others to follow.

Rainbow Plastics—The El Monte, California company which molded the American Trends Pluto Platters for Fred Morrison in 1955 and 1956.

Republic Tool and Die Company—Mold makers used by SCP.

Retooling—Revising a mold to alter the design or to correct a flaw or problem.

Ribs—Another commonly used name for the design patterns on the Observation Domes of the ATPP through WPP2 discs and their mimics which simulate window panes. (See BBQ recipes elsewhere)

Ridges—(See Flight Rings)

Rim—The outermost (usually rounded) edge of a disc; the leading edge of the airfoil shape.

Glossary of Terms

RKI—(See Royale Kraft International)

Roswell—The town in New Mexico near where a UFO was reported to have crashed in 1947.

Rotary Fingernail Clipper—Fred's in-house pet name for the original Flyin-Saucers earned by their habit of punishing the digits of errant catchers. The term was *never* used in public.

Royale Kraft International—The company which appears to have bought the Flyin Saucer mold from SCP and probably produced its FS10 Saucers beginning about 1970.

Royalties—A share in the proceeds paid to an inventor for the right to sell or use his/her invention.

Saucer—A dish-shaped object. (See Flyin, Flyin-, Flying Saucer)

SCF—Short for Self-Caught Flight. A competitive event consisting of two parts: MTA (Maximum Time Aloft), in which a competitor's throw is timed from the moment of release until the disc is caught with a clean one-handed catch, and TRC (Throw, Run, Catch) in which the distance is measured from the point of release to the point at which a clean one-handed catch is made. Some tournaments include only one or the other component of SCF.

SCP—(See Southern California Plastic Company)

Silk Screening—The method of applying an ink-based decoration to a disc using a screen-printing process.

Sky Pie—A non-saucer flying disc designed to be caught with a hand-held, metal wire device; produced by Hall Mfg. in 1949 and patented in 1954 by Teller Hall. (See pg. 260)

Slingshot—The first product manufactured and sold by Wamo in 1948. Projectiles, when fired against a hard object, were thought by company owners to produce a "wamo" sound.

Southern California Plastic Company—The Glendale, CA business that produced the original Flyin-Saucers in 1948 for PIPCO. In 1953 they reacquired the mold from Warren Franscioni and began producing Flyin Saucers using polyethylene plastic. In the 1960s SCP finally removed the PIPCO graphics, replacing them with their own logo.

Originally run by Stan Gray, Edward Kennedy became president in 1952 upon Gray's death. SCP went bankrupt sometime between the late-1960s and 1971 when its assets were bought by Molding Corporation of America, then in Glendale (presently in Burbank), CA.

Space Saucer—A flying disc originally hand built by Ernest (Bill) Robes in his New Hampshire log cabin. A variety of injection-molded Styles were sold principally in New England college campus outlets from 1955 until the early 1960s. (See page 261)

Sprue—Extra plastic remaining attached to a molded disc at the injection point, usually at the top or bottom center.

Steel Ring—An early idea to increase the weight and stability first of cake pans, and then the Flyin-Saucer's rim, it was abandoned as impractical by SCP before production began. (See Whirlo-Way drawing on page 50)

Style—The term used in the Kennedy System for each unique molded disc design without regard to how long it was produced or how many were made…thus single examples and prototypes (but not flawed or malformed discs) as well as designs produced over many years are counted as Styles. Applied decorations are not considered. (See Period)

Templates—Patterns constructed from working drawings used (in this case) as a guide for creating injection molds.

Tenite—Early hard plastic suitable for lathe-forming prototypes.

Tin—(See Lid and Pie Pan)

Tip—An individual or a group of people being sold to; often aggressively. (See Pitch)

Torque—The moment of a force; the measure of a force's tendency to produce torsion and rotation about an axis, equal to the vector product of the radius vector from the axis of rotation to the point of application of the force.
(All right, all right…a twisting action.)

Ultimate (Frisbee)—A two-team game played on a rectangular field with two end zones. Play is continuous, as in soccer.

Utility Patent—(See Patent, Utility)

Vanes—(See Arcuate Vanes)

Variegated-Color Disc—A multi-colored disc resulting from the mixing of different colored plastic pellets, sometimes intentional, often as disc color changes are made during a nonstop mold run. (See Vomit Model)

Vomit Model—Fred's term for a Variegated-Color Disc. (He claims they came in Airsick, Carsick, and Seasick!)

Wamo Manufacturing Company—The original spelling (which changed to "Wham-O" early in 1957) appearing on small labels adhered to the underside of early-1957 WPP1 discs, on the wooden stakes included in early Horseshoe Games, and printed on early cardboard boxes containing the Horseshoe Games, and various product literature.

Wham-O Manufacturing Company—The spelling after early-1957. Founded in 1948 by Rich Nerr and Arthur "Spud" Melin the company has produced many unusual products and spawned numerous fads. On January 23, 1957 (then still) Wamo bought the production and promotional rights to the Pluto Platter from Fred and Lu Morrison, and soon renamed it the Frisbee. Today the company is called Wham-O, Inc.

Whirlo-Way—The name Fred chose for the world's first flying disc design. The name appears on a draftsman's drawing developed from Fred's original conceptual design sketches in 1946…one year before the term "flying saucer" was coined by a news reporter. The name honors the legendary 1940s racehorse Whirlaway.

WPP—The designation used in the Kennedy System for the Wham-O Pluto Platter (i.e. WPP5).

Yellow Pages, The—Name coined for Fred's bound copies of Warren Franscioni's business records; a portion of the "yellowing letters" referred to by Coszette Eneix, daughter of Warren Franscioni.

BIBLIOGRAPHY

BOOKS & CHAPTERS IN GENERAL WORKS

Bloeme, Peter. *Frisbee Dogs: How to Raise, Train and Compete.* Atlanta, GA: PRB and Associates, 1991, 1994.

Caney, Steven. "The Invention of the Frisbee." In Steven Caney's *Invention Book,* pages 97–102. New York, NY: Workman Publishing Co., Inc., 1999.

Danna, Mark and Dan Poynter. *Frisbee Players Handbook.* Parachuting Publications, 1978.

Dickson, Paul. *The Mature Person's Guide to Kites, Yo Yos, Frisbees and Other Childlike Diversions,* pages 116–131. The New American Library. Plume Books, 1977.

Horowitz, Judy and Billy Bloom. *Frisbee, More Than Just a Game of Catch.* Champagne, IL: Leisure Press, 1983.

Johnson, Stancil, E.D. *FRISBEE: A Practitioner's Manual and Definitive Treatise.* New York, NY: Workman Publishing Co., Inc., 1975.

Kalb, Irv and Tom Kennedy. *Ultimate: Fundamentals of the Sport.* Santa Barbara, CA: Revolutionary Publications, 1982.

Lander, Irv. *Ashley Whippet.* Van Nuys, CA: PAWSitive Publishing, 1996.

Malafronte, Victor A. *The Complete Book of Frisbee: The History of the Sport & The First Official Price Guide.* Alameda, CA: American Trends Publishing Co., 1998.

Moran, Tom. *Frisbee Disc Flying Is For Me.* Minneapolis, MN: Lerner Publications, 1982.

New Frisbee—The New Games Book, pages 28–29. New York, NY: Doubleday & Co. Inc., A Headlands Press Book, 1976.

Norton, Goldy. *The Official Frisbee Handbook.* New York, NY: Bantam Books, 1972.

Olney, Ross R. *Tricky Discs: Frisbee Saucer Flying.* New York, NY: Lothrop, Lee & Shepard Company div., William Morrow & Co., 1979.

Panati, Charles. "Frisbee: Pre-1957, Connecticut." in *Extraordinary Origins of Everyday Things,* pages 372–373. New York, NY: Harper & Row, 1987.

Parinella, James and Eric Zazlow. *Ultimate: Techniques and Tactics.* Champaign, IL: Human Kinetics, 2004.

Poynter, Margaret. *Frisbee Fun.* New York, NY: Julian Messner div., Simon & Schuster, 1977.

Pryor, Karen. *How to Teach Your Dog to Play Frisbee.* New York, NY: Simon and Schuster, 1985.

Roddick, Dan. *Frisbee Disc Basics.* Englewood Cliffs, NJ: Prentice-Hall, 1980.

Roddick, Dan. *The Discourse.* San Gabriel, CA: Wham-O, Inc., 1978, 1986, 1989

Schmitz, Dorothy Childers. *Fabulous Frisbee.* Mankato, MN: Crestwood House, Inc., 1978.

Tips, Charles. *Frisbee by the Masters.* Millbrae, CA: Celestial Arts, 1977.

Tips, Charles and Dan Roddick. *Frisbee Sports & Games.* Millbrae, CA: Celestial Arts, 1979.

Wallechinsky, David and Irving Wallace. "Tossing The Discus." In *The People's Almanac #2,* page 1091. New York, NY: William Morrow and Company, Inc., 1978.

Walsh, Tim. "Wham-O Frisbee" in *The Playmakers: Amazing Origins of Timeless Toys,* pages 137–141. Sarasota, FL: Keys Publishing, 2004.

MAGAZINE & NEWSPAPER ARTICLES

Cooper, Corinne. "The Frisbee Frenzy: Whole New World." *American Collector*, August 1978, pages 12–13 & 31.

Danna, Mark. "After 30 High-Flying Years, The Frisbee Still Soars." *Sports Illustrated,* May 11, 1987.

Danna, Mark. "How and Why a Frisbee Flies." *Muppet Magazine,* Spring 1983, page 52.

Flagg, M. J. "Aerodynamics: Secret of the Frisbee Toss." *Science Digest,* June 1978, pages 73, 74–75.

Leonard, George. "Flat Flip Flies Straight." *Esquire Magazine,* February 1988, pages 138–141, 143–146.

Flint, Frank P. "Frisbee: Manners And Morals." *Sports Illustrated,* June 3, 1957, "Letters," page 79.

Flying Disc Magazine. 1980 (3 issues).

Flying Disc World. 1974–1975 (9 issues).

"Flying Frisbees." *Sports Illustrated,* May 13, 1957, "Events & Discoveries," page 22.

"Flying Saucers." *People and Places,* June, 1958, page 22. (DeSoto dealer publication)

"Frisbee." *National Lampoon Magazine,* July 1979, page 32.

Frisbee Disc World. 1976–1981 (31 issues).

"Frisbee Fiasco; Navy Research." *Time Magazine,* November 6, 1978, page 85.

"Frisbee for Fanatics." *Esquire,* October 1976, pages 88–89.

"Frisbee: Historians Report." *Princeton Alumni Weekly,* July 1, 1975, "Letters," page 79.

"Frisbee: Ohio Version." *Sports Illustrated,* May 27, 1957, "19th Hole, Readers Take Over" (letters), pages 78–79.

"Frisbee: Phrisbee." *Princeton Alumni Weekly,* July 1, 1975, "Letters," page 79.

"Frisbee Sports & Games." *Boy's Life,* August 1979, page 15.

"From Pie Tin to Frisbee." *National Geographic World,* December 1987.

"Games Kids Play." *Sport Illustrated For Kids,* May 1990, pages 66–70.

Gold, Michael. "Fairy Tale Physics of Frisbees." *Science '82,* June 1982, pages 76–77.

Gott, Peter H. "The First Frisbee." *Princeton Alumni Weekly,* July 1, 1975, "Letters," page 7.

Higdon, Hal. "Gentlemen, Start Your Frisbees!" *Ford Times* (Dearborn, MI), April 1970, pages 39–43.

Hindman, Darwin A. "Summer Games." *Young Athlete Magazine,* August 1981, pages 41–42.

IFA News. 1968–1974 (20 issues).

Jares, Joe. "It's Beer, Bratwurst and a Guts Game." *Sports Illustrated,* August 1970, pages 48–49.

Johnson, Stancil. "A Slightly Slanted Pitch on Frisbees." *Smithsonian,* September 1976, pages 179–180.

Katz, Paul. "The Free Flight of a Rotating Disc." *Israel Journal of Technology.* 1968, Volume 6, No. 1–2, pages 150–155.

Koon, Bruce. "How to Keep Sales of a Toy Up: Build a Sport Around It." *The Wall Street Journal,* August 17, 1979, page 19.

Makower, Joel. "Pie in the Sky." *New York Post,* October 31, 1985, page 41.

McMahon, Jeff. "Where The Frisbee First Flew." *New Times Weekly,* San Luis Obispo, CA, July 24-31, 1997, pages 10–13.

Morrison, Shelley. "From Pie Tin to Rose Bowl." *Young Athlete,* March 1976, pages 70–73.

"Name's Frisbee, The." *Newsweek,* July 8, 1957, "Life And Leisure-Games," page 85.

"One Man's Toy." *Sports Illustrated,* February 26, 1990, page 85.

O'Rourke, P. J. "Play it Where it Lays: Frisbee Golf in Central Park." *New York Times,* June 12, 1977, pages 24–25.

Page, Anita. "Pie in the Sky." *La Verne Magazine*, April 1977, page 14. (Feature article on Fred Morrison)

Palmeri, Jim. "Collecting the Pluto Platter." *Flying Disc Magazine,* February 1980, pages 18–22.

Palmeri, Jim. "The Space Saucer." *Flying Disc Magazine,* April/May 1980, pages 46–47.

Peterson, James R. "Zen and the Art of Frisbee." *Oui Magazine,* May 1975, page 88.

Reed, J. D. "They Are My Life and My Wife." *Sports Illustrated,* February 24, 1975, pages 62–72.

Riggs, Carol R. "Wham-O! Mad Fads and Big Profits." *D & B Report,* January/February 1982, pages 9–15.

Roddick, Dan. "Frisbee Disc Sports—A Game for Everyone." *Journal of the National Intramural Recreational Sports Association,* May 1979, pages 45–47.

Sabin, Lou. "Frisbee's on the Rise." *Boy's Life,* 1975.

Talese, Gay. "Frisbees, Yo Yos, Goo-Goos, Etc." *New York Times Magazine,* August 11, 1957, page 24.

Tidyman, Kathryn. "Frisbee." *Boys Life Magazine,* March 1978, pages 30–33.

Tips, Charles. "Frisbee—Play it Your Way." *Young Athlete,* June 1977, pages 53–55.

Wegman, David H., M.D. and John M. Peters, M.D. "Frisbee Finger." Harvard School of Public Health, *The New England Journal of Medicine*, October 2, 1975, Vol. 293, No. 14, pages 725–726.

"What's Next? Why, Frisbee Golf." *Mechanix Illustrated,* March 1978, page 80.

Widel, Ron. "Frisbee: A Humanistic Sport." *The Humanist* (NY), January/February 1981, pages 37–41.

Wilhelm, Douglas. "Famed Flying Frisbee Feted on its 50th." *The Boston Globe,* June 4, 1989, pages 29–30.

WEB SITES

50 Years of Flying Discs. *The Christian Science Monitor*:
http://www.csmonitor.com/durable/1998/11/03/p8s1.htm

Bloomfield, Louis A. "Flight of the Frisbee, The." *Scientific American*. Article reprinted from April, 1997:
http://www.sciam.com/article.cfm?articleID=000155A0-6D59-1C71-9EB7809EC588F2D7&pageNumber=1&catID=2

Fascinating facts about the invention of the Frisbee by Walter Frederick Morrison in 1950. *The Great Idea Finder*:
http://www.ideafinder.com/history/inventions/story008.htm

First Flight of the Frisbee, The: http://www.airfairways.com/history.htm

Flying Disc, The. *MIT Inventor of the Week*:
http://web.mit.edu/invent/www/inventorsA-H/flyingdisk.html

Frisbee. *Bad Fads Museum*:
http://www.badfads.com/pages/collectibles/frisbee.html

Frisbie. *GCFDA Newsletter*: http://www.discsports.com/gcfda/fn/fn98.htm

Frisbee. *Flaghouse Activity Guide*, page 2:
http://216.239.51.100/search?q=cache:tFIz2UydQS0C:
www.flaghouse.com/Ideas/DiscActivities.pdf+flyin+saucer&hl=en&ie=UTF-8

Frisbee. *Strong Museum*: http://www.strongmuseum.org/NTHoF/frisbee.html

Frisbee. *Wikipedia*:
http://www.wikipedia.org/w/wiki.phtml?title=Frisbee&redirect=no

Frisbee. *The Fifties Web Index*: http://www.fiftiesweb.com/pop/frisbee.htm

Frisbee Physics. *Mansfield CT Middle School* (From Newton's Apple):
http://www.mansfieldct.org/schools/mms/staff/hand/Flightfrisbee.htm

Frisbee Physics. *PBS*: http://www.pbs.org/ktca/newtons/9/frisbee.html

Frisbee, The. *About.com/Inventors*:
http://inventors.about.com/gi/dynamic/offsite.htm?site=http://muttley.ucdavis.edu/Book/Sports/instructor/frisbee%2D01.html

Frisbee. *YesterdayLand*:
http://www.yesterdayland.com/popopedia/shows/toys/ty1022.php

Frisbee. *Wham-O*: http://www.whamo.com/content/aboutfrisbee.html

History of Invention, The. *CBC.ca 4/Kids*:
http://www.cbc4kids.cbc.ca/general/the-lab/history-of-invention/frisbee.html

History of the Frisbee, The. *About.com/Inventors*:
http://inventors.about.com/library/weekly/aa980218.htm

Bibliography

History of the Frisbee, The. *UK Ultimate Association*:
http://www.ukultimate.com/history.asp

International Frisbee Hall of Fame:
http://www.sas.it.mtu.edu/~dkwalika/frisbee/Hall.html

Invention of the Frisbee, The. *Lost Tribe Disc*, New Zealand:
http://ngatai.orcon.net.nz/ltd/otherdiscsports.html

Kottmeyer, Martin. The Saucer Error. *The Reall News, The Official Newsletter of the Rational Examination Association of Lincoln Land*. Vol. 1, number 4: http://www.debunker.com/texts/SaucerError.html

McMahon, Jeff. "Where the Frisbee First Flew." *The Ultimate Handbook*:
http://www.ultimatehandbook.com/Webpages/History/histdisc.html

Patent for the Pluto Platter, September 30, 1958. *U. S. Patent Office*:
http://patimg1.uspto.gov/.piw?Docid=D0183626&homeurl=http%3A%2F%2Fpatft.uspto.gov%2Fnetacgi%2FnphParser%3FSect1%3DPTO1%2526Sect2%3DHITOFF%2526d%3DPALL%2526p%3D1%2526u%3D%25252Fnetahtml%25252Fsrchnum.htm%2526r%3D1%2526f%3DG%2526l%3D50%2526s1%3DD183626.WKU.%2526OS%3DPN%2FD183626%2526RS%3DPN%2FD183626&PageNum=&Rtype=&SectionNum=&idkey=B20FFBDBAD34

Pluto Platter. *About.com/Inventors*:
http://inventors.about.com/gi/dynamic/offsite.htm?site=http://irafs1.ira.uka.de/%7Ethgries/disc/articles/pluto%2Dplatter

Pluto Platter, The. *Thomas Griesbaum's International Frisbee Sport*:
http://www.ira.uka.de/~thgries/disc/articles/pluto-platter

Slipped Disc. *Outside Online*: http://www.frisbee.ee/eng/mis.html

Tallinn Frisbee Club: http://www.frisbee.ee/eng/mis.html

Toys Were Us. *Discovery Online*:
http://www.discovery.com/stories/history/toys/FRISBEE/birthday1.html

Walter Frederick [sic] Inventor of the Frisbee. *Inventors Museum*:
http://www.inventorsmuseum.com/frisbee.htm

Walter Frederick Morrison. *About.com/Inventors*:
http://inventors.about.com/gi/dynamic/offsite.htm?site=http://www.ira.uka.de/%257Ethgries/disc/articles/morrison

Walter Frederick Morrison. *Thomas Griesbaum's International Frisbee Sport*: http://www.ira.uka.de/~thgries/disc/articles/morrison

World Wide Words. http://www.quinion.com/words/topicalwords/tw-fri1.htm

Young, Josh. "Oh, the Joy of a Good Toy for a Boy." *Long Creek News*, http://www.longcreekherbs.com/columns/Josh/native/7.26.02.html

INDEX — Book One

Text references are in lightface, photo references are in **boldface**.

Air Force: 43, **44**, 45, 49, 58, 88, 127, 139, 159, 173, 183, 213.
Airfoil: 49, 58, 62.
Airport, Richfield, UT: 139, 143.
Aluminum Pans: 42.
Anaheim, CA: 74.
Arcuate Vanes: 49, 62, 189, 194.
Ashley Whippet: **241**.
"Awesome Foursome, The": 92, 101.

Bags, Product Display: 71.
Bakelite Plastic: 42.
Bakersfield, CA: 45.
Baywood Park, CA: 40, 52, 89.
BB Guns: 218.
Bernoulli's Principle: 58.
Bower, James S.: 185.
"Boys, The": 106, 108, 113, 115, 120, 125–126, 128, 130, 132, 216, 225.
Builder's Buddy: 125.
Building Inspector: 127, 133.
Burandt, Robert: 169.
Butane Business: 54–55, 173.

Caco Engineering: 98, 100.
Cahow, Jo: **239**.
Cake Pan: 18, 38, **39**, 42, 49, 56, 171, 174, 187.
CalPoly Students: 188.
Capp, Al: 178, 181–182, 213–214.
Carpenter: 47, 90, 101, 121, 134.
Christy, Parker and Hale: 120.
Complete Book of Frisbee, The: 30, 239.
Conejo Drive, SLO, CA: 161.
Connally, John: 220.
Cook, on Shark Boat: 90.
Cove Mountain, UT: 151.
Crooked Arrow Horse Ranch: 151.
Cropper, Jerry: 152.
Crossbows: 108.
Cup 'n Sticks: 123, 125.
Cuyama, CA: 89.

Davis, Jon: 239.
Dawn of Discdom: 62.
Dedication Disc, Hall of Fame: 236, **337**.
Des Moines, IA: 102, 201.
"Diaphragm for Elephants": 60.
Disc Design, First: 51.
Disc Golf: 240–241.

Disc Golf Hall of Fame: 238, 240.
Disc Golf PoleHole: 199, 229.
Disneyland: 203.
Doc: 181.
Dodger Convention Room: 231.
Douglas Aircraft: 43.

Eagle Harbor, MI: 210, 238.
Eastman Plastics: 56.
Employment Registration Form: 166, **167**.
Eneix, Coszette: 24, 160–161, 179, 198, 203, 205, 242.

FAIRS:
 Arizona State Fair: 81, 83, 95, 100.
 Del Mar: 101, 108.
 Florida Fairs: 83.
 Iowa State Fair: 102.
 L.A. County Fair: 74, 83, 92, 100, 121, 200.
 Nebraska State Fair: 84.
 Pomona Fair: 108, 112, 202.
 San Bernardino County Orange Show: 84, 113, 122.
 San Diego County Fair: 101.
 Ventura County Fair: 81.
"Flat Flip Flies Straight": 19, 158.
Floating Free: 235.
FLYIN SAUCERS (FS4–FS13):
 Account, Disneyland: 203.
 Accounts, SCP: 201–202.
 Competition, Pluto Platters: 201.
 Demonstrations: 93.
 Expense of, 1954: 97.
 L.A. County Fair, 1954: 92.
 Ordering, Fred: 93, 95.
 Paid for COD: 93, 202.
 Polyethylene: 93, 183.
 Sales Commissions, Fred: 202.
 Sales Commissions, Warren: 202.
FLYIN-SAUCERS (FS1–FS3):
 Bags, Product Display: 71, 177.
 Cardboard Templates: 59.
 Demonstrating: 74.
 Design Claim, Warren's: 213.
 Designing: 59.
 Film, 16mm: 170.
 Financing the Mold: 57, 215.
 First Plastic Flying Disc: 18, 59.
 First Production Run: 67.

428

INDEX—Book One

Injection Mold: 62.
Inserts: 177.
Interest in Relinquished, Fred's: 97.
Invisible Wire: 78.
Mold: 174.
Mold, Dual-Cavity: 182, 200.
Mold Ownership: 92, 159.
Mold, Single-Cavity: 183, 200.
Molding Process: 68.
Molding Time: 67.
Naming: 62.
Not Patentable: 188.
Original Idea: 97.
Patent Application: 187–188, 190.
Patent Application Abandoned: 192.
Patent Attorneys: 188–189, 190.
Pitch, Sales: 78.
Powder Blue Saucers: 67.
Prototypes: 56, 59, 61, 62.
"Rotary Fingernail Clippers": 63.
Unpatented: 97.
Vomits: 68, **69**.
Wire in Rim: 58.
Woolworths: 72.
Flying Disc Magazine: 240.
"Flying Saucer" Term: 62.
Food Stamps: 141, 145, 229.
FRANSCIONI:
   Children: 161.
   Family: 198, 215.
   Lawsuit Considered: 160, 162, 213.
   Major (in Air Force): 183.
   Mother: 57, 164, 179.
   Mother-in-Law: 57, 164, 179, 182.
   Warren: 20, 25, 31, 54–55, 57, 62, 67, 78, 92, 159–161, 164, 166, 169, 177, 181, 186–188, 190, 192, 196, 198, 200, 205, 212, 242.
Franscioni & Davis: 54, 173.
Franz & Rothrock: 174, 176, 182.
Franz, Chuck: 171, 184, 200.
Frisbee World: 238.
FRISBEE:
   Headrick, Ed: 130–133, 224–230, **224, 228–230**.
   Origins: 18, 54.
   Origins of Name: 119, 219.
   Promotions: **132**, 231.
FRISBEE: A Practitioner's Manual and Definitive Treatise: 212.
Frisbie Pie Company: 119.
Furman, Tony: 235.

Glendale, CA: 64, 72.
Go-Fer Hardware: **135**.
Guts Frisbee: 228.

Hall of Fame Installation Disc: **237**.
Hall of Fame Installation: 29, 210, 227, 236.
Hardware Store: 134, 146, 209.
Harry (lawyer) Letter: 164, **165**.
Harvest Moon Street: 91.
Headrick, Ed: **130**–133, 208, 224–230, **224, 228–230**.
Headrick, Ed's Ashes: 230.
Healy Brothers: 238.
Hoornbeek, Marge Nay: 93, **94**.
Hoornbeek, Paul: 93, **94**, 100, 105, 110, 112.
Horse Ranch: 151.
Houghton, MI: 29, 210, 227, 236, 239.
"How To" instructions: 18, 71, 99.
Hula Hoops: 113–114, 120, 122, 125, 218.

IFA: 208, 238–239, 240.
IFT: 238–239.
Injection Molding: 56.
Inserts, Li'l Abner: **178-180**.
Internet: 22, 159, 162, 212, 236, 242.
Inventions, Fred's Other: 121.
Invisible Wire: 20, 77.

Joe: 34.
John Marshall High School: 34.
Johnson, Stancil: 25, 208, **209-211**, 236.
Joys of Impotence, The: 243.
Julius T. Nachazel Cup: 238.

KENNEDY:
   Ed(ward) L.: 56, 58, 67, 71–72, 92, 97, 183–185, 199–204.
   Pat: 199.
   Phil: 156, 159, 188, **199**, 233, 244, **Back Cover**.
King Features: 169.
Kirkland, John 'Friz Whiz': 208, 239.
Knerr, Rich: 105, 108, 119, 128, 216–223, **219, 223**.
Korean War: 46.
Koufax, Sandy: 130, 225.
Kransco: 143, **144**, 146, 150, 152.
Kransco Lawsuit: 143–150, 229.
Krazy Eight Bowling Balls: 113, 121, **123**, 125.

INDEX—Book One

L.A., CA: 90.
La Verne, CA: 134.
Lander, Irv: 240.
Lathe Operator: 59–60.
Li'l Abner: 178, **178-180**, 213–214.
Lockheed Aircraft: 41.

Malafronte, Victor: 29, **33**, 206, 227, 239.
Mallard, Ken: 109, 222.
Mangone, Dan: 241.
Marriages, Fred: 137–138, 140.
McIff, Kay L.: 146–150.
McMahon, Jeff: 23–24, 105, 108, 140, 153, 159, 162, 178, 198, 205, 212–213, 242, 244.
Melin, Spud: 105, 108, 216–223, **221, 223**.
Monroe, UT: 140.
MORRISON:
  Dr. Walter F.: 40, 42, 49, 51, 204.
  Family: 41, **127**.
  Fred: **12**, **34**, **41**, **44**, 62, **113**, **139**, 160, 171, 182–183, 186, 188, 191, 195–196, 200, 202–203, **209**, 214, **223**, **226–227**, 233, 240, **Back Cover**.
  Fred's Mom: 40.
  Fred, Later Marriages: 138.
  Lu: **6**, 18, **19**, 31, 49, 62, 85, 87, 94, 99, 108, 117, 122, **127**, 132, 134, 137, 142–143, 146, 172.
  Marriage, Fred & Lu: 40, 137.
  Walter "Bill": 91, **127**.
  Walter Fredrick (birth name): 24.
Morrison's Modulus: 174.
Morro Bay City, CA: 52.
Motel, Richfield, UT: 140, 143, 146.
Muller, A.V., Patent Attorney: 190.

Nay, Clarence: 36, 47, 52.
Nay, Lu(cile): 34.
Norton, Goldy: 231–235, **231, 234**, 236.

O'Brien & Jacobson, Patent Attorneys: 190.
Official FRISBEE Handbook, The: 233.
Olympic Games: 231.
Olympic Rings: 131.
O'Neal, Tatum: **227**.

P-47 Pilot, WWII: 43, **44**.
Pacific Plastics: 175.
Palmeri, Jim: 240.
Paper Cup Contest: 116.
Parking Lot: 105.
"Partners In Plastic": 66.
Paso Robles, CA: 172.
PATENTS:
  Application Papers: 196.
  Application, Flyin-Saucer: 187–188.
  Application, Pluto Platter: 120.
  Attorneys, Flyin-Saucer: 188.
  Date Conceived, Whirlo-Way: 187.
  Date of, Pluto Platter: 120.
  Design Patent: 189, 194–195.
  Engineering Data: 191.
  Flyin Saucer Application, New: 192.
  Flyin-Saucer Application: 190, 198.
  Flyin-Saucer Application Abandoned: 192.
  Muller, A.V., Attorney: 190.
  Not Patentable, Flyin-Saucer: 188.
  O'Brien & Jacobson, Attorneys: 190.
  Patent Office: 120, 188, 192, 195–196.
  Patentable Structures: 189, 194, 196.
  Signature, Lack of Fred's: 192, 196, 198.
  Signatures Required: 188.
  Utility Patent: 189.
  Vanes: 189, 194.
  Whirlo-Way Drawing: 192.
Phoenix, AZ: 81, 95.
Pie Tin: 38, 213.
PIPCO:
  Acronym, Meaning: 64.
  Agreement, First: 57.
  Agreement, Lack of Written: 88.
  Contract Negotiations: 164.
  Contract, None: 57.
  Corporation: 164, 181, 184, 198.
  Corporation, Demise: 184, 213.
  Film, 16mm: 170.
  Financial Backers, Potential: 87, 171.
  Flyin-Saucer Mold: 88.
  Logo: **65**.
  Office: 65.
  "Partners In Plastic": 66.
  Partners, Later: 176, 182, 203.
  Partnership: 164.
  Split, Fred & Warren: 87, 159, 164, 175, 177, 181, 183, 200, 214.
  Split, Date of: 166.
Pitch, Sales: 78, 93, 100, 124.

PLASTICS:
  Bakelite: 42.
  Brittle: 62.
  Flexible: 43, 56, 93.
  Granules: 68.
  Hard: 56, 59.
  Lathe-Compatible: 56.
  Polyethylene: 93, 97, 183.
  Tenite: 57, 62.
  Turning Characteristics: 61.
  Use of for Discs: 56.
  Variegated Colors: 68.
  Vs Metal: 56, 61.
PLUTO PLATTERS:
  Caco Engineering: 98, 100.
  Contract Signed: 111, 201.
  Cost of, 1955: 97.
  Debut: 100.
  Designing: 98.
  Distributors for: 107.
  Fairs, 1955–1956: 100.
  First Seen by Wham-O: 108.
  Frisbee: 131.
  "Frisbee" Name Origin: 119.
  "How to Instructions": 99.
  Mold, New: 97.
  Mold Ownership: 110.
  Mold Retooled to Pro Model: 131.
  Morrison's Second Disc: 18.
  Name Changed: 119–120.
  Naming of: 98.
  Ordering: 100.
  Packaging, Wham-O: 112.
  Parking Lot: 105.
  Patent, Date of: 120.
  Patent Expired: 128.
  "Pluto's Platter": 200.
  Pomona Fair, 1955: 98.
  Promotion, Morrisons': 112.
  Promotion, Wham-O's: 112.
  Rainbow Plastics: 97, 100.
  Redesign of: 225.
  Royalties Percentage: 109.
  "Stranger, A": 106.
  Success: 216.
  Test-Marketed by Wham-O: 117.
Pomona, CA: 92.
Popcorn Can Lid: **14**, 18, 34, 38.
Popsicle Machines: 123, **124**, 125.
POW, WWII: 44, 173.
Pro Model Frisbee: **131**, 225.
Prototypes: 63.

Rainbow Plastics: 97, 100.
Recession, 1986: 143.
Reiter, Charlotte & Ray: 153.
Richardson, Paul 'Sky King': 208, 239.
Richfield, UT: 138–139, 143.
Rings, Rim: 131.
Roddick, Dan 'Stork': 208, **238**.
Rodondo Beach, CA: 185.
Roller Skate: 126.
Rose Bowl: 27, 220, 222, 225, 227.
"Rotary Fingernail Clippers": **63**.
Rothrock: 181, 184, 186.
Royalties: 109, 112, 121, 126–127, 132, 134, 137–138, 143, 146, 150–151, 184, 213, 219, 225, 244.

Sacramento, CA: 87, 171.
Salt Lake City, UT: 146.
San Diego, CA: 201.
San Dimas, CA: 91.
San Francisco, CA: 147, 170, 184.
San Gabriel, CA: 217.
San Luis Obispo, CA: 24, 52, 60, 90, 161, 190.
Santa Anita, CA: 222.
Santa Monica, CA: 38, 45.
SCP (Southern California Plastic Co.): 56, 58, 62, 67–68, 92, 183, 185, 200, 202, 206.
Settlement, Kransco: 150.
Sevier Valley, UT: 151.
Shark Boat: 90.
Shelton, Jay: 240.
Shipyard: 43.
Slingshots: 107–108, **217**.
Soup-Fin Sharks' Livers: 90.
South Dakota, Franscioni in: 183.
Southern California Plastic Co. (See SCP)
Southern California Sports Writers' Association: 231.
Spin: 58.
"Spin-Thimble": **30**
Split, PIPCO: 177, 181, 183, 214.
Split, PIPCO, Date of: 166.
Sporting-Goods Stores: 72, 112, 169, 218.
'Stork,' Roddick, Dan: 238.

INDEX—Book One

Tenite Plastic: 57.
Tent: 52.
Thanksgiving, November 25, 1937: 34, 38.
Third Degree, The (TV show): **229**.
Tin Pans: 42.
Torque: 58.
Turbine: 49, 62.

UFOs: 62.
USC: 217.

Variegated Discs: 68, **69**.
Vomit Models: 68, **69**.

Walt'z Hardware: 134.
Washington, DC: 190.
Water Wiggles: 222.
WHAM-O:
  Advertising: **132**.
  "Boys, The": 106, 108, 114–115, 119, 125–126, 128, 130, 216, 225.
  Competitive Events: 208.
  Contract: 114.
  Contract Negotiations: 109, 128.
  Contract Signed: 111.
  Contract Lawsuit, Kransco: 146.
  Contract, Frisbee: 143.
  Contract, Pluto Platter: 201, 203.
  Crossbows: 108.
  Disc of Their Own: 107, 129.
  Entertainment, In-House: 116.
  "Frisbee" Name, Use of: 119, **120**.
  "Frisbee" Name Origin: 219.
  Frisbee PR: 231.
  Frisbee Success: 224.
  Furman, Tony: 235.
  Headrick, Ed: 224.
  Headrick, Ed, Hired: 130.
  Hula Hoops: 120, 122.
  Hula Hoops, First Demo of: 113.
  Inventors, Other: 115.
  Knerr, Rich: 216–223, **219, 223**.
  Kransco, Wham-O Acquired by: 143.
  Krazy Eight Bowling Balls: 113, 121, **123**.
  Mallard, Ken, Attorney: 109, 222.
  Melin, "Spud": 216–223, **221, 223**.
  Mold Ownership: 110.
  Norton, Goldy: 231.
  Packaging: 112.
  Patent Attorneys: 120.
  Patent Expired: 128.
  Pluto Platter Redesigned: 225.
  Pluto Platters First Seen by: 108.
  Pluto Platters Renamed: 18.
  Popsicle Machines: 123.
  Pro Model Frisbee: 225, **131**.
  Pro Model, Introduction of: 131.
  Promotion of Pluto Platter: 112.
  Redesign of Pluto Platter: 225.
  Roddick, Dan 'Stork': 238.
  Roller Skates: 126.
  Royalties: 109.
  Royalties Reduction: 127.
  Sales Test-Marketing: 112, 117.
  Settlement, Kransco: 149, 152.
  Slingshots: 107, 217.
  Store Display: **118**.
  "Stranger, A": 106–107.
  TV Commercial: 112.
  "Wamo," Original Name: 217.
  Water Wiggles: 222.
"Where the Frisbee First Flew": 23, 162.
Whirlaway (Racehorse): 51.
Whirlo-Way: **50**, 51, 56, 58, 98, 127, 187, 188, 192, 213, 215.
Wide World of Sports: 235.
Wire Rim: 49, 58.
Woolworths: 72.
World Junior Championships: 238.
WWII: 43, 88.

Yellow Pages, The: 158–159, 164, 166, 181, 188, 190, 200, 212.
Yellowing Letters: 162.

INDEX — Book Two & Color "Plates"

Text references are in lightface, photo references are in **boldface**.

All-American Pro Frisbee: **272**.
Amherst, MA: 283.
Antique Dealers: 281, 288.

Bags, Plastic: **253**, **257**, **263–271**, 299.
Barrett, Roger: 283.
Boxes: 299.
Buck Rogers Flying Saucers: **260**, 293.
Budgets, Setting: 295.

Cake Pan: **247**.
Candy Tin Lid: **246**.
Capp, Al: 283, 286–287.
ChemToy Super Zinger: **275**.
Cleaning Discs: 299.
Collectors: 281.
Complete Book of Frisbee, The: 281, 284, 301, 309.
Condition Categories: 323, **327–329**.
Condition of Disc, Grading: 309.
Connections, Getting: 295.
C.P.I. Saucer Tosser: **275**.
Cross-Section Comparisons of Discs: **276**.
Curiosity: 301.

Damage Categories: 311, **311–321**.
DISC COLLECTING:
 Interest in: 290.
 Sources: 291.
 Specialty Categories: 292.
Disc Collectors Anonymous: 308.
Disc Golf: 293.
Displaying Discs: 307.
Double-Esker: **270**, 279.
Duplicates: 297.

EBay®: 281, 283, 287, 291, 308.
Ejector Pins: 305.
Elliott, Daryl: 283.
Eskers: **265**, **270**, 302, 340.
Estate-Sellers: 281, 286.
Expectations of Collecting: 308.

FACT FINDERS: 348–349.
Flea Markets: 283, 291.
Fly-Marts: 295.
FLYIN-SAUCERS:
 FACT FINDER: 348.
 FS1: **248–249**, 279, 281, 284–285.
 FS2: **250**, 283, 285–286, 293.
 FS3: **250**.
 FS4: **252**.
 FS5: **252**.
 FS5/AT: **253**.
 FS6: **254**.
 FS7: **254**.
 FS7/AT: **255**.
 FS7/D: **256.**
 FS8/D: **257.**
 FS9: **258**.
 FS10: **258**.
 FS11: **258**.
 FS12: **259**.
 FS13: **259**.
 Identify, How to: 342.
 Powder Blue: **248–249**, 287, 288.
 Prototype: **249**, 286.
Flying Disc Magazine: 309.
Flying Saucer (Wham-O): **273**.
Franscioni, Warren: 279, 286.
Frisbee World Magazine: 283.
Frisbee: A Practitioner's Manual and Definitive Treatise: 278, 283.
FRISBEES:
 Ancestors of: 334.
 Misspelling the Name of: 287, 289.
Frisbie Pie Tin: **247**.

Garage Sales: 291.
Giant Mystery-Y (Empire Plastics): **275**.
Goo Gone®: 300.
Google: 291.

Hartford, CT: 278, 282.
History of Discs, Early: 280.
"Holy Grails": 282, 287, 289.
Horseshoe Model Frisbee: **273**.
Horseshoe Set: **266**.
Hot-Stamp: 314.

Identifying a Pluto Platter: 338.
Important Discs, List of: 331.
Information, Getting: 296.
Internet: 280, 291.

Johnson, Dave: **291**.
Johnson, Stancil: 278, 283.
Jumping Jupiter (Irwin Corp.): **275**.

KENNEDY:
 Pat: 278.
 Phil: **278**, **Back Cover**
 Shannon: 435.
 Shawn: 278, 279.
Kennedy System: 338.

433

Li'l Abner: **250–251**, 279, 283, 287, 293.
Li'l Abner Insert: **251**, 285.
Loupe: 306.

Malafronte, Victor: 281, 309.
Mangone, Dan: 305.
Mars Platters: **274**, 293, 301–302.
Master Model Frisbee: **273**.
Misto Disc Ship: **260**.
Molding Process: 302, 310.
Moonlighter Pro Frisbee: **272**.
More Than One: 297.
Morrison, Fred: 279–280, 286, 290, 334.
Mystery-Y (Empire Plastics): **275**.

Nipple, The: **264**, 303.
Nozzle, The: **264**, 303.

Palmeri, Jim: 309.
Photographing Discs: 335.
Pie Tins: **247**.
PIPCO: 283–284, 286–287, 293.
PIPCO Logo: **249**.
PLUTO PLATTERS:
 American Trends (ATPP): **262–263**, 279, 281, 286, 297, 300, 303–305, 308, 339.
 American Trends Labels: **255**.
 American Trends Reorder Forms: **263**, **370**.
 American Trends Packaging: **263**.
 ANATOMY (Schematics): **350**.
 Colors: 298.
 Double-Esker: **270**, 330.
 Eskers: **265**, **270**.
 FACT FINDER: 349.
 Horseshoe Set: **266**.
 Identify, How to: 338.
 Label for, Wamo/Wham-O: **265**.
 Packaging: **265–266, 268, 271**.
 Styles of: 338.
 WPP1: **264–266**, 278, 282, 290, 292, 303, 305, 326, 339.
 WPP2: **267**, 301, 303, 340.
 WPP3: **268**, 303–305, 340.
 WPP4: **269**, 304–305, 310, 340.
 WPP5: **270**, 304, 330, 341.
 WPP6: **270**, 304, 341.
 WPP7: **271**, 302–304, 341.
 WPP7R: **271**, 341.
 ® Symbol: **269**, 305.
Popcorn Can: **246**.
Premier Products: 301.

Pricing: 281.
Pro(fessional) Model Frisbee: **272**.
Prototypes: 286.
Puddle, The: **271**, 303.

Regular Model Frisbee: **273**.
Restoration, Disc: 305.

Sailing Satellite: **273**.
SCP (Southern California Plastic Co.): 286, 287.
Selling & Trading Tips: 337.
Shipping: 299.
Silk-Screening: 314.
Skeptical, Being: 296.
Sky Pie: **260**.
Southern California Plastic Co. (See SCP)
Space Saucer: **261**.
Spokes: **264**, 303.
Storage: 299, 306.
Story, Documenting the: 297.
Swap Meets: 291.

Tag Sales: 291.
Tape: 306.
Thrift Shops: 291.
TOOLS OF THE TRADE:
 Fact Finder, Flyin-Saucer: 348.
 Fact Finder, Pluto Platter: 349.
 Identifying a Flyin-Saucer: 342
 Identifying a Pluto Platter: 338.
 Photographing Discs: 335.
 Selling & Trading Tips: 337.
Tracking Number: 299.

Unscrupulous Bastards: 296.

Web Sites: 307.
WHAM-O:
 "Frisbee" Name: **267**, 302, 305.
 Pluto Platter, Interest in: 286.
Whiffle Flying Saucer: **275**.
Whirlo-Way: 334.
Window Panes: **264**, 303.
World's Oldest Plastic Flying Disc: **248**, 289.

X-Acto® Knife: 306.

Zo-lar (Empire Plastics): **274**.

Acknowledgements

A special thank-you to all those who provided essential research information and/or graphic materials for this book:

Dan "Stork" Roddick—For opening up his extraordinary archives of photographs, articles, Wham-O memorabilia, personal Discography (bibliography), and especially for being a life-long inspiration to all of us in the flying disc community.

Dan Mangone—For his help with disc molding production details.

Jo Cahow—For sharing her priceless scrapbooks.

Jeff McMahon—For permission to reprint his newspaper article… (which originally "inspired" Fred to write this book!)

GRAPHIC MATERIALS
Credit for photography and illustrations (when known) has been listed next to the images.

Back cover photo of Fred and Phil, by Shannon Kennedy, 2002.

All photos of discs, the front cover photo, and the photo on page 245 are ©Phil Kennedy. Digital images taken with a Canon EOS 350D. Cover and page 245 photo taken with a Mamiya RZ on Provia 100 and digitally scanned on a UMAX PowerLook 3000 at 300ppi. Most images have been digitally enhanced in Adobe Photoshop 7.

DESIGN & PRODUCTION
This book was designed and produced in QuarkXPress 4.1 on an Apple G4 Macintosh desktop computer (still) running OS9.2.

Most type fonts are from the Zapf Humanist family.

EXTRA SPECIAL APPRECIATION
Pat Kennedy—for her essential proofreading and editing assistance. Her emotional support, encouragement and (especially) *patience* throughout this incredibly exciting four-year project were critical!

A FINAL NOTE: While we've endeavored tirelessly to create the perfect masterpiece, inevitably flaws may be lurking. If you find an error or make a historical discovery, please alert us so that we can make the next edition even better!

Order Form
Use for purchases within the U.S. only*

FLAT FLIP FLIES STRAIGHT
True Origins of the Frisbee®

PLEASE PRINT CLEARLY

Name _____

Address _____

City _____ State _____ Zip _____

Telephone (For order contact only) _____

Email (For order contact only) _____

Please send _____ book(s) @ $29.95 each ....$_____

Shipping & handling: First book $5.50 ....$_____

                        Add'l books @$1.50 each ....$_____

                      Sub Total of above ....$_____

Add 6% Sales Tax for orders shipped to CT addresses .....$_____

                    TOTAL ....$_____

Please fill out a copy of this order form and send with payment to:

WORMHOLE PUBLISHERS
Ordering Dept., 181 Ridge Road, Wethersfield, CT 06109-1045

Money Order / Certified Check allows next day shipping in most cases. Personal / Business check must clear before shipment (7 to 10 days).

Books will be sent Priority Mail.

Order by major credit card or PayPal at: www.FlatFlip.com

For special pricing for bookstores, dealers and distributors, please email FlatFlip@cox.net, or fax 860-571-0281.

* For international purchases, please contact: www.DTWorld.com